Chaplains of the
Revolutionary War

Chaplains of the Revolutionary War

Black Robed American Warriors

JACK DARRELL CROWDER

McFarland & Company, Inc., Publishers
Jefferson, North Carolina

LIBRARY OF CONGRESS CATALOGUING-IN-PUBLICATION DATA

Names: Crowder, Jack Darrell, 1944– author.
Title: Chaplains of the Revolutionary War : black robed American warriors / Jack Darrell Crowder.
Description: Jefferson, North Carolina : McFarland & Company, Inc., Publishers, 2017. | Includes bibliographical references and index.
Identifiers: LCCN 2017039338 | ISBN 9781476672090 (softcover : acid free paper) ∞
Subjects: LCSH: United States—History—Revolution, 1775–1783—Chaplains. | United States—History—Revolution, 1775–1783—Religious aspects. | Military chaplains—United States—History—18th century.
Classification: LCC E209 .C76 2017 | DDC 973.3/1—dc23
LC record available at https://lccn.loc.gov/2017039338

BRITISH LIBRARY CATALOGUING DATA ARE AVAILABLE

ISBN (print) 978-1-4766-7209-0
ISBN (ebook) 978-1-4766-3071-7

© 2017 Jack Darrell Crowder. All rights reserved

No part of this book may be reproduced or transmitted in any form or by any means, electronic or mechanical, including photocopying or recording, or by any information storage and retrieval system, without permission in writing from the publisher.

Front cover: *James Caldwell at the Battle of Springfield,* watercolor by Henry Alexander Ogden (Library of Congress)

Printed in the United States of America

McFarland & Company, Inc., Publishers
  Box 611, Jefferson, North Carolina 28640
    www.mcfarlandpub.com

To my wonderful wife Peggy
for her encouragement, belief in me,
and help with this book, and
to the important clergy in my life,
Father Donald Clark, Father Richard Judge,
and Brother Tony Pistone.

Table of Contents

Preface 1

Introduction 3

The Chaplains 7

Appendix: Other Chaplains Who Served in the American Revolution 151

Bibliography 169

Index 177

Preface

All books on the American Revolution discuss how leaders like George Washington, Nathanael Greene, and other great men inspired the troops and led them to victory. They also state that in the early part of the war troops were deserting, enlistments were down, and support for the war was waning.

I began to wonder why the army didn't completely fall apart, and why the people on the homefront didn't just give up. While researching another book on the Revolution I found the answers to my questions. The most influential man in each town and village was the pastor of the church. He was the glue that kept the town and the army together.

"Rebel pastors," as they were called by the British, would preach every week about freedom and resistance against tyranny. The pastors were the ones that would fire the people up for the cause of liberty and encourage the men of the town to join the cause. When the news on the battlefield was bad, they would bolster the morale of the people by telling them that their cause was just.

It was the pastors that kept the flow of men enlisting in the army. Many times army recruiters would come to town, and the pastor would be the first person they would talk with for help in recruiting. They knew the people were more likely to listen to the minister than a stranger. The pastors were the reason men enlisted, not the military leaders.

When the pastors became army chaplains it was their duty to nurse the physical and spiritual needs of the men. The troops looked to the chaplain to calm and encourage them before a battle. The Rev. William Emerson, with musket in hand, as the British advanced on Concord, turned to the frightened lad next to him and said, "Stand your ground, Harry! Your cause is just and God will bless you."

The men were inspired during battle when the chaplain stood next to them and faced danger and death. The Rev. Thomas Allen was standing on a fallen tree and facing the enemy as bullets whizzed by his black clerical robe. He turned to his brother, who was a lieutenant in the militia, and hollered, "Now give me a musket; you load, and I'll fire!"

Preface

I wrote this book to honor the forgotten warriors of the American Revolution. Since these men were educated, many of them wrote detailed letters and diaries about what they saw and went through while in the army. They gave important details of battles told from the viewpoint of the common man. These letters and diaries proved to be very valuable in my research. Their contribution toward our independence cannot be emphasized enough. Their names and deeds must be recorded or they will be forgotten.

Much of the information obtained on these men come from their own words in their pension applications, diaries, and letters. I have used their original wording and spelling, and they have not been changed. Some of the information is from sources written more than a hundred years ago and out of print.

Introduction

The memory of the just is blessed: but the name of the wicked shall rot.
—Proverbs 10:7

When the American Revolution began, the majority of the people in the colonies were Protestant. There were clusters of people in various regions that were members of the Jewish faith, which amounted to around 3,000 people. At the start of the war Maryland was the home to several thousand Catholics. Several years earlier there were strong anti-Catholic feelings in Congress. When the colonies sought their independence, these feelings changed in order to gain support from them.

Although the official state church in the colonies was the Church of England, the Anglicans were outnumbered by other groups that had broken away. The main groups included the Presbyterians, Lutherans, Baptists, Quakers, and Congregationalists. All of these groups had their own religious beliefs and cultural differences. There was, however, one belief many shared, which was the belief in civil and religious liberty.

Most of the time the sermons of the ministers stressed their political beliefs. Most believed that it was a sin to start a war, but they believed that it was justifiable to go to war in the case of self-defense. The ministers that supported the American cause preached that the British had forced the colonists into a defensive war. A preacher outspoken against the British held great power over the people in his congregation. These men in black robes were respected and usually considered the most important men in town. Their opinions carried a great deal of power and influence.

The preachers were great army recruiters as well. Since they commanded such respect in the community, the locals would follow their example or suggestions. Recruitment officers when visiting a town would many times ask the preacher to personally appeal to the men to join up. On some occasions the preacher would recruit men from the congregation and then lead them off to battle.

Introduction

The chaplains had no specific uniforms although some were given black material to make a replacement set of clothes. Many carried a firearm and the sword of an officer. Their duties included fighting at times, caring for the sick and wounded, and holding prayer services for the soldiers and the local community. At times they even preformed marriages in the camp or the surrounding community.

Normally, services were held out in the open or in a building if available. Sometimes a penalty, such as digging out tree stumps, was given for missing services. Chaplin Charles Beaty increased his attendance at services by giving out the daily rum ration to the soldiers in formation for prayers. Typical sermons involved the topics of temperance, cleanness, honesty, and re-enlistment.

When the fighting began some pastors believed that they needed to do more than just talk about fighting the British. Toward the end of 1775 the Rev. Peter Muhlenberg preached his sermon and at the end of it he took off his black robe. Under it he wore the uniform of a Continental officer. He gathered his rifle and encouraged his men to follow him as he walked from the pulpit. That day nearly 300 men in the area marched off to battle with him.

This action was repeated across New England when the fighting started. Pastor Jonathan Todd of Connecticut marched to Boston with 83 of the men from his church. They were followed by 100 men led by Pastor Benjamin Boardman and 100 more led by Pastor Eleazer May. As the British approached Lexington, Pastor Jonas Clark was asked if his men would fight. The pastor replied, "I have trained them for this very hour; they would fight, and, if need be, die, too, under the shadow of the house of God."

The ministers that supported the patriot cause, but did not join in the actual fighting, kept morale up back home with their patriotic sermons and actions. Pastor John Adams of Durham, New Hampshire, stored gunpowder under his pulpit and Pastor David Ely stored gunpowder in a bin in the attic of his house. Ely was so outspoken for independence that the local Tories said they would hang him if they got the chance. When Pastor Ely visited members of his church, he carried his Bible in one hand and a loaded musket in the other.

Pastor Ebenezer Prime was driven from his home at the age of 77 and his church was torn down because of his patriotism. Pastor Blackleach Burritt preached such fiery sermons against the British that he was cap-

Introduction

tured and confined to the Old Sugar House prison in New York City. John Nicholas Martin, the pastor of St. Johns Church in Charleston, South Carolina, was told to pray for the King and when he refused the British shelled his church. Pastor Samuel McClintock of New Hampshire lost three of his four sons in the fight for American freedom.

The sermons of the pastors would convince the congregation that their cause was just and that God would help them defeat the hated enemy. British General Cornwallis once said about Pastor Richard Furman, "I feared the prayers of that Godly man much more than the armies of Sumter and Marion."

The members of the Society of Friends or Quakers faced harder choices than the other religious groups. Traditionally, they were pacifists and were expected to remain neutral. Some Quakers believed that they could take up arms and fight and thus were referred to as "Free Quakers." Most remained pacifists, and the members that supported the Revolution faced discipline from the church.

George Gray held a political office that supported the war. He and his patriotic wife were expelled from the Society. Benjamin Fell offered his supplies and leather business to make shoes for the Americans at Valley Forge. For this he lost membership in the Society of Friends.

Some Quakers went so far as to take up arms against the British. John Dickerson would not vote for the Declaration of Independence, but he did accept a commission as an officer in the Pennsylvania militia. Nathanael Greene was raised a Quaker, and he rose from a private to the commander of the southern campaign.

General Washington and his commanders knew that a clergymen provided comfort and encouragement to the common soldier. This was especially true in the early years of the war when the cause looked hopeless. These men of the cloth could make the difference between defeat and victory. Their presence would encourage the soldiers to stay the course and not give up hope of an eventual victory.

In July of 1776 the Continental Congress voted to pay the chaplains $33⅓ per month and to give them the rank and rations of an army colonel. They each were assigned to a regiment and most bore arms and joined in the fighting. General Washington required the soldiers to attend Sunday service each week when possible. Washington also informed his officers that he wanted them to encourage the men to refrain from the wicked practice of cursing and swearing.

Introduction

Besides looking after the men's spiritual needs, ministers with some training in medicine also looked after the men's physical needs. Chaplain David Avery brought his own medicine and instruments when he joined the army. He was described as fearless in battle and untiring in his attention to the sick and wounded.

The Rev. James Caldwell was a Presbyterian minister who fought at the battle of Springfield. His church was burned to the ground, and after the battle he preached from a pulpit with his pistols lying on either side of the Bible. Baptist minister David Jones served under General Anthony Wayne. Jones was so heroic on the battlefield that British General Howe offered a reward for his capture. Of the more than 218 chaplains that served in the army, about 25 were killed or died during the war. This 11 percent casualty rate is the highest rate in the history of the chaplain corps.

If a chaplain was taken prisoner, he was sometimes treated with courtesy and consideration. Many times, however, this was not the case. The British hated them for the courage and passion they instilled in the men. As a result, many of the ministers were treated with brutal severity and punishment.

The clergy was so influential in the war effort that the British, and those loyal to the crown, referred to them as the Black Regiment because they wore black robes. This book contains many of the brave ministers that served in the army during the American Revolution. For every name mentioned in this book there may be several names that are not recognized and in some cases forgotten to history. This is a chronicle of dedication and sacrifice.

> *Great Father, we bow before thee, we invoke thy blessing, we deprecate they wrath, we thee return thanks for the past, we ask thy aid for the future; for we are in times of trouble, O Lord, and sore beset by foes, ... God prosper the cause. Amend.*
> —Prayer given by 25-year-old Chaplain Joab Trout, September 10, 1777, the day before his death at the Battle of Brandywine (California Society of the Sons of the Revolution, taken from the New Hampshire State Archives and transcribed at the U.S. 1875 Centennial)

The Chaplains

Amos Adams

Amos Adams was born on September 1, 1728, in Medfield, Massachusetts, and he died on October 5, 1775, in Suffolk County, Massachusetts. He married Elizabeth Prentice on October 18, 1753, and they had seven children. She died in 1769 and Amos married Sarah Chauncey.

Amos graduated from Harvard in 1752, and he was ordained on September 12, 1753. He served as minister of the First Church of Roxbury, which was a Congregational Church in Massachusetts. Amos was described by his parishioners as able and energetic. He was popular, even though some complained of the plainness of his speech and the length of his sermons.

Pastor Adams was a passionate patriot. He was appointed scribe of the Convention of Ministers at Watertown in May 1775. This convention recommended that the people take up arms against the British. After preaching to his congregation he would then preach to the soldiers in the area.

He was appointed the Chaplain of the 9th Massachusetts Militia under the command of Colonel David Brewer. He served from May 1775 until his death in October. He died from dysentery that was rampant in the camp and surrounding area. Amos was buried by his regiment with full military honors. In his will, written a few months before his death, Amos said he wanted his younger children to receive a liberal education.

Sources: 1. *History of the Adams Family* by Henry Whittemore, 1893, page 20. 2. *Known Military Deaths in the American Revolution 1775–1783* by Clarence Stewart Peterson, page 11. 3. *D.A.R. Lineage Book*, Vol. 3, page 276. 4. *Massachusetts, Wills & Probate Records 1635–1999*, Vol. 74–75. 5. *Sons of the American Revolution Application*. 6. *Massachusetts Soldiers & Sailors in the War of Revolution*, Vol. 1, page 36.

Moses Allen

Moses Allen was born on September 14, 1748, in Northampton, Massachusetts, and he died on February 8, 1779, in Charleston, South Carolina. He married Elizabeth Odingsell.

Moses was educated at Princeton and at the College of New Jersey. He was in the same class with future president James Madison. After graduation he preached at several churches and later became the pastor of the Midway Congregational Church in Georgia. The church had been trying to obtain a pastor for nearly four years, and they welcomed the new pastor when he preached his first sermon there on June 22, 1777. His church and the surrounding St. John's Parish became a hotbed of patriot feeling at the outbreak of the revolution.

In the latter part of 1778 his church was burned, and the congregation was scattered by British troops under General Prevost. Moses fled to Savannah and became a chaplain in a Georgia brigade. On December 29, 1778, Savannah was captured by the British, and since Pastor Allen was a vocal sympathizer for the American cause he was sent to the prison ship *Nancy* in Charleston Harbor. Many of the officers were pardoned and sent to Sunbury on parole. Pastor Allen, being a commissioned chaplain, was kept on board the prison ship.

While on board the prison ship *Nancy* he wrote a letter to his brother-in-law Benjamin Odingsell on January 20, 1779. In about three weeks Moses would attempt to escape.

> Dear Brother: Yours of the 16th, came to hand yesterday. It gives me great pleasure to hear of my family's arrival in Carolina, when I feared they were in the Enemy's Hand at Abercorn. I wrote five or six letters to you sister & others; am surprised that none have reached them; however, I hope this may come safe, & you will as soon as possible transmit it to Mrs. Allen. I wrote to her but two or three days since, whether it was permitted to pass or not I cannot tell. I believe Betty had better let out her negroes to a good master by the month. I feel no good Prospect of being exchanged soon, & many be confined many months, however, she is among friends & cannot suffer. Beg her not to be troubled on my account. Captivity agrees with my constitution much better than I could have expected. The mess I belong to is indulged the use of the Cabin & our friends in town supply us with necessaries not allowed in our daily rations, such as bread, coffee, Tea, sugar, Rum & the like, so that upon these considerations, our situation is very happy. By the kindness of friends I am also very well supplied with Linen, stockings, &c. It would, therefore, be irreligious in her to murmur or repine. I hope better things of her. She will dis-

cover faith & fortitude, she will be an example of patience & resignation. The Christian graces may be made to appear more conspicuous in adversity than in Days of prosperity.

If she has no Carolina Currency, She can get necessaries for her self & her little Companion upon Credit. I would not have here want for any Thing, but remember our late losses, & be frugal, I don't mean Stingy.

Remember me to Col. Elbert, Harris & all friends with you, too numerous to mention. I wish they may think of my exchange. Desire Mrs. Allen to remember me kindly to all friends with her. I have wrote Col. Harris, but have received no answer. Beg Col. Roberts to write, he was once in the same Predicament.

I am your Affectionate friend & Brother, Moses Allen

On February 8, 1779, Moses jumped overboard with two other men and swam for land three miles away. As he neared the shore he turned back to help one of the other men. A cramp suddenly seized him and he sank and drowned within 20 yards from the shore. His body was found and the prison ship's commander had it dumped in a nearby swamp and said, "The rebel preacher deserved only a traitor's grave."

His body was recovered by some friends who requested from a British officer some boards for a coffin. They were refused, so the body of Moses Allen was taken out to sea and given a burial. When his body was found, his friends found parts of his diary that survived in his pockets.

29th December 1778, Tuesday. A Battle at Savannah & the town taken by ye English. Number lost not known.

30th. Between three and four hundred prisoners shut up in ye State house.

31st. Citizens & soldiers drove into a prison ship, no distinction between ye Gentlemen of property, & a rascal at the—

Jan'y 1st:—Officers allowed their Parole, Chaplain [himself] exempted. Parole signed by all except the chaplain & he ordered to the common jail.

2nd. Ordered on board ye ship Nancy, a prison ship. It is a happiness that Mr Sheftall is a fellow sufferer, he bears it with such fortitude at is an example to me. His case is peculiarly hard, & his son suffers with him. The Cap'n seems willing to serve us, gives us a room between the Cabin & ye steerage. We are thankful for the distinction made between us &—[Mordecai Sheftall (1735–1797) was a prominent Jew from Savannah, and reputed among the British: "a very great rebel"].

3rd. Sunday. Our allowance, three gills of rice [about 1½ cups] & eleven ounces of beef per [day]. Some officers on board spoke ill-natured things of Mr. Sheftall the Cap'n ordered us out of the steerage into ye hole with ye common prisoners. A man dead onboard, the Chaplain not allowed to bury him.

4th. Nothing particular. I pity Mr. Bryan.

5th. Cap'n of transport called to Agent [Noles]. The question asked the Cap'n of the Nancy by ye Agent Noles, "Have you a Parson Allen on board?" "Yes." "Take

> care of him, he's ye damnedest rebel upon the continent." Poor consolation for a man in distress & denied a hearing.
> 6th. Ordered to Cockspur [Island]. A man dead on board. The Lieutenant of ye Vigilant forbid ye Chaplain's burying him.
> 7th. Head wind. Moved but little today. Got down to Tybee [Island]. Buried another.

Here the daily record is broken. On January 20 Moses Allen wrote his brother-in-law, Benjamin Odingsell, in which he expresses a more positive picture of his captivity.

> Jan'y 28th. Jail six days for saying that Parson Allen was used very ill at the time of captivity.
> 29th. A corpse buried. Seven dead since we went on board. Went on board ye Whitby.
> 30th. A Bit of pork for dinner. The Jews Mr. Sheftall & son refused to eat their pieces & their knives and forks were ordered to be greased with it.
> 31st. Sergeant Bond came aboard. They have lost five men belonging to the Vigilant.—News by a Woman that Col. Brown is not killed, but his arm wounded & cut off. 17 men of his killed in the action at the time he was wounded, that the enemy's Light Infantry were all killed & taken on Sunday last at Briar Creek, etc. The Eleanora, a Hospital ship came down, took 70 sick.

The rest of the diary is not legible.

The following is a letter written by the prisoner Mr. Sheftall eleven years later. It gives a good description of the conditions that the men endured as prisoners and the death of Amos Allen.

> Savanna in Georgia, Feb. 4, 1790
> [to] Captain Joseph McLellan, of the Sloop *Falmouth* of Portland.
>
> SIR:—The other evening, entering into conversation with you respecting a man whom I had known during the late war, on board the prison ship Nancy, commanded by one Samuel Tate, heavens, what was my astonishment to find that that miscreant was now living in the town of Portland in the state of New Hampshire. Surely the good people of that place cannot be acquainted with the character of the man, or 'tis impossible that he should be permitted to reside amongst Americans, much less allowed to carry on trade, as I suppose that to be the case.
>
> I take the liberty of giving you a short detail of that man's conduct toward poor prisoners, that were put on board his ship.
>
> I was sent on board his ship on the 2nd of January 1779, with the Rev. Moses Allen, also a son of mine & several other gentlemen. Humanity must shudder at the thought of what immediately presented itself to view, which was nothing less than one of our poor countrymen, stretched out on the deck of the ship, in the agonies of death, without the least medical assistance, or even the smallest nourishment, when the hell-born monster, in order I have supposed to show us what we had to expect from his clemency, kept taunting the poor fellow (who retained his senses to the last) in the following manner: "Why now, you are mighty bad! I

am glad of it! I wish there was ten thousand of you in the same way, and your d—d rebel Congress, too!"

The next thing I took notice of that I thought material was the scanty allowance of provisions, with which we were served, which was two pints & a half & a half a gill of rice, served out to each mess, together with seven ounces of beef for each man for 24 hours.

Judge you what an allowance this,—not quite half a pound of rice a man for 24 hours & that not half boiled. This lasted for 12 days, when Captain Henry of the Man-of-War, who then acted as Commodore, (Captain Hyde Parker being at that time in Savannah,) assisting in regulating their police, permitted us to write to town (as we then lay at Cockspur,) for assistance to my friends, which I did & in a very pointed manner described the situation of the poor prisoners, well knowing that my letter would be read by the Commander-in-chief, who was Colonel Campbell, who was a man of humanity & a gentleman, although an enemy. My letter had the desired effect, & orders were given to send out 21 quarts of rice to each mess, consisting of six men. This was some relief to us poor prisoners, though it served our monster of a captain also, for he was steward or commissary, & he took care that if we were benefited by the late order, he would be profited by it, for his gallon pot wich we were served out of, only held five pints & a gill [½ cup]. This evil, though often complained of, was never remedied, & this font of malice permitted to enrich his coffers at the expense & blood of numbers of our worthy citizens, for from the scanty allowance of provisions the poor fellows were induced to take large draughts of water, & that frequently brackish, which brought on dysentreries, and occasioned the death of many much better men that the wretch I am writing about.

Before taking my leave of this citizen (or alien) I must mention two or three acts of his, one, that I have seen him take a bottle of fresh water from one of our soldiers who was carrying it between decks to his companion, who the soldier said was very ill, but this brute divested of every feeling of humanity, threw the bottle over board, & told the soldier if his companion wanted water, he must come & fetch it.

The poor man was accordingly brought up by two of his companions, when I held the can to his mouth & the poor creature drank, I suppose a quart of water. The next morning the poor man was brought up dead from between decks.

The next thing that I would wish to remind him of is, that the Rev. Moses Allen, brother of the Rev. Thomas Allen of Pittsfield, Mass., being tired & fretted almost to death (being a man of high spirits) at the treatment we received from this hero of a captain, had endeavored to make his escape from the ship by swimming, in which attempt he was unfortunately drowned. Some few days after he was picked up, & though there was a quantity of boards on board the ship, which this man caused his boats to pick up & bring on board, & I offered him two half Johanneses [gold Portuguese coins] out of three that I had, for a as many boards as would make a coffin; yet this fellow refused to let me have the boards, saying Rebels had no business with coffins.

To enumerate all that I know of this said Capt. Samuel Tate, late master of the prison ship Nancy, in the service of the British Tyrant, would take more of my time than I could wish to bestow. Therefore, I shall conclude with assuring you, that you have my liberty to show this to anybody you please, & to publish it in the newspaper of Portland or any other place you like.

I wish you good voyage and happy sight of your friends & family, & am, Sir, Your obedient servant, Mordecai Sheftall.

Sources: 1. *South Carolina Historical and Genealogy Magazine*, 58:44, 1957. 2. Excerpt from "Betty Allen" in *The Magazine of History with Notes and Queries*, pages 197–202. 3. *The Biography of Elizabeth "Betty" Parsons-Allen*. 4. *History and Published Records of the Midway Congregational Church, Liberty County, Georgia* by James Stacey. 5. *Betty Allen and Her Six Sons* by Mary H. Emerson.

Thomas Allen

Thomas Allen was born on January 17, 1743, in Northampton, Massachusetts, and he died on February 11, 1810, in Pittsfield, Massachusetts. He married a minister's daughter Elizabeth Lee on February 18, 1768, and they had 12 children.

Thomas graduated from Harvard at the age of 19. The expense of his education was paid for by his grand-uncle Thomas. When Thomas became the first pastor of the Pittsfield Congregational Church, the town consisted of six houses not built with logs. The church was not finished until 1770.

After the Americans were defeated at Long Island and New York fell into the hands of the British, discouragement spread throughout New England. Thomas decided that actions rather than words were needed, so he became an army chaplain. He died not believing that his only duty as chaplain was to preach and pray with the men, rather he should furnish an example of courage to them.

Pastor Allen served as a chaplain from October 3, 1776, until January 23, 1777, and he was at the Battle of White Plains. He kept a diary of his service at White Plains and gave his description of the battle.

> Oct. 27. Arrived at break of day at White Plains, having performed a march of above twelve miles in the night. Lay down after daylight for sleep on the ground.

When the battle began on the 28th Thomas was in position to see every movement of the British line. When the Americans began to flee he rushed forward to offer his service as a volunteer.

> Oct 28. About 9 o'clock, A.M. the enemy and our out parties were engaged; about 10, they appeared in Plain sight, falling off towards our right wing. A strong cannonade ensued from both armies. A great part of the enemy's strength seemed

bent towards our right wing, but no additional force of ours was as yet directed that way.

At length the enemy came up with our right wing, and a most furious engagement ensued by cannonade and small arms, which lasted towards two hours. Our wing was situated on a hill, and consisted of, perhaps, something more than a brigade of Maryland forces. The cannonades and small arms played most furiously without cessation—I judge more than twenty-three cannon a minute.

At length a reinforcement of Gen. Bell's brigade was ordered from an adjacent hill, where I was. I had an inclination to go with them to the hill, that I might more distinctly see the battle, and perhaps contribute my mite to our success. Just as we began to ascend the hill, we found our men had given way, and were moving off the hill in some confusion, at which some elevated shots from the enemy came into the valley where we were very thick—one of which took off the fore part of a man's foot in about three rods of me. I saw the ball strike, and the man fall; as none appeared for his help, I desired five or six of those who had been in battle to carry him off. Others I saw carrying off wounded in different directions. With the rest retreated to the main body. Our men fought with great bravery; they were sore galled by the enemy's field-pieces.

Thomas again served as a chaplain in June and July of 1777, and he was at the surrender of Fort Ticonderoga in July of 1777. Before the fort was surrendered, Thomas gave a stirring sermon to the soldiers to inspire them. The sermon began with "Yonder are the enemies of your country, who have come to lay waste and destroy, and spread havoc and devastation through this pleasant land. They are mercenaries, hired to do the work of death, and have no motives to animate them in their undertaking. You have every consideration to induce you to play the men, and act the part of valiant soldiers."

Unfortunately, the soldiers never had the chance to show their courage, because General St. Clair gave up the fort after only a few shots were fired. After the fall of the fort, Thomas left the army and returned home in disgust. He believed that the surrender of the fort by General St. Clair with very little resistance was a disgrace. Thomas wrote: "In about five hours afterwards the garrison was evacuated, and our vast army fleeing before their enemies with the utmost precipitation and irregularity, leaving behind, for the use of the enemy, an immense amount of baggage, artillery, ammunition, provisions, and every warlike necessary. The fate of America must depend on the treatment of those five general officers who gave up Ticonderoga."

Many Americans shared the feelings expressed by Thomas. John Adams later wrote, "I think we shall never be able to defend a post until we shoot a general." King George of England did not, however, share in that opinion. It was said that he ran into the Queen's chambers as she was dressing and shouted, "I have beat them! I have beat all the Americans."

British General Burgoyne sent about 1,200 troops, mostly Hessians, to raid Bennington which was about 34 miles north of Pittsfield. The General believed the town was lightly defended and it contained supplies needed for the British army. He was not aware that he would meet nearly 2,000 militiamen and the very angry Rev. Thomas Allen.

After Thomas Allen had returned to Pittsfield he learned that the British were marching toward Bennington. When the alarm to assemble reached Pittsfield the men assembled including Pastor Allen on his old horse he used to visit his congregation. The men had been assembled before for alarms, which turned out to be false. The men were in no mood to stand around so they marched to Bennington.

It was raining when they reached the army camp of General John Stark at one in the morning. Thomas had the General aroused from his sleep and said to him, "The people of Berkshire have often turned out to fight the enemy, but have not been permitted to do so. We have resolved that if you do not let us fight now, never to come again."

The General replied, "Would you go now, in this dark and rainy night? No; go to your people; tell them to rest if they can; and if God sends us sunshine tomorrow, and I do not give you fighting enough, I will never call upon you to come again."

It was reported that before the battle the next day on August 16, 1777, General Stark inspired his men with the cry, "There are your enemies, the Red Coats and the Tories. They are ours, or this night Molly Stark sleeps a widow."

As the regiment to which Thomas Allen was in approached the Tory outworks, the pastor knew that some of his neighbors must be there on the enemy's side. Feeling a sense of duty to these men, he stood on a fallen tree in his black clerical robe in full view of the enemy line and tried to get the men to join the American side. He warned them of consequences if they failed to do so.

"There's Parson Allen, let's pop him" was the reply. Some began to fire at him resulting in a shower of bullets flying around the preacher. Thomas, satisfied that he had done his duty to these men, turned to his brother Lieutenant Joseph Allen, and being the better shot said, "Now give me a musket; you load, and I'll fire!" At the final charge Thomas led it and was one of the first to scale the breastworks. Once the battle ended the pastor began tending to the wounded.

When the battle had ended the Americans had killed and captured over 1,000 British troops. This victory would help the Americans defeat General Burgoyne in the fall at Saratoga. Later, when Thomas was asked if he actually killed any man during the battle, the pastor replied that he did not know. He said he observed a flash often repeated from a certain bush, and it was usually followed by the fall of one of the Americans. Thomas said he fired at the bush and put the flash out. Three days after the battle, Thomas returned home to his parish and the next day he preached to his congregation.

In February of 1779 he learned that his brother Pastor Moses Allen of Georgia had escaped from his prison ship and drowned. Even though the journey to Savannah was very dangerous, he went and returned to Pittsfield with the wife of Moses and her young child. After the war Thomas kept up his interest in state and national affairs.

Sources: 1. *Memoir and Official Correspondence of General Stark* by Caleb Stark, 1860, page 494. 2. *Sons of the American Revolution Application.* 3. *D.A.R. Lineage Book*, Vol. 17, page 334. 4. *The Congregational Quarterly*, Vol. 19, pages 476–490. 5. Tombstone.

James Francis Armstrong

James Armstrong was born on April 3, 1750, in West Nottingham, Maryland, and he died January 19, 1816, in Trenton, New Jersey. He was married to Susannah Livingston on August 22, 1782, and they had six children. Susannah received a widow's pension of $600 a year for his service.

He attended the College of New Jersey, now called Princeton, and lived with the family of John Witherspoon the college president. When the British invaded New Jersey, he joined as a private in Peter Gordon's Company, 1st Regiment of Hunterdon County. He decided that he could better serve the cause as a chaplain, so he continued his studies in theology. In January of 1777 he received his licensed to preach. He became chaplain of the 2nd Maryland brigade on July 17, 1778.

He marched with the army to the south, and he was supposed to have remained in the service until the victory at Yorktown. He contracted a rheumatic disease and was forced to return home. He left the army in

1782 and became pastor at a church in Elizabeth, New Jersey. He later served as the minister of the First Presbyterian church in Trenton from 1787 until his death in 1816.

Sources: 1. *The Magazine of American History with Notes and Queries*, Vol. 6. 2. *Annals of the American Pulpit* by William Buell Sprague, 1856, Vol. 3, pages 289–391. 3. *Brief Sketches of the New Jersey Chaplains in the Continental Army* by F.R. Brace, 1909, pages 8–9. 4. Tombstone. 5. Pension Application W5638.

David Avery

David Avery was born on 5 April 1746 in Norwich, Connecticut, and he died on February 16, 1818, in Hanover, New Hampshire. He married Hannah Chaplin on October 10, 1782, and they had four children.

David did not have the money to attend school, so he appealed to his family to loan him the money. They were unable to help, so he worked to earn the tuition and later entered Dr. Eliezer Wheelock's Indian Charity School. He earned money while in school by spending part of the year teaching Indians the basics of education.

When the Lexington alarm went out in the spring of 1775, he preached his sermon and then told his congregation, "God will take care of you, as for myself I am going to join the army." Pastor Avery with about 20 of his parishioners marched to the army head-quarters at Cambridge, and on April 22, 1775, David was made the chaplain of Colonel Patterson's regiment.

In June of 1775 the regiment was present at the Battle of Bunker Hill. As the British attacked Breed's Hill, David Avery stood on nearby Bunker Hill watching and praying. He later wrote in his diary, "Early in the morning of June 18th the enemy attacked our entrenchments, but was driven back. After repeated trials they succeeded in dislodging the troops. In the retreat many of Col. Sherbourne's men were killed. My dear friend, Dr. Warren, was shot dead. I stood on a neighboring hill with hands uplifted, supplicating the blessing of Heaven to crown our unworthy arms with success. The enemy burned Charlestown that they might be benefited by the smoke."

After the battle Pastor Avery dressed the wounds of the soldiers and attended to their spiritual needs. The British had won the battle but at the great cost of over a thousand men killed or wounded. The Americans suffered a little over 400 killed or wounded. Washington's army then retreated through New York and New Jersey. Avery wrote in his diary, "The lustre of our commander's [Washington] presence and magnanimity gave a charm to our gloomy misfortunes, it animated and raised our spirits above the power of undue fear."

On Christmas night 1776 David Avery crossed the Delaware River and marched with the army to attack the Hessians at Trenton. During the battle he grabbed the musket of a soldier that fell by his side and began firing at the enemy. He received an injury to his hip which took him off his feet for several weeks. The man that had treated so many wounded soldiers was now going to be the patient.

Crossing back across the Delaware River was a difficult experience he described in his diary, "We were greatly distressed with a very cold storm of rain, hail, and snow, which blew with great violence. I was extremely chilled, and came near perishing before I could get to a fire."

In June of 1777 Avery was helping to build the fortifications at Fort Ticonderoga, which soon fell to British General Burgoyne. He was with the army when the Americans captured the army of General Burgoyne at the Battle of Saratoga in the fall of 1777. During the winter of 1777–78 he suffered with Washington's army at Valley Forge.

In October of 1780 he was active in trying to capture Benedict Arnold who he knew. Avery stood by the side of General Washington when the general signed the death warrant of Major Andre and Avery later saw the British officer hung.

After the war Avery preached in several places and again became a missionary to the New York Indians. On May 25, 1786, he became pastor of the Congregational Church in Wrentham, Massachusetts. It was not a happy arrangement and problems soon developed. One problem was the fact that Pastor Avery had a slave in his family, which was contrary to the wishes of his church. There were also some questions about his theology and his overbearing manner in the pulpit.

In 1794 several ecclesiastical were called, and they dismissed him from the pastorate. He appealed to the law courts but was overruled. The court said this his principles of church government were arbitrary. He began to hold services in his home and finally moved around 1796 to Connecticut. For the next few years he preached at various churches and preformed some missionary work. In 1817 he visited his youngest daughter in Virginia and preached in the area for several weeks. He was invited to become pastor of a church in Middletown, Virginia. He accepted the position, but before he joined the church he was stricken with typhus fever and died on February 16, 1818.

During the time he served with General Washington the two men grew close. David often rode with the General and at times shared meals with him. He was described as a large portly man, of fine personal appearance and manners, and a commanding presence. It was said that Pastor Avery was "everything Washington wanted in a chaplain. His voice was so clear and sonorous, and his articulation so distinct, that it was a common saying in the army, that every soldier in a brigade could hear all that he said. Intrepid and fearless in battle, Unwearied in his attentions to the sick and wounded, nursing them with care and faithful to souls as if they were of his own Parish. He had a Love of Country so strong that it became a passion, was cheerful under privation, ready for any hardship, and never lost, in the turmoil of camp, that warmth and glowing piety which characterized the devoted minister of God."

Source: *The Groton Avery Clan, Vol. 1* by Elroy McKendree Avery and Catherine Hitchcock (Tilden) Avery, 1912, pages 329–331. 2. *God of Liberty: A Religious History of the American Revolution* by Thomas S. Kidd, pages 1–4. 3. Sons of the American Revolution Application. 4. *Biographical Sketches of the Graduates of Yale College*, Vol. III, Annals 1768–69, pages 305–310. 5. *D.A.R. Lineage Book*, Vol. 20, page 242. 6. *The Chaplains and Clergy of the Revolution by Joel Tyler Headley*, 1864, pages 287–299. 7. Tombstone.

Benjamin Balch

Benjamin Balch was born on February 12, 1743, in Dedham, Massachusetts, and he died on May 4, 1816, in Barrington, New Hampshire. He married Joanna O'Brien on May 4, 1765, and they had 12 children. He received a pension of $135 a year for his service.

Benjamin graduated from Harvard in 1763 and spent time studying theology with his father, who was a pastor. In 1765 Benjamin was pastor of the South Precinct Church in Mendon, New Hampshire. Soon after his marriage in 1765 he returned to Dedham and served at a church. Five years later he had a dispute over his pay, so he sold his property to a Quaker and moved to New Mills. At this time selling to a Quaker was considered almost a sin by the locals.

In 1775 he joined the army as a chaplain with the rank of Lieutenant and served under the command of Captain Edmund Putnam. On April

19, 1775, his company marched to Lexington and participated in the Battle of Lexington. Seventeen men marched to battle from Danvers and seven were killed that day. The company, along with other militia units encountered the British at Arlington as the British retreated. The half mile outside of Arlington proved to be the bloodiest half mile of the retreat, and more than 20 Americans were killed and as many British soldiers.

After Lexington, Benjamin served as chaplain in the Massachusetts militia under Colonel Ephraim Doolittle. He continued to preach in churches in the area for the next couple of years. On October 28, 1778, he went to Boston and joined the navy and served as chaplain on the frigate *Boston*. Despite the navy regulations that a chaplain serve on every ship, Benjamin and the Rev. James Geagen were the only chaplains known to have served in the Continental Navy. He was paid the rate of 90 shillings per month.

After the *Boston* was captured, Benjamin served on the frigate *Alliance* with his two young sons Benjamin and Thomas. The two boys together received the pay of a full man, and they served as powder boys. Another son, William, would become the first chaplain in the United States Navy in 1798. During a voyage to France the *Alliance* came under fire from two British ships. During the battle, Benjamin seized a musket and began firing it with such fury that he was later given the nickname "The Fighting Parson."

At the end of the war Benjamin became minister of a church in Barrington, New Hampshire. He remained there preaching for 30 years and in 1815 he preached a farewell sermon and retired from the ministry. A few days later he died suddenly while walking through town.

Sources: 1. Tombstone. 2. *D.A.R. Lineage Book*, Vol. 12, page 225. 3. Pension List of 1792–1795. 4. *The History of the Chaplain Corps, United States Navy* by Clifford Drury, Vol. 1, 1778–1939, pages 4–5 and 257. 5. *Answering the Call: The Story of the U.S. Military Chaplaincy from the Revolution through the Civil War* by William E. Dickens, Jr., page 20.

Abraham Baldwin

Abraham Baldwin was born on November 23, 1754, in Guilford, Connecticut, and he died on March 4, 1807, in Washington, D.C., while serving as a U.S. Senator from Georgia. He was married and had 12 children. He graduated from Yale in 1772 and received his license to preach in 1775. Instead of becoming a pastor, he stayed at Yale as a teacher. He became known as an educator with the skill for directing and motivating young men at Yale.

Abraham served as a part-time chaplain with Connecticut forces during the early part of the war. In February of 1779 he was appointed one of two brigade chaplains allotted to the Connecticut forces. He served as chaplain in General Samuel H. Parsons' brigade until June of 1783. While in the army he studied law and was later admitted to the Connecticut bar.

He had major responsibilities as chaplain, such as caring for the spiritual needs of over 1,500 soldiers, maintaining the men's moral, being a political advisor to the brigade, and having certain educational duties. Of his duties, Baldwin wrote, "I read French, write, and make visits from morning till night, and then sleep from night till morning."

Baldwin did not participate in combat, and he was stationed at a garrison near West Point assuming a defensive nature. Many army units experienced desertions, but Baldwin had educated his men to the nation's war aims and the need for the men to "stay the course." While at West Point he witnessed the betrayal by Major General Benedict Arnold.

During the hard winter of 1779–80 near Morristown, Baldwin wrote, "and I think is very like to continue for the winter—nothing to eat or drink for men or cattle or at least not half allowance and no prospect of that much longer." When there was talk of mutiny by some of the troops, Baldwin preached a strong sermon about the obligation to defend liberty.

After the war Baldwin was influenced by General Nathanael Greene to move with him to Georgia. Abraham did this and entered the law profession. After the adoption of the Constitution, which Abraham Baldwin signed, he went on to serve five terms in the House and two terms in the senate. He was also the Father of the University of Georgia.

Sources: 1. *From Its European Antecedents to 1791—The United States Army Chaplaincy* by Parker C. Thompson, 1978, pages 205, 215–216. 2. *Soldier-Statesman of the Constitution* by Robert K. Wright, Jr., and Morris J. MacGregor, Jr., 1987, pages 64–66.

Joel Barlow

Joel Barlow was born on March 24, 1754, in Redding, Connecticut, and he died on December 26, 1812, in Poland while trying to meet with Napoleon.

He was born into a large family and received formal education from the local minister. When Joel was 18 his father sent him in 1774 to Moor's Indian School (now called Dartmouth). When his father died, Joel was forced to return home to help support the family. In 1775 he entered Yale and showed an interest in writing and in moral and political philosophy.

His first published poem was a satire about the bad food served in the Yale lunch hall. While at Yale he saw the outbreak of the Revolutionary War. The Connecticut Militia was called out, and Joel joined the camp where four of his brothers were serving. He marched and carried a musket during his college vacations and fought in several skirmishes. At the battle of White Plains in the fall of 1776 he distinguished himself by his bravery.

Joel graduated in 1778 and began to study law, but because the Massachusetts line was in need of chaplains he dropped law for theology. After six weeks of study he had a license to preach, so he entered the army as chaplain of the 4th Massachusetts Brigade under Colonel Bailey. He preached a sermon at West Point on the treason of Arnold and proclaimed, "The vengeance of God was proclaimed against all those who dared to lift a traitorous hand against their oppressed county." General Washington was impressed with his fiery sermon and invited the chaplain for dinner placing him at his right side.

He continued to write poetry, and in 1779 he became secretly engaged to Ruth Baldwin. Her father wished for her to select a more practical mate. However, by 1781 they were married. When the war ended Joel was not interested in becoming a parish minister so he returned to the study of law.

During the rest of his life he was a businessman, politician, writer, and diplomat. He provided backing for Fulton's steamboat, referring to his friend as "Old Toot." As a diplomat he negotiated for the lives of American hostages held by the Barbary Coast pirates. He was appointed Ambassador to France by President James Monroe.

Sources: 1. *Biographical Sketches of the Graduates of Yale College.* 2. *Connecticut Men in the Revolutionary War*, pages 144 and 376. 3. *D.A.R. Lineage Book*, Vol. 2, page 262.

John Barnet (Barnett)

John Barnet was born on June 26, 1753, in Windsor, Connecticut, and he died on December 4, 1837, in Durham, New York. He married

Tryphena Spencer around 1785. He was a graduate of Yale. By the early 1800's he had developed serious lung problems and could no longer preach, and he was almost incapable of normal conservation. This problem began while he was in the army. He was said to have injured his voice permanently by open-air preaching in camp.

He first served as chaplain in Colonel Roswell Hopkin's Regiment of Amenia at Saratoga, and later he was chaplain of the 2nd Brigade Massachusetts Militia under command of General Patterson and later General Greaton. His appointment to the 2nd Brigade was made by Congress, so that all the Massachusetts' chaplains were at that time graduates of Yale.

John received a yearly pension for his service in the amount of $480. In his pension application he states, "I entered the service in the State of New York at West Point on or about the first day of June 1782 as chaplain to the Second Massachusetts Brigade of Infantry commanded by Brigadier General Paterson and that I continued to serve in said corps. In the service of the United States as chaplain until the army was disbanded in November 1783."

Pastor Barnet's preaching was described as "didactic and logical, rather than practical; instructive to a certain class, but not effective with the many." He did not consider himself the pastor of the congregation but only a hired preacher. Because of this he did not perform the normal duties of a pastor which is required to be a successful pastor. From 1790 to 1795 he was at Middlebury, Vermont, and as his health began to decline he moved to Durham, New York.

Sources: 1. *Yale and Her Honor-roll in the American Revolution, 1775–1783* by Henry Phelps Johnson, page 344. 2. *The Early History of Amenia by Newton Reed*, page 4. 3. Sons of the American Revolution Application. 4. Pension Application S44311.

Caleb Barnum

Caleb Barnum was born on June 30, 1737, and he died on August 23, 1776, in Pittsfield, Massachusetts. He received his degree from the College of New Jersey (later Princeton) in 1757 and his masters from Harvard in 1768. He was a pastor of the First Congregational Society in Franklin, Massachusetts, from 1760 until 1763. On February 2, 1769, he became pastor at Taunton, Massachusetts.

When news of the Battle at Lexington reached Taunton, he announced the intelligence from his pulpit, and roused the people by an address, in animation and eloquent terms, invoking their patriotism and firmness. On May 3, 1775, he entered the army as a chaplain. He served first under Colonel Walker's Regiment and then under Colonel Greaton in the 24th Regiment. In 1776 he served in New York under Colonel Loammi Baldwin.

After the evacuation of Boston by the British in March of 1776, he accompanied his regiment to New York and then to Montreal. While in Montreal there was a smallpox outbreak and Pastor Caleb was inoculated for it. The American army began a retreat from Canada, and while Caleb was at Fort Ticonderoga he was seized with a bilious disorder which hurt his health so much that he was discharged from the army on July 24, 1776.

He began his trip home to Pittsfield, which was a distance of about 120 miles. He arrived home on August 2, 1776, in a much weakened condition. He got worse until he died on 23 August at the age of 39. On his deathbed he said, "That if I had a thousand lives I would willing lay them all down in my country's cause."

Sources: 1. *Quarter Millennial Celebration of the City of Taunton, Massachusetts,* 1889, page 64. 2. *Sermon on the 25th Anniversary of His Settlement as Pastor by Erastus Maltby,* 1851, page 32. 3. *Princeton Alumni Weekly,* Vol. 65, December 1, 1964, page 20. 4. *D.A.R. Lineage Book,* Vol. 16, page 223. 5. *Princeton College During the 18th Century* by Samuel Davies Alexander, 1872, page 43. 6. *A Centurial History of the Mendon Association of Congregational Ministers* by Rev. Mortimer Blake, 1853, page 100.

Nathaniel Bartlett

Nathaniel Bartlett was born on April 22, 1726, in Redding, Connecticut, and he died there on January 11, 1810. He married Eunice Russell on June 13, 1753, and they had six children. He studied theology at Yale and graduated in 1749.

He preached in different churches for several years until in 1753 he was appointed pastor of the Congregational Church in Redding. He served as pastor for the next 57 years, which was the longest any pastor served at the same church.

He was such a fiery preacher for the cause of independence that local Tories threatened to hang him if they ever caught him. He made the rounds to his parish with a Bible in one hand and a musket in the other. He even allowed gunpowder to be stored in a special bin in the attic of his house.

He frequently served as chaplain to General Putnam's division of the Continental Army with them camped near his town. He was described as "a gentleman of the old school, of an equable temper, a just man, a fine scholar, and an eloquent preacher."

Sources: 1. *Biographical Sketches of the Graduates of Yale College*, Vol. III, Annals 1768–69, pages 100–201. 2. Tombstone 3. *Connecticut Men in the Revolutionary War*, page 585.

Daniel Beck

Daniel Beck was born on August 18, 1748, in Boston, Massachusetts, and he died on August 12, 1845, in Hartford, Vermont. He married Hannah Porter on February 19, 1786, and they had nine children.

He graduated from Princeton in 1785 and served in the army for one year. Daniel enlisted as a chaplain in Colonel Elisha Porter's Regiment. Daniel received a pension of $281.66 a year for his service. The following is from his pension application: "The Reg. was a reinforcement to the army at Quebec after the defeat of Gen. Montgomery that having effected a retreat from Quebec and were stationed in the course of the summer and principal part of the fall at Crown Point, Ticonderoga and several other places near Lake Champlain. In the winter ensuing I was discharged."

When General Benedict Arnold failed to capture Quebec he stayed in the area during the harsh winter. The arrival of British reinforcements, and an outbreak of smallpox forced the Americans to retreat to Fort Ticonderoga.

While Colonel Porter was at the fort, he kept a diary and he mentioned Daniel Beck several times:

> July 7th. Sunday. Very still for a camp this morning. Gave orders for public worship to be attended at 10 o'clock—rained some in the morning. Had a sermon at the time appointed in the forenoon, by Mr. Breck, from James 4:10—a good one. Afternoon adjourned the time to five o'c.—had orders to attend the Genl. At that time. The Genl. Informed us that the Genl. had determined we should remove to Ticonderoga and then take Post—this news gave universal uneasiness in the Camp.
>
> July 14th. In consequence of yesterday's orders for the sick to be sent to Fort George, this morning about 50 were returned by ye Sergt., &c., to go—ordered an examination by the doctor and 10 were returned and ordered to go immediately. Mr. Avery preached to us and Col. Greatorex's Regt. in ye forenoon from Ezekiel

18:31—a good sermon. In ye afternoon Mr. Beck preached from Gal. 4:18 and an excellent discourse. Mr. Avery and Mr. Varnum present all day. Afterwards went into the Fort and heard Mr. Robbins preach a fine sermon from Isaiah 8:9, 10, with suitable application. Soon after had news from New York of beating off ye Regulars from Long Island and ye Jerseys, ye sinking a tender and taking a sloop with Intrenching Tools, &c.

[The Mr. Avery the Colonel mentions is probably Rev. David Avery previously mentioned in this book. Avery was at the fort at this time working on building the fortifications.]

28th. Obliged to attend upon Court Martial again. This day procured a discharge for Stoughton Dickinson, and leave for his brother to attend him to Pittsfield, who set our accordingly. Mr. Beck preached to ye few of ye Regt. who could attend. Got a futlough for ye Adjutant and Ensign Snow for 3 weeks.

4th. Mr. Beck preached two sermons to ye Regt. and others today. The news of yesterday again confirmed by another officer who came from Canada, and that an account of a French fleet being in the river was ye occasion.

25th. Mr. Davids, Chaplain of Col. Bond's Regt. preached a sermon to the Brigade in ye afternoon. Mr. Beck returned from Fort George –lost his pack with all his clothes after he landed, found it again at the landing in evening. At night was taken with a fever. Had a very restless night.

Sources: 1. Diary of Colonel Porter. 2. Pension application S23552. 3. *Soldiers of the Revolutionary War Buried in Vermont* by Walter Hill Crockell, 1904, page 65. 3. *General Catalogues of Princeton University 1746-1906*, 1908, page 97. 4. *Hartland in the Revolutionary War* by Dennis Flower, 1914, page 19. 5. *D.A.R. Lineage Book*, Vol. 13, page 102.

James Beebe

James Beebe was born c. 1718 in Danbury, Connecticut, and he died on August 3, 1785. He married Ruth Curtiss on July 13, 1749, and they had seven children. He studied theology at Yale and was ordained on May 6, 1747. He became pastor of a church in Trumbull, Connecticut.

He served as an army chaplain in the 3rd Regiment of the Connecticut militia in 1760 in the French and Indian War. In 1776, nearly 60 years old, he again served as a chaplain in the local militia. In addition to his church duties he ran a large farm, had part ownership in a local grist and sawmills, and he owned several slaves. They were freed after his death.

One night he organized a public meeting at his house to talk about the Revolution. While he was addressing the people, gunfire was heard and fires were seen in the distance as if the British were coming. Beebe suspected this was a trick. So he sent a small party by a back road to check it out and to cut off the retreat of this scouting party. They captured the culprits, who turned out to be young men from the town who had burned some cornstalks and were playing a joke on the people at the meeting to test their patriotism.

Sources: 1. *History of Stratford, Connecticut 1639–1939* by Wm. Howard Wilcoxson, 1939, pages 663–665. 2. *Biographical Sketches of the Graduates of Yale College*, Vol. II, page 20. 3. *D.A.R. Lineage Book*, Vol. 23, page 197. 4. *History of Stratford Connecticut 1639–1939*, page 664.

Abner Benedict

Abner Benedict was born on November 9, 1740, in North Salem, New York, and he died on November 19, 1818, in Roxbury, New York. He married Lois Northrup on October 30, 1770.

He graduated from Yale in 1769 and he was ordained in 1772 and settled in Middlefield, New York. He was a part-time volunteer chaplain in the army of one of the Connecticut Regiments in New York in 1776. On August 2, 1777, Abner was in the Brooklyn Heights standing on the ramparts and watching the troops form before the Battle of Long Island the next day.

He wrote that around 7 in the evening the sky became as black as ink and it began to rain. He said, "The lightnting fell in masses and sheets of fire to the earth, and seemed to be striking incessantly and on every side." By morning it was mild and peaceful as if nothing had happen. Reports began to come in of the results of the lightning. Abner recorded, "A captain and two lieutenants belonging to McDougal's regiment, were killed by one thunderbolt. The points of their swords melted off, and the coin melted in their pockets. Ten men encamped outside of the fort near the river, and occupying one tent, were killed by a single flash." Numerous reports of death and destruction came in during the morning.

Abner conducted religious services, and as soon as they were finished troops from General Washington's army began to move into the area. "In a short time the whole country, to the front and right, as far as the eye could reach, was covered with the smoke of battle, and shook to the thunder of cannon." Abner said his heart filled with sorrow because the Americans had not only lost the battle, but it looked as if Washington's army would be destroyed.

Under the cover of the rain and night and fog, Washington began to slip his men into boats and cross the East River to safety. Abner watched as one by one boat loads of men were ferried across the river. He chose to stay and cross on one of the last boats. He later witnessed the Battle of White Plains on October 28, 1776, and the fall of Fort Washington a month later. With winter setting in he returned to his parish.

Sources: 1. *Biographical Sketches of the Graduates of Yale College*, Vol. III, page 304. 2. *D.A.R. Lineage Book*, Vol. 55, page 144. 3. *Prominent Families of New York*, edited by Lyman Horace Weeks, 1897, page 55. 4. *Connecticut Men in the Revolutionary War*, page 631.

Benjamin Boardman

Benjamin Boardman was born on August 3, 1731, in Glastonbury, Connecticut, and he died on February 8, 1802. He married Anna Johnson on February 11, 1762.

He graduated from Yale in 1758, and he received a Berkeley Scholarship to study theology. He received his license to preach on February 5, 1760. He answered the Lexington alarm in 1775 and was in the militia as a chaplain for five days in Captain Comfort Sage's horse troop. Later in April of 1775 he was appointed chaplain of the 8th Company commanded by Captain Levi Welles in the 2nd Regiment under Colonel Joseph Spencer. He later served in Colonel Durkee's Regiment in the 20th Continental Army.

Another way he showed his patriotism was by accepting very little payment of his salary from his parish. From 1777 to 1782 his stipulated salary was 95 pounds per year, but during this time he accepted a total of only 36 pounds and 18 shillings.

His great booming voice won him the nickname "Big Gun of the Gospel Boardman." Boardman genealogy reported that "while chaplain in the army, he once made a prayer that was heard across the water at a distance of more than a mile." This happened while he was serving near Boston, and it was the British who heard him praying for an American victory.

While serving in Durkee's Regiment, when New York was captured by the British, Benjamin kept a diary during this time. Here are some excerpts:

Sept. 15th 1776: After Long Island was evacuated, it was judged impossible to hold the city of New York, and for several days the artillery and stores of every kind had been removing, and last night the sick were ordered to Newark. About 11 o'clock a furious cannonade was heard above New York, and before night numbers came over from the city and informed us that it was evacuated by our troops, and about sunset we saw the tyrant's flag floating on Fort George.

Sept 16th: About two o'clock this morning an attempt was made to burn the ships that passed up by the North River yesterday, and anchored about three miles above us.

Sept 17th: This day a quantity of lead, musket ball and buck shot was discovered in a suspected house about a mile and a half above us, and brought down to this place and properly secured for the United States.

Sept. 18th: The brave Lieutenant Col. Knowlton, of our regiment was killed in the action that happen a little below Kingsbridge. The joy of the success that action would have occasioned was greatly lessened in this department by the less of an officer so greatly respected and beloved.

Sept. 21st: At two we were waked up by the guards who informed us that New York was on fire. As the fire began at the south-east end of the city, a little east of the grand battery, it was spread by a strong south wind, first on the East River, and then northward, across the Broadway opposite to the old English church, from thence it consumed all before Broadway and the North River.

Sept 22nd: We received orders this morning to remove our artillery, stores, and baggage, and hold ourselves in readiness to retreat; before night most of them were removed.

Sept. 23rd: We were ordered to retreat from the Hook. Our little battalion retreated with drums beating, and colors flying to Bergen and before night the Britons ventured on shore and took possession of our evacuated works.

After the war Benjamin became pastor of the South Church in Hartford with a salary of 120 pounds a year. He died from complications of diseases in 1809.

Sources: 1. *Historical Collection of the Part Sustained by Connecticut during the War of the Revolution*, complied by Royal Hinman, 1842, pages 45 and 106. 2. *Connecticut Town Birth Records Pre–1870*, page 11. 3. *Connecticut Men in the Revolutionary War*, page 17. 4. *Yankee Township* by Carl F. Price, pages 114–115. 5. *Biographical Sketches of the Graduates of Yale College*, Vol. II, pages 380–388. 6. *Record of Service of Connecticut Men in the War of the Revolution* by Henry Phelps Johnston, 1889, page 45.

Edmund Botsford

Edmund Botsford was born on November 1, 1745, in Woburn, England, and he died on December 25, 1819, in South Carolina. He married three times: 1. Susanna Nunn who died in 1790. 2. Catherine McIver who died in 1796. 3. Ann Deliesseline.

He was left an orphan at the age of seven and placed under the care of his aunt. He was sent to America with Mrs. Barnes a friend of Edmund's mother, and he arrived at Charleston, South Carolina, on January 28, 1766. The Rev. Oliver Hart gave him instructions to prepare for the ministry and Edmund was licensed to preach in February of 1771. He settled in Tuckaseeking in Georgia and began preaching.

Pastor Botsford wrote, "In the month of August 1773 I rode 650 miles, preached 42 sermons, baptized 21 persons, and administered the Lord's Supper twice. Indeed I travelled so much this year, that some used to call me the flying preacher."

After the fall of Savannah in 1778 Edmund and his family, like so many others, became refugees and moved into South Carolina. They had to leave so quickly that they had time to only take two horses and a cart containing a single bed, one blanket, and a sheet. For the next couple of years they lived a nomadic life.

Pastor Botsford received an invitation from General Williamson of the South Carolina Militia to be their chaplain. Edmund accepted the invitation and served for several months. On one occasion the troops were assembled in a grove, and Pastor Botsford began preaching his sermon. One of the sentries posted nearby was listening to the preacher and he became drowsy. As he began to drop his head and nod off, a large goat nibbling grass near him noticed the man nodding off. The goat interpreted the nodding as a challenge to battle. The goat charged the man and hit him low. Many of the men listening to the sermon observed the collision and began to laugh. Pastor Botsford could not find it in his heart to criticize the laughter.

While serving as chaplain Edmund received an invitation to become pastor of a church in Welsh Neck, which he accepted. He later became pastor of a church in Georgetown, South Carolina. In 1803 he was seized with the disease Tic Douloureux, a severe stabbing pain to one side of the face. It is considered one of the most painful conditions to affect people. He had very few pain free periods of time and the disease finally wore him down. Edmund died in 1819 at the age of 79.

Sources: 1. Tombstone. 2. *Roster of Revolutionary Soldiers in Georgia*, Vol. III, page 32. 3. *Materials Towards a History of the Baptists* by Morgan Edwards, Vol. 2, page 164. 4. *A General History of the Baptist Denomination in America* by David Benedict, page 723. 5. *Memoirs of Elder Botsford* by Charles D. Mallory, 1832, pages 45–55. 6.

Georgia Baptist: Historical and Biographical by Jesse Harrison Campbell. 7. *South Carolina Baptists, 1670–1805* by Leah Townsend, page 177.

Hugh Henry Brackenridge

Hugh Brackenridge was born on October 4, 1748, in Kintyre, Scotland, and he died on June 25, 1816, in Carlisle, Pennsylvania. One night on his way home he stopped at a tavern of a German farmer named Wolf in Washington County to rest and feed his horse. When he was leaving the tavern, the German's daughter Sabina Wolf brought his horse to the door. Hugh was so taken with her appearance, that after riding several miles, he rode back and asked her father for her hand in marriage. After convincing the father that the proposal was serious, the father agreed to the marriage. After they were married, Hugh sent his wife to Philadelphia to be educated in "ways polite."

Hugh came to America when he was five years old and settled in Pennsylvania. He was educated by a local clergyman and became a country school teacher. By saving and working hard he earned enough money to attend Princeton College. While at Princeton he earned money teaching two classes, and after graduation he tutored and then took charge of an academy in Maryland. He later moved to Philadelphia and studied theology.

In 1777 he served as a chaplain in a Pennsylvania during the New Jersey campaign. After the war he was elected to the legislature. In 1794 he sided with the insurgents in the Whiskey Insurrection. This was a protest against the government taxing the production of whiskey for the purpose of paying off the war debt of the Revolution. The rebellion was broken with the arrival of the militia under President Washington and Secretary of the Treasury Alexander Hamilton. In 1799 Hugh was appointed to the Supreme Court of Pennsylvania.

Sources: 1. *D.A.R. Lineage Book*, Vol. 5, page 233. 2. *The Pennsylvania Magazine of History & Biography*, Vol. XIII, 1889, pages 7–10.

Matthew Bridge

Matthew Bridge was born on July 18, 1721, in Lexington, Massachusetts, and he died on September 2, 1775, in Framingham, Massachusetts.

He married Anna Perkins on September 29, 1747. He graduated from Harvard in 1741 and was ordained on February 19, 1746. For 30 years he served as pastor of the Church of Christ in Framingham.

He was considered a good man and a good pastor though not a great preacher. It was said of him, "Good himself, he wished everybody else so." When the Revolution began he was among the first of the ministers to volunteer. He came to the aid of General Washington under the Great Elm at Cambridge. A popular myth developed that under this tree George Washington first took command of the American Army.

Pastor Bridge resembled Washington in physical appearance, and it was said that upon horseback it was difficult to tell them apart. The pastor was over six feet tall, with very black hair that fell in curls over the collar of his coat. He was said to have piercing black eyes and an erect form. Matthew was one of the first to join and became one of the first to die. He developed camp disease and died in September of 1775.

Sources: 1. "Harvard Soldiers and Sailors in the American Revolution," *Harvard Alumni Graduates Magazine*, 1920. 2. *Genealogy of the John Bridge Family in America* by William Dawson Bridge, 1924, page 79. 3. *Index of Obituaries 1740–1800*, page 130.

Thomas Brockway

Thomas Brockway was born on 20 January c. 1744 in Lyme, Connecticut, and he died there on July 5, 1807. He married Eunice Lathrop on December 8, 1772, and they had 12 children.

Thomas attended Yale College and graduated in 1768 and was ordained as pastor of the church of Lebanon, Connecticut, on June 24, 1772. He started with 69 people in his church, and during his ministry 139 were added. He served that church for 39 years until his health forced him to return to Lyme.

He served as chaplain in 1776 in the 4th Battalion, under the command of General Wadsworth, and in Colonel Samuel Selden's 4th Regiment. This Regiment was caught in the retreat and panic on 15 September, when the city of New York was invaded and captured by the British. Thomas served from July 15, 1776, until November 14, 1776. The regiment had many men killed and taken prisoner including Colonel Shelden who was captured. Thomas who was sick in camp at the time was removed in a horse cart by a boy. Later in the war when word reached him that the British landed at New London in September of 1781, he grabbed his musket and power horn and road off to battle. He rode the distance of 13 miles and arrived too late to be of service.

Sources: 1. *Magazine of the D.A.R.*, Vol. 2, Issues 2–4, page 30. 2. Sons of the American Revolution Application. 3. Tombstone. 4. *Connecticut Men in the Revolutionary War*, page 403. 5. *New England Families, Genealogical & Memorial* by William Richard Cutter, Vol. 3, 1914, page 1465. 6. *Yale and Her Honor Roll in the American Revolution 1775–1783* by Henry Phelps Johnston, 1888, page 252. 7. *D.A.R. Lineage Book*, Vol. 116, page 130.

John Conrad Bucher

John Bucher was born on June 10, 1730, in Switzerland, and he died on August 15, 1780, in Annville, Pennsylvania. He married Maria Magdalena Hoch on February 26, 1760. He came to America as an officer in the British Army in 1755. John served in the French-Indian War and was promoted several times.

In 1769 he became pastor of the German Reformed Church in Carlisle, Pennsylvania. He preached in English, French, and German languages. He never wrote out his sermons in full, rather he used briefs or notes, mainly in German.

When the Revolution began he was in ill health due to his previous service in the French and Indian War. He served as chaplain in a German Regiment in Pennsylvania. Because of his health he received a leave of absence from the regiment. He later received this letter from Colonel Baron Von Arnt, "High Honored Sir Chaplain—At my entry into the Regiment it came to my knowledge that you were attached to it as Chaplain, but are now at home on leave, but as I cannot have anybody belonging to the Regiment absent without the greatest necessity, I herewith give you the order to return to it without further delay, otherwise your resignation will be required, and someone else take your place, so I do hope to have the pleasure of seeing you with us soon. Baron Von Arnt, Colonel of the German Regiment." It is not known if Chaplain Bucher obeyed the summons or not.

Sources: 1. "Famous Pennsylvania Germans: Rev. John Conrad Bucher," *The Pennsylvania German*, Vol. IV, July 1903. 2. D.A.R. Lineage Book, Vol. 27, page 92. 3. *The Pennsylvania German Society*, Vol. XII, 1901, page 24. 4. Sons of the American Revolution Application.

Blackleach Burritt

Blackleach Burritt was born c. 1740 in Huntington, Connecticut, and he died on August 27, 1794, in Winhall, Vermont. After he graduated from Yale in 1765 he married Martha Welles and they had 12 children. After her death he married her sister Deborah in 1788, and they had two children.

Little is known of his childhood except of stories of his aerobatic performances on the roofs of buildings which he seemed to enjoy. He wanted to further his education, and his college tuition was paid for from money he inherited from his grandfather's estate. Upon graduation he studied theology and was licensed to preach in the Congregational Church on February 24, 1768.

In 1779 he was made pastor of the Congregational Church in Greenwich, Connecticut, and he became very outspoken for the American cause. On many occasions he took his musket into the pulpit for defense if necessary. Early in the morning of June 18, 1779, he was captured and taken to the Sugar House Prison in New York City.

A Tory account of his capture was found in Frank Moore's *Diary of the Revolution*, and it was credited to the *New Hampshire Gazette* of the issue of July 13, 1779:

> July 19.—Yesterday morning about 4 o'clock 32 Refugees [displaced Tories] commanded by Capt. Bonnell and other officers landed at Greenwich, in Connecticut. A thick fog favored their entrance, and they marched through the town undiscovered; but the Rebel guard being at length alarmed, and imagining the Refugees to be more numerous than in fact they were, fled with precipitation before them, and so close was the pursuit that some were overtaken and secured. The inhabitants of the town refused to open their doors to the Refugees, and reduced them to the necessity of entering the windows; notwithstanding which they plundered the houses of nothing but arms and ammunition, their principal object being horned cattle, of which they brought off 38, also 4 horses and 10 or 12 prisoners. Among the latter is a mist pestiferous Rebel Priest and preacher of sedition, who when taken swore that there was no firearms in his house, but upon his being cautioned against equivocation and threatened with the consequences which would result from persisting in it., his timid spouse produced his firelock and a cartouch box with eighteen rounds in it.

They later referred to the Rev. Blackleach Burritt as "an egregious Rebel who has frequently taken up arms and is of great repute in the Colony."

It is interesting to compare the above Tory account of the invasion of Greenwich with the account recorded in the patriot newspaper *Connecticut Gazette of New London* issue of July 8, 1779:

> New Haven, June 23.—Wednesday night last a party of the enemy from Long Island, landed at Green's Farms in Fairfield and plundered the house of Dr. Jessup of all they could carry off. The next night a considerable party landed at Stamford, who before the inhabitants could collect in force, made prisoners of 8 or 10 persons, among whom was a Mr. Blackleach Burritt, an ordained preacher, and took off 30 or 40 head of cattle, which they got on board under cover of the fire of a privateer which landed close in under a point. They likewise plundered all they could lay their hands on, broke windows, &c., committed many outrages.

The following is an account of the capture of the Reverend Burritt by Mrs. D.E. Sackett, the granddaughter of the Reverend Burritt: "He used often to take his musket into the pulpit for defence, and if need be, for ready joining in offensive warfare. At the seizure, some privates burst into the room. Grandmother sprang between the raised bayonets and her husband, holding them at bay, till an officer ordered them to desist. As they did not then allow him time enough, or had not enough of human kindness to let him dress, his poor wife followed, clothes in hand, bagging a chance for him to put some on, which finally they granted with rough oaths. She then followed to the water pleading for her two cows. They left her have one cow which she drove it back to her desolated home, grief for her lost husband and pity for her helpless children dividing her heart."

He was kept in prison for around 14 months. During this time he became very ill and was nursed by William Irving, the father of Washington Irving. He was released a few days before General Washington entered the city in 1780. It was reported that he expected to be released on a certain Monday. So he prepared a very spicy sermon for the Sunday before. The officers in charge of the prison were determined to prevent the sermon so they released him the Saturday night before. He was ordered to leave at once, which to his regret he did.

Blackleach served as pastor of several Presbyterian churches until his death from a fever in 1794. He was described as a person of physical strength and agility. As a preacher he was noted for fluency and a love of an argument.

Sources: 1. Sons of the American Revolution Application. 2. *D.A.R. Lineage Book*, Vol. 8, page 37. 3. *Gray Genealogy: Being a Genealogical Record and History of the Descendants of John Gray of Beverly, Mass* by Marcius Denison Raymond, 1887, page 17. 4. *Biographical Sketches of the Graduates of Yale College with Annals of the College*

History, Vol. 3, 1903, pages 103–105. *Sketch of Rev. Blackleach Burritt and Related Stratford Families: a Paper Read before the Fairfield Historical Society, 1892* by Raymond Marcius Denison, pages 13–27.

James Caldwell

James Caldwell was born on April 17, 1734, in Charlotte County, Virginia, and he died on November 24, 1781, in Elizabethtown, New Jersey. He married Hannah Ogden on March 14, 1763.

He was a man of middle height and powerfully made. His voice was described as a contrast. On usual occasions it was low, sweet and musical, but when he stood in front of a regiment, it rose to a clear and distinct roar over the roll of the drum and piercing notes of the fife.

James graduated from Princeton in 1759 and was licensed to preach in 1760. After his ordination in 1761 he joined the First Presbyterian Church of Elizabethtown, New Jersey. When New Jersey was called to arms at the beginning of the Revolution, Pastor Caldwell was elected the chaplain of the militia brigade under the command of Colonel Elias Dayton. Eighty-three men in his church joined the army with him.

Caldwell would preach at his church on Sunday and the rest of the week be with the army. His great popularity and influence filled the local Tories with rage, and his name was well-known to the British. Large rewards were offered for his capture. As a precaution, James traveled well-armed. When preaching he would walk up to the pulpit and place two loaded pistols before him. One of the common themes in his sermons was "There are times it is righteous to fight as well as to pray."

On July 15, 1776, news of the Declaration of Independence reached Caldwell and his regiment encamped at Johnstown, New York. Colonel Ebenezer Elmer gave the following account: "At twelve o'clock assemble was beat that the men might parade in order to receive a treat, and drink the State's health. When having made a barrel of grog, the declaration was read, and the following toast was given by parson Cardwell: 'Harmony, honor, and all prosperity to the free and independent United States of America; wise legislators, brave and victorious armies, both by sea and land, to the United States of America.' When three hearty cheers were given, and the grog flew round a-main."

For the next several years Elizabethtown became a target for various raids by the British. The people would flee to the countryside and return home to repair the damage caused by the British. In January of 1780 a Tory set fire to Caldwell's church. When the man confessed of his deed he added, "I am sorry that the black coated rebel was not burned in his own pulpit."

By the spring of 1780 the British had gained victories in the south and the Tories called upon the British to increase their presence in New Jersey and New York. General Cornwallis agreed, and in June he sent General Clinton towards Elizabethtown with nearly 6,000 troops. The war had finally reached the home of James Caldwell.

James relocated his family to Connecticut Farms, a few miles outside of Elizabethtown, where he thought they would be safe from the British. The British plan was to march through Elizabethtown, then through Connecticut Farms, then to Springfield, and from there to Morristown to engage General Washington's army. When news reached Caldwell that the British were approaching, he rode off to headquarters to alert the militia.

After he had ridden a short distance he began to fear for the safety of his family, so he rode back. When he reached home he told his wife Hannah that she and the children should accompany him to headquarters. She told him that they would be fine staying in their home. She went to the kitchen and brought him a cup of coffee, which he drank while on his horse. Before he finished the drink the British came in sight. His wife said they would be fine, so James rode off to headquarters.

Hannah soon became alarmed, when she began to see smoke rising in the distance and the screams of frightened women and children running through the streets. She began to straighten up her house and put on one of her best dresses, as she remarked, "to receive the British as a lady." She also took the time to lower some of their valuables into the well.

She took her baby into the bedroom, and as she gave the child to her nurse Katy, Hannah noticed a British soldier climbing over the fence and heading toward the house. She began saying to herself, "they will respect a mother, they will respect a mother." She was not aware that she was in plain sight of the window.

The soldier walked by the window and looked in and realized that this was the wife of the "Rebel Priest" James Caldwell. He raised the musket to the glass and fired. Mrs. Caldwell was hit in the heart and fell to the floor dead. The soldiers then entered the house and searched through Hannah's dress looking for valuables. They then torched the house and dragged her body outside and into the street where it laid for several hours. A neighbor later moved the body into one of the few buildings left standing.

Pastor Caldwell was a short distance away at Short Hills while his wife was being murdered. He was standing beside General Lafayette looking through an eyeglass toward Connecticut Farms. Looking at the smoking buildings he exclaimed, "Thank God, the fire is not in the direction of my house." He did not learn the fate of his wife until that evening when he passed by two soldiers talking in whispers, and he heard the name of "Mrs. Caldwell." When he was told what happened to his wife, it was reported that he "staggered like a smitten ox under the sudden blow, and turned pale as death." The next morning under a flag of truce he went to Connecticut Farms and found the body of his wife and his crying children. The small town was a heap of smoking ruins.

After the burial of his wife, James joined the army at Springfield and faced the advancing British army. During the battle he was in the hottest part of the fight. He noticed that one of the companies was running out of wadding for their muskets. (When the musket was being loaded and the musket ball was inserted into the muzzle, paper was shoved into the muzzle. This wadding stopped the ball and powder from falling out if the muzzle was lowered.)

Pastor Caldwell rode to the nearby Presbyterian Church, ran in, and went from pew to pew gathering up all the hymn books he could carry. The books were hymnals by the English minister Isaac Watts. He rode back to his men and gave them the books and said, "Giv'em Watts boys! Put Watts into 'em." With a laugh the soldiers began to tear pages out of the books and rammed them into their muskets. The Americans eventually turned the British back.

In November of 1781 a family by the name of Murray, who had relatives in Elizabethtown, had shown kindness to New Jersey prisoners held in New York. They came to the American fort near Elizabethtown under a flag of truce to share news with the prisoners' families. James Caldwell met them at the wharf to escort them to the fort. There was an American sentry at the entrance of the fort, and James passed the man several times. The third time James was carrying a small package, and the guard ordered him to stop thinking the package contained there was contraband in the bundle. James said it belonged to Mrs. Murray, and when he was told by the sentry that it must be opened, James turned to take it back to the ship to be opened there. The sentry fired hitting James in the chest and killing him.

The man who killed the pastor was James Morgan, a person who when he drank had a mean streak about him. Neighbors that knew him told a story about his temper. They said, "One day his child fell from a wall around a well and drowned. When Mr. Morgan found the dead child he took the dead child by the arms and beat the broken-hearted mother with the dead body of her own child until the neighbors rescued her."

Morgan was arrested and placed on trial. Most agreed that Morgan had been paid by the British to assassinate the pastor. Morgan was convicted of murder and sentenced to hang on January 28, 1782. Nicholas Murray kept a record of the execution: "The day appointed for his execution arrived. His grave was made in the northwestern corner of the churchyard in Westfield, away from all other graves; some even objecting to have his remains placed within the enclosure."

Morgan was taken to see his grave by the Sheriff, and then he was taken to church. The Reverend Elmer preached a sermon while the convicted man was seated in a chair in front of the pulpit. After the service he was taken away and hung.

After the death of James Caldwell there was great concern for his nine orphaned children. Many people donated money to care for them, including a donation of $100, from General George Washington a very large amount at the time. Friends stepped forward and helped raise the children, and General Lafayette took the third child, John, and educated him in France. James was buried next to his wife.

Sources: 1. Sons of the American Revolution Application. 2. *The Chaplains and Clergy of the Revolution* by Joel Tyler Headley, 1864, pages 217–232. 3. *D.A.R. Lineage Book*, Vol. 2, page 61. 4. *From Its European Antecedents to 1791—The United States Army Chaplaincy* by Parker C. Thompson, 1978, pages 195–196.

Jonas Clark

Jonas Clark was born on December 14, 1730, in Newton, Massachusetts, and he died on November 15, 1805, in Lexington, Massachusetts. He married Lucy Bowes, a cousin to John Hancock, on September 21, 1757, and they had 13 children. He graduated from Harvard in 1752 and entered into studies of theology. He was ordained and became pastor of a church in Lexington in 1755.

Jonas quickly settled into the simple life for a country pastor earning

80 pounds a year and 20 cords of wood. A member of his congregation described his voice: "His voice was powerful and agreeable, and when excited by his subject, which was often the case, it extended far and beyond the bounds of the meeting house, and could be heard distinctly by those who were anywhere in the immediate neighborhood."

When trouble between the colonies and England began to develop, Jonas quickly chose a side. He was no longer the obscure country preacher, but he became known through the region as an uncompromising patriot. Long before the talk of war began to fill the air, he thoroughly indoctrinated his people to be ready for a fight and to die rather than yield to arbitrary force.

John Hancock was a frequent visitor to his home, and it is not known if the pastor influenced Hancock, or if Hancock influenced the pastor. The Rev. William Ware of Cambridge wrote to Dr. Sprague and said, "It would not be beyond the truth to assert that there was no person at that time and in that vicinity—not only no clergyman, but no other person of whatever calling or profession, who took a firmer stand for the liberties of the county, or was more ready to perform the duties and endure the sacrifices of a patriot, than the minister of Lexington."

On April 18, 1775, after attending the Provincial Congress, John Hancock and Sam Adams were staying at the home of Jonas Clark. They were not aware that the British had landed and were marching toward Lexington. Paul Revere was riding to alert the countryside that the British were coming. A little after midnight Revere had reached the home of Pastor Clark and he was halted by Sergeant Munroe who was guarding the house. Munroe refused to allow Revere into the house, because the guard did not know Revere. Munroe said that the men inside the house had retired for the evening, and he did not want them disturbed by any noise in the house.

"Noise!" shouted Revere, "you'll have noise enough before long. The British troops are on their march and will disturb you all." Revere pushed by the sentry and knocked on the door. An upstairs window opened and John Hancock looked out and recognizing Paul Revere he told him to enter the house.

The big question with Hancock and Adams was if the people would fight. Would a bunch of shop keepers and farmers with very little military training, if any, stand up to the highly professional best trained army in the world? When Pastor Clark was asked if they would fight his reply was

"I have trained them. They would fight, and if need be die, too, under the shadow of the house of God."

It was decided that the militia needed to be alarmed, and for better security Hancock and Adams needed to be moved to safety. Hancock objected, saying, "it should never be said of him, that he had turned his back upon the British." He was then convinced of the importance of his preservation to the country, so he agreed to leave. The two men were escorted about two miles the north of Pastor Clark's home. Paul Revere rode on to warn Concord and was later captured by the British. After questioning, he was released and he walked back to Lexington as the battle was about to take place.

The militia was summoned to meet on the Lexington green beside the church, where the men listened to the sermons of Jonas Clark every Sunday. The home of Jonas Clark was about a five minute walk to the Lexington green, and you could see the green from a front window. At 2 in the morning of the 19th of April Captain John Parker called roll and about 130 men answered to their names. According to Jonas Clark, "The militia assembled and sent out observers to collect intelligence on the British movements; after a while one of them returned and reported that all was quiet, at which point the militia dispersed." Captain Parker dismissed them with orders to appear again with the beat of a drum. Some men went back home, and a large group of them went into Buckman's tavern.

The British troops by day break were near Lexington, when they were spotted by a patriot who rode to warn Captain Parker. The militia had earlier sent out several patrols, but they had been captured by the British. When the news of the advancing British reached Captain Parker, he ordered alarm guns to be fired and the drum beat to arms. In a matter of minutes the British would be in Lexington. Pastor Clark and about 70 of his male congregants stood with their muskets on Lexington green ready to face the British. There were also some 30 or 40 spectators standing nearby and a few with muskets. Around 5 in the morning these 70 ill-trained citizen soldiers were facing about 400 of the finest trained soldiers in the world.

Captain John Parker ordered his men, "do not fire unless fired upon." One of the men present said years later that Parker's order was "Stand your ground. Don't fire unless fired upon, but if they mean to have a war, let it began here." Paul Revere recalled the order as having been "Let the soldiers pass by. Do not molest them without they begin first." Regardless what was the correct order given, it was clear that Captain Parker did not want to have the Americans fire the first shot.

When the British entered the green their commander told his men to hold their fire. He then shouted to the Americans, "Disperse, ye rebels; lay down your arms and disperse!" The Americans stood their ground. The British officer repeated his order with a curse. Some accounts say that the officer then ordered his men to fire upon the rebels. Most accounts say that some unknown person fired the first shot.

When the unknown shot was fired many of the British opened fired. None of the Americans were hit, and they believed that the first British volley was just powder with no shot. When the British fired a second volley some Americans began to fall. John Munroe recalled, "Seeing no one I said to my relative, Ebenezer Munroe, Jr., that they had fired nothing but powder. On the second discharge, Ebenezer replied, 'They have fired something besides powder now, for I am wounded in the arm.'"

The militia began to pull back, when Captain Parker realized he was out numbered and ordered his men to disperse. Scattered firing on both sides continued as the Americans left the field. After the firing had stopped and the combatants had left the field, Pastor Clark surveyed the green by his church. He saw eight of his congregation dead and 10 wounded. The British had one man wounded in the leg and another man wounded in the hand. Pastor Clark later said, "From this day, will be dated the liberty of the world."

The following men died at Lexington in the first battle of the Revolution:

1. Jonathon Harrington was fatally wounded by a musket ball and crawled back to his home. His wife at the window saw him crawling across the road to their home. She came outside to help him and he died at her feet.
2. Caleb Harrington who had been sent to the meeting house before the battle to obtain a quantity of powder stored there was attempting to escape from the meeting house when he was shot and killed.
3. Jonas Parker was wounded and was attempting to reload after firing his first shot. He frequently had said, "I will never run from British troops." Jonas was bayoneted to death as he faced the enemy.
4. Isaac Muzzy was killed on the green near where the line was formed.
5. Robert Munroe was bayonetted on the green near where the line was formed. He was the oldest to die at the age of 63.

6. John Brown was killed off the green.
7. Samuel Hadley was killed off the green.
8. Asahel Porter had been taken prisoner on the march to Lexington and saw a chance to escape, and he was shot near the green.

On the first anniversary of the Battle of Lexington, Clark preached a sermon based upon his eyewitness testimony of the event. He called his sermon "The Fate of Blood-Thirsty Oppressors and God's Tender Care of His Distressed People." He added this narrative to his printed sermon: "So far from firing first upon the King's troops, upon the most careful enquiry, it appears that but a very few of our people fired upon the troops, they were wounded themselves, or saw others killed, or wounded by them; and looking upon it as next to impossible for them to escape."

Sources: 1. Sons of the American Revolution Application. 2. *The Chaplains and Clergy of the Revolution* by Joel Tyler Headley, 1864, pages 74–82. 3. *D.A.R. Lineage Book*, Vol. 3, page 60. 4. *The New England Clergy and the Revolution* by Alice Baldwin, 1928, pages 94–95. 5. *History of the Battle of Lexington: On the Morning of the 19th April 1775* by Elias Phinney, pages 10–22. 6. *History of Lexington* by Charles Hudson, 140–154. 7. Sermon preached by Jonas Clark April 19, 1776.

Ebenezer Cleveland

Ebenezer Cleveland was born on January 5, 1725, in Canterbury, Connecticut, and he died on July 4, 1805, in Rockport, Massachusetts. He married Abigail Stevens in 1746, and they had 12 children. While in college at Yale Ebenezer and his younger brother John Cleveland (also in this book) had a conflict with the administration. The two boys had refused to repent for attending a Separatist congregation, so they were expelled from college in 1745. Ebenezer received his degree from Yale in 1748. (The Separatists were English Protestants who made up the extreme wing of Puritanism. The Separatists were severely critical of the Church of England and wanted to either destroy it or separate from it.)

Ebenezer was ordained in 1755 and served at the church in Sandy Bay in the same year. He served as a chaplain to a Massachusetts' Regiment in the French and Indian War from 1756 to 1760. His brother John also served as a chaplain. They were both at Ticonderoga on July 8, 1758, and the expedition to Canada. At Ticonderoga the American militiamen fought with the British troops and were soundly defeated by the French.

Ebenezer fought at the Battle of Bunker Hill in June of 1775. He served as chaplain under the command of Colonel Jonathan Ward's 21st Infantry Regiment from January 1, 1776, until the end of the year. His regiment was with General Washington at the Battle of Long Island. He may have also been at the Battle of Trenton.

Sources: 1. *Biographical Sketches of the Graduates of Yale College with Annals of the College History, Vol. II May 1745–May 1763*, 1896, pages 196–197. 2. Tombstone 3. *The History of Woburn, Middlesex County, Mass.* by Samuel Sewall, 1868, page 604.

John Cleveland

John Cleveland was born on April 12, 1722, in Dartmouth, Massachusetts, and he died on April 22, 1799, in Ipswich, Massachusetts. He married Mary Dodge on July 31, 1747, and they had seven children. Mary died of cancer on April 21, 1768, and he then married Mary Neal. He was going to become a farmer, but an accident when he was young disabled him from hard physical labor so he sought a college education. While in college at Yale, he and his brother Ebenezer (also in this book) had a conflict with the administration. The two boys had refused to repent for attending a Separatist congregation so they were expelled from college in 1745.

After his expulsion, John served two years as a minister to a Separatist society in Boston before becoming pastor of a new Separatist church at Chebacco, Massachusetts. He was ordained on February 25, 1747. John served in the French and Indian War as a chaplain to Colonel Jonathan Bagley. He was in the battle at Fort Ticonderoga on July 8, 1758.

When the Revolution began, he joined the army from June to November 1775 as chaplain in Colonel Little's Regiment, 17th Infantry. His four sons also served in the war. For a short time in the fall of 1776 John served as chaplain in Colonel Jonathan Cogswell's Essex County Regiment around New York. It was said with some exaggeration that he preached all the men of his parish into the army. While in the army Pastor Cleveland once complained that "profane swearing seems to be the naturalized language of the regulars. Their gaming, robbery, and thievery epitomized the immorality and corruption that colonists feared was rampant in English society."

A sermon at death by the Rev. Elijah Parish was printed, and it bears ample testimony to his character. As thus commemorated, "tho' of a mild spirit, he was decided in his opinions; tho' gentle in his manner, he was independent in his conduct.... We recollect his pleasing address, his meekness of temper, the suavity of his manners, and the uniform propriety of his deportment.... Charity and good nature were prominent features of his character."

Sources: 1. John Cleveland Papers at the Peabody Essex Museum. 2. *New World Faiths: Religion in Colonial America* by Jon Butler. 3. *The History of Woburn, Middlesex County, Mass.* by Samuel Sewall, 1868, pages 603–604. 4. *Cleveland Genealogy* by Cleveland & Cleveland. 5. *Biographical Sketches of the Graduates of Yale College with Annals of the College History, Vol. II May 1745–May 1763*, 1896, pages 29–35.

John Cleveland

John Cleveland was born on March 26, 1738, in Blue Run, Virginia, and he died on March 25, 1825, in Cleveland Ferry, South Carolina. He married Mary Martha McCann in 1759 and they had seven children. He was known as "the Father of Baptist Principles."

He served as a chaplain with the rank of Lieutenant in the North Carolina Militia in the Revolution under his brother Colonel Benjamin Cleveland. John Cleveland is mentioned in the pension application of Thomas Majors as serving as an Ensign in 1780 under the command of Colonel Benjamin Cleveland. John was at the Battle of Kings Mountain on October 7, 1780. His regiment attacked the main Tory force at the base of the mountain. This was a bloody fight, often hand-to hand against the militias of both sides. Some of the combatants were neighbors. The battle lasted a little over an hour, and it resulted in an important patriot victory. John received 25 pounds and 12 shillings for his service as chaplain.

After the war, John moved and was one of the first settlers in Pickens District of South Carolina. He preached at the Chauga Baptist Church in Oconee County, South Carolina. It was said of him, "he was good to his neighbors and the poor, kind to his many darkies, who thought their master better than any other man." He later preached in Franklin County, Georgia.

One person said of his preaching, "When he would preach, the wicked people would take him out of the house and beat him, but he would preach on, and when they let him go, would mount a stump or log and finish his sermon."

As he got older and after the death of his wife, Pastor John went to live with his son-in-law in South Carolina. He died there in 1825.

Sources: 1. *The Genealogy of the Cleveland and Cleaveland Families* by Edmund J. Cleveland and Horace G. Cleveland, 1899, Vol. III, pages 2058–2059. 2. State of North Carolina Archives, Revolutionary Army Accounts, Vol. A, page 193. 3. Tombstone. 4. U.S. Census 1820. 5. Pension Application of Thomas Majors S30564.

Noah Cooke

Noah Cooke was born on October 8, 1749, in Hadley, Massachusetts, and he died on October 15, 1829, in Keene, New Hampshire. He married Mary Rockwood on January 11, 1784, in New Hampshire. He graduated from Harvard in 1769 and received his license to preach in 1771.

Pastor Cooke served in the army as a chaplain from 1775 until 1780 and achieved the rank of Colonel. He served in the 5th Infantry of the Continental Army under Colonel John Starks. He later served in the 8th Infantry under Colonel Enoch Poor. In September of 1777 he was assigned to hospital chaplaincy by Congress.

When he left the army in 1780 he moved to Keene, New Hampshire, and studied law. He practiced law for several years in Keene, was appointed librarian of the Social Library, and was the first president of the General Monadnock Society for the promotion of Morals.

Sources: 1. *The United States Army Chaplaincy* by Parker Thompson, Vol. 1, page 171. 2. New Hampshire, Death & Burial Records 1654–1949. 3. *Keene's Revolutionary Soldiers*, 1897.

Robert Cooper

Robert Cooper was born in 1732 in Ireland, and he died on April 5, 1805, in Pennsylvania. He married Elizabeth Kearsley and they had four children. At the age of nine he came to America with his widowed mother. He graduated from the College of New Jersey in 1763 and was ordained a pastor on November 21, 1765. He preached at the Middle Spring Congregation church near Shippensburg, Pennsylvania, for 31 years.

His personal appearance was not commanding. He was described as "low in stature and of a thin, spare habit. His face considerably resembled a print of melancholy." Pastor Cooper accompanied his men to the front as their chaplain, and when failing health forced him to resign his commission he stated in his resignation letter, "I bore arms, marched and countermarched through the Jerseys on foot, so long as I was able, and stood in line of battle at Trenton."

Sources: 1. *History of Middle Spring Presbyterian Church, Middle Spring, Pa. 1738–1900*, 1900, pages 31 and 208–209. 2. *Annals of the American Pulpit, Vol. III* by the Rev. William B. Sprague, 1860. 3. *Rev. C. P. Wing's History of Cumberland County*, 1879, page 242.

John Cordell

John Cordell was born in 1749 in Wiltshire, England. And he died in April of 1800 in Virginia. He married Judith Blackwell on June 19, 1779. He was ordained in the Episcopal Church.

He served as chaplain with the rank of a Captain under the command of General Morgan in the 11th Virginia Regiment. He was captured at the Battle of Brandywine on September 11, 1777, and he may have been taken to the Walnut Street Prison in Philadelphia. Judith filed for a widow's pension, writing, "I am the widow of the late Rev'd. John Cordell who was first a Captain & then a Chaplain in the Virginia Line in the army of the Revolution, but whether of the Continental or State lines I do not know—he entered the army at an early period of the war, but at what precise time I do not know—that by reason of the loss of my memory through age & recent illness I cannot remember many particulars respecting his services—but I know that he went to the North & was in the army & was captured at the battle of Brandywine, as he always stated, & was confined some months in Philadelphia, in prison, & that he came home to Fauquier Co Virginia in the year 1779. Shortly afterwards he returned to the army & went [ink blot covers several words] the army several times, & sometimes was gone several months before he returned, and that he continued to do so for two or three years after we were married."

After John was released, he continued to serve various times until he was discharged on February 10, 1781. He received 4,000 acres of land for his service and his wife received a yearly widow's pension of $480.

Sources: 1. Pension application W9814. 2. *From Its European Antecedents to 1791—The United States Army Chaplaincy* by Parker C. Thompson, 1978, page 156.

John Craighead

John Craighead was born in 1742 in Cumberland County, Pennsylvania, and he died on April 20, 1799, in Franklin County, Pennsylvania. He married Jenny Jane Boyd before 1775. He graduated at the College of New Jersey in 1763 and was ordained to preach in the Presbytery of Donegal around 1767. He was installed as pastor of Rocky Spring Church near Chambersburg, Pennsylvania on April 13, 1768. He preached there until 1798.

One biographer of Pastor Craighead wrote that he preached "in glowing terms, Jesus Christ, the only hope of salvation, and after the delivery of the message, in eloquent and patriotic strains exhorted the youth of his congregation to rise up and join the noble band, then engaged under the immortal Washington, in struggling to free our beloved country from British oppression." After the speech was given the whole congregation rose and declared their willingness to march to the conflict.

The story was told that Pastor Craighead was once reprimanded, while he was preaching a sermon about joining the cause of liberty by a concerned mother who told him, "Yer always preaching to the boys about it, but I dinna think ye'd be very likely to go yerself." So the pastor organized the men in his congregation and went through the entire war with them as their chaplain and captain. He fought with Washington at Trenton and Princeton.

Sources: 1. *Centennial Memorial of the Presbytery of Carlisle*, Vol. 2, pages 47–48. 2. *Nevin's Encyclopedia*, page 162. 3. Tombstone. 4. *History of Middle Spring Presbyterian Church, Middle Spring, Pa. 1738-1900*, 1900, pages 208 and 217. 5. *Pennsylvania Province and State History, 1609-1790*, Vol. II, pages 416-417.

Charles Cummings

Charles Cummings was born in 1732 in Donegal County, Ireland, and he died on March 25, 1812, in Washington County, Virginia. He married Mildred Millicent Carter around 1775. He came to America at the age of 18 and entered Carlisle College in Pennsylvania. When he graduated he went to Lancaster County, Virginia, and he taught school and studied theology with the Rev. James Waddell. He was licensed to preach by

Hanover Presbytery on April 17, 1766. He became pastor of Brown's meeting-house congregation in 1767. In 1773 he was called to minister to two congregations on the Holston, and he settled near Abingdon.

While there Pastor Cummings was known as a fighter. Because of the fear of Indian attacks he always carried a gun, even to church. Every Sunday he would "put on his shot-pouch, shoulder his rifle, mount his horse and ride to church." After placing his weapons within reach, he would preach two sermons with a short interval between.

One story is told how he saved the town from an Indian attack by self-scalping. As the story goes, Indians attacked while the pastor was riding in a wagon, and as he jumped to safety his wig caught in the brush. The Indians were so surprised to see a "scalp" hanging on a limb that they hesitated to attack the town. This provided time for Cummings to organize a defense.

Another time occurred in 1776 when Cummings was living in a fort with his family. He with a servant and three neighbors went by wagon to a farm on an errand, and they were attacked by a party of Indians. The Indians opened fire from the woods that bordered the road. Pastor Cummings and the others returned fire and a skirmish began. Cummings was out in the open and two of the men were shot dead. The pastor told his servant to follow him, and they ran into some bushes. The Indians began to yell and raced toward the two men. Fortunately, men from the fort heard the shots and came to the relief of the attacked party. They got there just as the Indians had turned on Cummings and his servant. Now outnumbered, the Indians fled.

In 1776 he accompanied the troops under Colonel Christian in their expedition against the Cherokees. Colonel William Christian commanded the 1st Battalion of Virginia Militia, and they marched on the Cherokee Indians on October 6, 1776. They found most of the Indian towns abandoned, and later the Indians came in and sued for peace. Those towns that did not ask for peace were destroyed. When the expedition was completed Colonel Christian, along with Pastor Cummings, returned to the Long Islands of Holston.

In the 1780s Southwestern Virginians had felt overlooked by the state government, and a secessionist movement began to grow. Pastor Cummings supported those that wanted to withdraw from Virginia and join with east Tennessee to create a "Greater State of Franklin." They named the new state after Benjamin Franklin hoping to gain favor. Virginia Governor Patrick Henry learned of the movement and suppressed it.

The will of Pastor Cummings reveals that he owned two slaves and that he was a widower: "In the Name of God Amen. I Charles Cumming of Washington County and State of Virginia minister of the Gospel being of perfect and disposing mind and memory do make and ordain this my last will and testament. I give and bequeath to my son John all the personal property which he has now in his possession. To my son James my negro Sam. After John gets the two ewes and lambs which I have given him. To my daughter Mary Swingle and her heirs forever one tract of land, two hundred acres lying in Washington County, known by the name of Boswells place. To my son Charles my silver shoebuckles, 1 knee buckles and stock buckle. To each of my sons and daughters one chair. To my daughter Amelia Balfour my riding mare. To my grand daughter Amelia Carter Cummings sixty pounds Virginia currency to be paid her by her father when she arrives at the age of twenty one years of age or when she marries which ever may first happen. I empower and authorize my son James to sell a negro girl named Hannah which I had intended for my said grand daughter.My books in the care of my son James and should any of my grandsons study Latin or Greek languages or divinity my will and pleasure is that they may have such of my books as they may need for that purpose. I do hereby appoint my sons Jams and Robert and my son in law John Gibson Executors. Remove all former wills and testaments by me. This second day of May in the year of our Lord 1807, Edward Campbell, John Campbell, James Piper. 17th day of December 1818."

Sources: 1. Presbyterian Heritage Center at Montreat website. 2. *Encyclopedia of the Presbyterian Church in the United States of America*, page 653. 3. *The Chaplains and Clergy of the Revolution* by Joel Tyler Headley, 1864, pages 273-275. 4. *Annals of Augusta County* by Jos. A. Waddell, 1886, pages 52-53. 5. *A Popular History of the Presbyterian Church* by Jacob Harris Patton, 1990, page 216.

Manassah Cutler

Manassah Cutler was born on May 13, 1742, in Killingly, Connecticut, and he died on July 28, 1823, in Hamilton, Connecticut. He married Mary Balch on September 1, 1766. Manassah graduated from Yale in 1765, taught school, then ran a merchant business, and at times practiced law. He entered the ministry in 1771 and became pastor of a Congregational Church in Ipswich, Massachusetts.

In 1776 he served as a chaplain for a few months in the 11th Massachusetts Regiment commanded by Colonel Francis. In 1778 he became chaplain to General Jonathan Titcomb's Brigade, and he took part in General John Sullivan's expedition to Rhode Island. When he returned from Rhode Island, he trained in medicine to supplement his income as a minister.

He was also forced to take up medicine, because the colonial's money was practically worthless during the war. By May of 1781 the Continental dollar had become so worthless that they ceased to circulate it as money. Pastor Cutler wrote, "In 1777 money had depreciated as much, at least, as five for one, but in 1779 it was nearer twenty to one. I have spent considerable of an estate in the support of my family, and now am driven to the practice of physic."

During much of the Revolutionary War Manassah kept a journal of his daily activities. Various pages have been lost over the years, but what remains gives an interesting account of things he did and saw during the war. Certain entries are included here while he was a chaplain

Only part of this entry exists for April 19, 1775, which is the day of the Battle of Lexington and Concord:

> At sunset we got almost into Cambridge, and met our people just after they fired their last gun. The British fought upon a retreat from Concord to Cambridge, where they had boats to take them on board for Boston. It is not known how many were killed on either side. Mr. Willard and I went to College, and from thence to Mr. Holyoke's, where we lodged.
>
> Apr. 2, Thurs. A vast number of men in Cambridge, and coming in from all quarters. We went to Metomeny to see the dead. The regulars [British troops] lay principally in the streets, but our men in homes and barns. It was supposed that about 30 provincials and 50 regulars were killed. In the afternoon we returned home. Mr. Jackson and Brother Balch and family came to our house.
>
> Apr. 21, Fri. Set out for Cambridge again. Rode to Newell's in Lynn. Upon hearing that the soldiers were making such movements that it was thought that they would strike upon Salem or Marblehead we returned. This night an alarm from Ipswich, but nothing more.
>
> May 3, Wed. This morning viewed Boston from Dorchester Hill. Saw the Regulars at work fortifying Beacon Hill and the Neck. We came to Roxbury, and went as far as the Georges Tavern. The Regular sentinels and ours were about forty rods asunder. Lodged at Watertown.
>
> May 8, Mon. By this time we obtained an exact account of the number of the Provincials that were killed and wounded in the battle of the 19th: 40 killed and 20 wounded. The number of Regulars that went out was 800 in the first brigade, and 1,200 in the second, who met first at Lexington. It is pretty certain that near

800 regulars were taken, killed, or wounded, and many more were surfeited, so that their loss upon the whole is said to be at least 500. It is not supposed that more than 300 of our men were actually engaged in battle at a time for the whole day, but yet the Regulars, who had two field pieces, fled with surprising precipitation. They took only two prisoners, but what they killed or let go again.

June 17, Saturday [the battle of Bunker Hill begins]. Heard that there was an engagement at Charlestown. In the afternoon saw a very great smoke, and at night saw the light of the fire which was the burning of Charlestown by the Regular forces. At the same time there was a very smart engagement at a small breastwork raided by our people upon Bunker's Hill. The fire was said to be the heaviest for near two hours ever known in America. There was constant cannonading from Boston, and three or four large ships. They forced the entrenchments and obliged our people to retreat. It was supposed that there were 5,000 Regulars, and not more than 2,000 or 3,000 of our men that actually engaged in the fight. Our loss is supposed to be about 50 killed and 20 or 30 taken prisoners. The enemy's loss is said to be 1,400 privates killed and wounded and 84 officers.

June 19, Monday. Went to the army. Went down upon a hill between Winter Hill and Bunker Hill, when a shot from a twelve pounder came very near us and fell beyond us. In the afternoon another shot from the same cannon fell within the breastwork at Ran's Hill. I was very near where it fell. Lodged at Watertown.

June 24, Sat. Prayed this morning with the soldiers. Viewed the ground with a glass where the late battle was on Bunker Hill.

In September of 1775 Colonel Benedict Arnold led an army of 1,100 men from Cambridge to the gates of Quebec City in Canada.

Sept. 13, Wed. This morning two or three companies of Riflemen marched by on their way to Quebec.

Sept. 14, Thurs. About 1,000 men marched by on their way to Quebec, under command of Colonel Arnold.

The Siege of Boston was from April 19, 1775, to March 17, 1776. It began after the Battles of Lexington and Concord, when the militia from the surrounding communities around Boston blocked the land access to Boston while leaving the British forces inside the city.

The Americans needed siege guns to force the British out of Boston. Washington sent Colonel Henry Knox and his men to retrieve the heavy artillery that the Americans had captured at Fort Ticonderoga. In the dead of winter Henry Knox did the impossible and brought the heavy guns across the frozen Hudson and Connecticut rivers and arrived at Cambridge on January 24, 1776.

By March the guns were in place and a bombardment of Boston began. The British decided it was time to leave Boston and began to make preparations to leave by ships in the harbor. On 17 March 1776 the winds were favorable and British General Howe began to board the ships. By 9 a.m. 120 ships had departed with more than 11,000 people aboard.

> Mar. 3, Lord's Day. Preached at Topsfield for Mr. Shaw. Heard that our troops began Saturday to bombard Boston.
>
> Mar. 4, Mon. Set out for Cambridge, but went no farther than Salem. A very heavy firing at Boston all night.
>
> Mar. 17, Lord's Day. Preached. This day the Regular Troops, under command of General Howe, evacuated Boston in a surprising manner. They went off in so great haste that they left a large number of their cannon and several of their best mortars, with many other valuable articles. The King's stores that are left are computed at three hundred thousand pounds sterling. What was the occasion of so precipitate a flight is not certainly known. It is generally compared to the flight of the Assyrians.

When Manassah was commissioned as a chaplain in the Massachusetts on September 5, 1776, his commission read:

> We, being informed of your Exemplary Life and Manners, and reposing special Trust and Confidence in your Abilities and good Conduct, Do by these Presence, constitute and appoint you, the said Manasseh Cutler to be Chaplain of the Regiment drafted out of the Militia of this State on the Continental Establishment for the defense and security of the Town and Harbor of Boston, whereof Ebenezer Francis, Esq. is Colonel.
>
> You are therefore carefully and diligently to inculcate in the minds of the Soldiers of said Regiment, as well by Example as Precept, the Duties of Religion and Morality, & a fervent Love of their Country, and in all respects discharge the Duty of a Chaplain in said Regiment—Observing, from time to time, such Orders and Instructions as you shall receive from your superior Officers. In pursuance if the Trust reposed in you, for which this shall be your Sufficient Warrant.

After Manassah received his commission he wrote in his diary about leaving his congregation and assuming his new position as an army chaplain.

> Aug. 25, Lord's Day. Preached. Received a message from Colonel Francis to go to Dorchester and supply his regiment as Chaplain, with which I acquainted the church and congregation after meeting, and there was no objection.
>
> Sept. 3, Tues. Went to Dorchester. Prayed with the regiment.
>
> Sept. 4, Wed. live in the same barracks with the field officers.
>
> Sept. 8, Lord's Day. Preached to the regiment. Found it hard to speak abroad.
>
> Oct. 13, Lord's Day. Our regiment marched up to the Meeting House. It being sacrament, I administered the ordinance.
>
> Oct. 16, Wed. Our regiment was reviewed by the General attended by his Aids-de-camp. I went on to the parade with the others, and took my post on the right wing. As the General began to march I paid the first salute with the fire-lock. The regiment made a very handsome appearance.

Oct. 27. Lord's Day. The regiment marched up to the Meeting House. I preached, and in the afternoon preached a sermon to the soldiers.

Nov. 30, Sat. Very rainy. The Regiment breaking up. All taken off duty. I set out for home with Captain Dodge about 12 o'clock, and got home about 9 o'clock in the evening, very wet, and much fatigued.

The Saratoga campaign from September 19, 1777, to October 7, 1777, was an important victory by the Americans over General Burgoyne and the British army. This American victory marked a turning point in the Revolutionary War. Burgoyne's defeat convinced the French that the Americans could win this war. French King Louis XVI began to send soldiers, supplies, and loans to the Americans. Congress declared December 18, 1777, as a national day of Thanksgiving and praise. This became the nation's first official observance of a holiday with that name.

Oct. 23, Thurs. Mr. Forbes here to dine. Received the agreeable intelligence of the surrender of General Burgoyne and his whole army to General Gates as prisoners of war. A general discharge of cannon at Boston, Marblehead, Salem, Beverly, Cape Ann, Newbury, and Portsmouth, and all the ships and vessels of force in all those harbors.

Nov. 5, Wed. Set out for Boston, in order to see Burgoyne's army come into Cambridge. Brother Balch went with me. We dined at Newell's and lodged at Mr. Everett's.

Nov. 7, Fri. Rode to Cambridge. Saw, in the barracks the regular troops who came in yesterday. About 12 o'clock Burgoyne came into town, attended by a party of the American Light Horse as a guard. General Glover rode with him, and two British generals, Phillips and Hamilton. Immediately after the Hessian troops came in, preceded and followed by a large guard of militia. They appeared to be as dull, heavy molded, and dirty a pack as ever I saw. The procession reached near three miles. I saw, likewise, General Riedesel, the commander of the Hessians, a very fine man. He was accompanied with two or three more Hessian generals. They barracked at Winter Hill, the Regulars at Prospect Hill. Returned home much fatigued.

The Battle of Rhode Island took place on August 29, 1778. American General John Sullivan began to withdraw his forces after abandoning their siege of Newport, Rhode Island. British forces supported by their navy attacked the Americans as they retreated. The battle ended in a draw however, and the Americans withdrew from the area.

Aug. 4, Tuesday. General Titcomb called on me on his way to Rhode Island, and invited me to go with him as Chaplain to his brigade on the present expedition.

Aug. 7, Friday. Preparing to set out for Rhode Island, tomorrow.

Aug. 8, Sat. Set out for Rhode Island with Captain Brown and Cabot. Crossed Winnissimet Ferry. Dined in Boston at Mr. Williams. The day exceeding hot. Set out from Boston at 5 o'clock; made our next stage beyond Milton Meeting House, at sunset, where we oated and drank coffee. Rode on to Noyes, at Stotenham; refreshed ourselves and horses about 12 o'clock, but did not go into the house. A very fine evening, cool and comfortable, far better riding than in the day time. Rode on seven miles further; stopped at a farmer's house, but the house was filled with soldiers, and we were obliged to turn into the barn. I slept on straw, between Captains Cabot and Brown, and very sound, until five in the morning, when the mustering of the soldiers waked us, and we immediately rose.

Aug. 10, Monday. This morning I crossed on to Rhode Island, and joined General Titcomb's brigade. Dined with him and a number of gentlemen on the ground abroad, not having any quarters. Slept this night in the officer's room at the barracks in the fort taken up by Colonel Wade. Last evening a fleet was seen off the harbor, of about eighteen or twenty sail, which came up near the Lighthouse and anchored. Several ships of the line, but unknown who, or where whence. About 10 o'clock the French fleet, that lay above the town of Newport, came to sail, and went out in pursuit of them. As they passed the town and forts, the ships began and kept up an incessant fire, until they all passed. The roar of the cannon at times was such as to make but one continued sound, with at any distinction of guns. The fleet in the offing, which proved to be a fleet from New York, immediately put to sea, and by dark the French fleet in pursuit of them was out of sight of land.

The British ships were commanded by Lord Howe and had departed New York. The French fleet engaged them, and as they prepared for battle a major storm broke out. It raged for two days and scattered both fleets. On August 11, 1778, General Sullivan began siege operations and began to move closer to the British lines on the 15th.

Aug. 11, Tuesday. The General procured a chamber for quarters at one of Browning's, a Quaker. Invited me to live with him. This morning the wind at N.E. blew pretty hard; cloudy and rainy. At 4 o'clock the whole army paraded, and was reviewed by the general officers. The order of battle and encampment: Front line, Varnum's and Cornell's Brigades on the right, Glover's and Colonel Commanding Greene's do, on the left. The second line, commanded by Major-General Hancock, Lovel's Brigade on the right, Titcomb's on the left. The light corps, consisting of Jackson's Corps, Boston Independents and Light Infantry, and 50 men from each brigade in the front line, commanded by Colonel Commanding Leviston. The reserve, consisting of Holden's and Brown's regiments, commanded by Colonel Commanding West. A flanking division on each wing of the army, and a flanking party to each wing of each line, consisting of volunteers and militia. A body of horse, commanded by General Whipple. The right wing of the whole army commanded by Major-General Greene; the left by the Marquis de la Fayette.

Aug. 12, Wednesday. This morning, orders for the whole army to be paraded at 6 o'clock for advancing toward the enemy's lines. The storm increasing violently, prevented. A great number of the militia, having no tents, were obliged to continue out in the storm without any shelter. Colonel Thorndike resigned, and

Colonel Wadsworth appointed. Captains Brown and Cabot took lodgings at our quarters.

Aug. 15, Saturday. At 6 o'clock a signal gun from the right fired as a signal for the whole army to parade. Half after six two cannons were fired for signals for forming into columns. Three cannons the signal for marching. The front line advanced in four columns, and the second line in two columns, commanded by their respective Brigadiers. Flanking divisions and flanking partie marched in their respective stations. The Light-corps advanced. Pioneers marched advanced of each division to remove walls, etc. The artillery and ammunition wagons between the first and second line; the baggage between the second line and the reserves. The reserved moved in one column. I had a fine prospect of the whole army as it moved off from Butt's Hill, where we first encamped. Then made a very good appearance. The army marched about three miles and halted. A council of war was held by the general officers, who advanced, and marked out the ground for encamping. No appearance of an attack from the enemy. The army extended quite across the Island from water to water. At 2 o'clock advanced and came upon the ground, about a mile and a half from the enemy's lines, directly in their front. They fired a few cannon. As soon as our brigade was halted on the ground, I returned to our old quarters and tarried the night. Was much pleased with the kindness and benevolence of Mr. Thomas Browning at whose house we quartered.

Aug. 17, Monday. Morning foggy. After it cleared away rode down to the lines with Colonel Thorndike. Had a fine view of the enemy's lines from the top of the house, about a quarter of a mile distance, and little advanced of our picket. The enemy had fired for some time in the morning, but had ceased for some hours. While we were on the house they begun their fire again from the redoubts. Several shots passed us on each side and fell beyond us. Made a shocking whistling. Soon after we left the house a shot came through it. Found our situation not very safe or agreeable. Stood by the Marquis when a cannon ball just passed us. Was pleased with his firmness, bit found I had nothing to boast on my won, and as I had no business in danger concluded to stay no longer lest I should happen to pay too dear for my curiosity.

Aug. 18, Tuesday. Morning foggy. As soon as it cleared off the enemy began to fire on the works thrown up last night, which were considerable, but our men were so covered that they continued the works for the whole day—no damage done except one man wounded. One man had his cartouch-box carried away. Nine arms belonging to our brigade paraded on the grounds near the entrenchment carried away by two balls. Captain Dodge escaped narrowly.

Aug. 19, Wednesday. Foggy morning. Our first battery opened. A steady fire from both sides. Three hundred cannon fired by 10 o'clock. The enemy evacuated one redoubt before 12 o'clock. At the great rock on our left had a fine view secure from danger. Rode in the afternoon in pursuit of a fishing boat. A man in one of the trenches had his thigh cut off by a cannon ball and expired in an hour and a half.

Aug. 21, Friday. The French fleet returned and came to anchor off the lighthouse, greatly damaged by the storm.

The French fleet was so damaged that they sailed off to Boston to make repairs. The Americans felt that the French had deserted them and were very angry. One American wrote that the French "left us in a most Rascally manner." The American officers felt they had no other choice but to withdraw the army.

> Aug. 23, Lord's Day. Expected to preach and just prepared to go up to the brigade when the General received a letter from General Sullivan, informing him that the French fleet was so disastered they could by no means afford us any assistance, but were gone to Boston to refit. As the plan had ever been to take off eight thousand men from the left of the army and land them on Brenton's Neck, in the enemy's rear, undere cover of the French ships, for it was well known their lines were impregnable, this could not be excuted with any degree of safety or prospect of success, without any cover, all the generals were called upon to give their opinion whether an immediate retreat was not absolutely necessary. This unexpected desertion of the fleet, which was the mainspring of the expedition, cast a universal gloom on the arm. Put most sanguine hopes were cropped in the bud, and we expected immediate orders to prepare to move off the ground. This prevented the brigade's meeting for religious services. A very heavy firing from the batteries all day. Rode down the lines. Had a fine prospect of the enemy's lines.n Saw all our shot strike which were well directed. One man killed by a cannon ball at one of our guns; another died of the wound he received yesterday by the bursting of a shell.
>
> Aug. 26, Wed. Expected to retreat at six this morning. Brigade paraded. Sent all our baggage off the Island. Extremely hot, but remained on the ground. Concluded to get myself for Connecticut. Came off the Island at 4 o'clock p.m.; crossed at Bristol Ferry, rode to Providence, and lodged about a mile out of town.
>
> Aug. 29, Sat. Applied to, to supply the pulpit to-morrow. This day our army retreated to Butt's Hill. The enemy pursued. A pretty warm action, but the enemy repulsed. Our loss: 30 killed, 150 wounded, 20 taken prisoners.
>
> Aug. 30, Lord's Day. Preached for Mr. Foster. This evening our whole army came off the Island, without leaving any thing behind.
>
> Aug. 31, Mon. Set out home.

After the war Manassah established a private boarding school and ran it for nearly 25 years. In 1786 he joined with other war veterans to form the Ohio Company of Associates. He organized a contract with Congress for the associates to buy one and a half million acres of land in the territory of Ohio with their Certificates of Indebtedness for their war service.

In December of 1815 Manassah's wife of 50 years died. He wrote a moving letter to his children on the occasion of her death. He also discussed some of his own health problems.

The Chaplains — Cutler

Hamilton, Dec. 1, 1815

My dear Son and Daughter

I have the painful duty of informing you of the sudden and unexpected death of your Mother, at half past 5 the morning of the 2nd of Nov. and shall presently inform you why I have not written you before.

You are sensible of the injury she received by a fall a year ago last July. Of the effects of this injury she had never recovered, but had most of the time been tolerably comfortable. She was able with assistance of a crutch to go about the house and up and down the stairs communicating with the chambers. She had several times attended meeting on the Sabbath. But the last summer she had not been so well. At times she had considerable pain in the part that was injured. She found at length her appetite very much to fail and very sensibly lost flesh, but there appeared no affection of the lungs. Lately she became fond of Oisters which could readily be procured. They set well on her stomach and seemed to strengthen her. She preferred to sleep in the study—retired very early to rest and generally slept very quietly, excepting that commonly once in the night she had a short turn of coughing, and raising loose phlem. As I was obliged to be up a great portion of the nights I fully know how she rested. About a fortnight before her death Mrs. Berry came from Salem, and she concluded to sleep with her in her chamber, where we kept a fire and eat our meals. She constantly sat with us at table tho she could eat very little, but eat more or less of oisters daily. For several days before her death, she seemed to be better, and especially the day before. Just at sundown I went out to attend a wedding, and returned about 7, when I found her in her chair. I expressed my surprise that she had not retired to bed, as it was later than her usual hour. She said she felt very well and preferred sitting up as she had company. Mrs. Berry, Martha Brown and Nancy were sitting with her. I observed that I had brought her a piece of wedding cake and cheese. She appeared to be much pleased and must taste of them. In this cheerful frame I left her and retired to my study. Between 8 and 9 she and Mrs. Berry went to bed. She soon fell asleep and slept quietly untill about half after 5 when a pretty hard fit of coughing came on, and Mrs. Berry lit the candles. Presently her mouth appeared to be full and she took a bason into which she used to spit, and emptied what was in her mouth and set the bason down. She looked into it, and then turned her head on to her pillow—saying "I do not know but I am dying." Mrs. Berry screamed—and Martha Brown, in the opposite chamber, sprang from the bed, and was instantly in the chamber. She drew a few breaths after she got to the bed—and expired without a sob or groan. A woman in the back chamber got in just as she drew her last breath. I had gone to bed that night, and was instantly called, but before I got into the chamber her soul had departed to the world of spirits. We found the whole of the contents in the bason was fresh blood, perhaps nearly a pint....

This was Friday morning. The funeral was on Monday. I sent for most of my brethern of the Association to attend. The corpse was carried into the meeting house. The first prayer by Mr. Abbot of Beverly. An appropriate sermon was preached by Dr. Dana and the last prayer by Dr. Worcester of Salem. The collection of people was very large. The femail members of the church conducted by Capt.

Whipple and Capt. Joseph Patrick, walked first—the make members followed and then the ministers, who preceeded the corps. After the mourners a very long procession—first females—then males. It was observed that the whole was conducted with unusual solemnity and propriety. She was deposited in a brick grave. I have given you this minute account, presuming it would be acceptable.

I find my affliction to be heavy, tho. I have no doubt my loss is to her infinite gain. She had long been persuaded that she had a short time to be here and had wholly devoted herself to reading and devotion. Her passage from time to eternity was remarkably easy. Her natural countenance remarkably returned to her after death, and there seemed to be a smile upon it, as if she had gained the victory. Her death was sudden and unexpected to me, as if she had been in perfect health, and found my mind wholly unprepared for it. I had long had the impression that I would be called for first, and had not anticipated this unexpected event. I know however that I must very soon follow—and may God graciously quicken me to be daily and hourly ready to receive that last summon.

Having been previously much exercised with the Asthma, and extremely feeble, together with the weight of this affliction and having to prepare a discourse myself on this trying occasion, I did not make the attempt to write to any friend untill the following Monday; being unavoidably prevented till Tuesday evening, I was called out, and returning much chilled with cold. I warmed me at the fire in the front room, while one was kindled in my chamber. I then rose, and stepping toward the door, a faint turn, to which I have long been liable, came upon me and finding my eyesight gone, I placed my hand on the end of the shelf but instantly my senses wholly left me and I fell backward with my whole weight on the hearth. My right side came upon the andiron and broke two of my ribs. But my head, coming against Daniel, who stood before the fire, saved my head from a blow that might have proved fatal. In this perfectly senseless state I remained for a considerable space of time. When I came to my senses I found myself partly raised up on the floor and a number of people about me endevouring to recover me. I was brought up to my chamber where I have been confined to my chair to this time. I have been exercised with much pain, have had for most of the time two watchers in the night. My bones are so far united, and the pain so much abated that I am attempting to write to my friends. This letter is the first attempt I have made and I am in doubt whether you will be able to read it. It is remarkable that since my fall I have felt nothing of the Asthma. Last night Temple showed me a letter from you which I was very glad to see. Nancy is still with us and a great comfort to me. By a letter from her father, she finds little reason to expect to return this winter. I should not know now how to part with her. She is a most excellent girl. She takes the whole care of me in my helpless, distressed condition. Mrs. Berry is here but expects soon to return to Salem. I should be glad to receive a line from you. I have written a long letter but must omit much. I should have wished to have written. With my love to both of you and all your children.

I conclude

Your affectionate and afflicted Parent
M. Cutler

Sources: 1. *From Its European Antecedents to 1791—The United States Army Chaplaincy* by Parker C. Thompson, 1978, pages 191–193. 2. *Life Journals and Correspondence of Rev. Manasseh Cutler, LL.D.* by William Parker Cutler and Julia Perkins Cutler, Vol. 1, 1888, pages 48–72. 3. *D.A.R. Lineage Book*, Vol. 24, page 78.

Naphtali Daggett

Naphtali Daggett was born on September 8, 1727, in Attleboro, Massachusetts, and he died on November 25, 1780.

He graduated from Yale in 1748 and served as pastor of the Presbyterian Church in Smithtown, Long Island. In 1755 he became a professor at Yale University, and in 1766 he became president of Yale and remained so until 1777. He stayed as rector at Yale until his death in 1780.

On July 5, 1779, the British invaded New Haven and were met by small bodies of militia. Among the first militiamen to encounter the British was Capt. James Hillhouse, Yale class of 1773. With Captain Hillhouse were many of the Yale students. Colonel S.B. Webb later wrote of the attack, "The enemy, about 2,000, under the infamous Gov. Tryon, have been at New Haven. They took possession of the town on Monday last, there being only about 100 of the militia in oppose to them. The young men of the town and the collegians behaved gallantly—fought them as long as it could be of service."

Elizur Goodrich, Yale class of 1779, was in the skirmish with the British and later wrote about facing the British,

> I well remember the Surprise we felt the next morning, July 5th, as we were marching over West Bridge towards the enemy, to see Dr. Daggett [now 52 years old] riding furiously by us on his old black mare, with his long fowling-piece in his had ready for action. We knew the old gentleman had studied the matter thoroughly, and satisfied his own mind as to the right and propriety of fighting it out; but we were not quite prepared to see him come forth in so gallant a style to carry his principles into practice. Giving him a hearty cheer as he passed, we turned down towards West Haven, at the foot of the Milford Mills, while he ascended a little to the west, and took his station in a copse of wood, where he seemed to be reconnoitering the enemy, like one who was determine to "bide his time."
>
> As we passed on towards the south at a line of fence, we fired upon them several times, and then chased them the length of three or four fields as they retreated, until we suddenly found ourselves involved with the main body, and in danger of being surrounded. It was now our turn to run, and we did for our lives. Passing by Dr. Daggett in his station on the hill, we retreated rapidly across West Bridge, which was instantly taken down by persons who stood ready for the purpose to

prevent the enemy from entering the town by that road. In the meanwhile Dr. Daggett, as we heard the story afterwards, stood his ground manfully, while the British columns advanced along the foot of the hill, determined to have the battle himself as we had left him in the lurch, and using his fowling-piece now and then to excellent effect, as occasion offered, under the cover of the bushes. But this could not last long.

A detachment was sent up the hill-side to look into the matter, and the commanding officer, coming suddenly, to his great surprise, on a single individual in a black coat, blazing away in this style, cried out:

"What are you doing there, you old fool, firing on His Majesty's troops?"

"Exercising the rights of war," says the old gentleman.

The very audacity of the reply, and the mixture of drollery it contained, seemed to amuse the officer. If I let you go this time, you rascal, says he, will you ever fire on the troops of His Majesty?

Nothing more likely, said the old gentleman, in his dry way.

This was too much for flesh and blood to bear, and it is a wonder they did not put a bullet through him on the spot.

The British troops then dragged the old man down to the rest of the troops and drove him before them. It was in the afternoon and a very hot day, and they forced Daggett force march the five miles to town. His knees weakened due to the heat and exhaustion, and they would stick him with their bayonets to keep him moving.

When the soldiers finally reached town Daggett was covered in blood. A Tory, who had come out to welcome the British, saw Daggett covered in blood and dirt and requested the man to be released. The officer did so, and Daggett was taken to a nearby house more dead than alive. He survived the ordeal and was able to preach again, but he never fully recovered from what happened that day. Sixteen months later Pastor Daggett died.

Sources: 1. *The Chaplains and Clergy of the Revolution* by Joel Tyler Headley, 1864, pages 199–204. 2. *Yale and Her Honor-Roll in the American Revolution, 1775–1783* by Henry Phelps Johnson, pages 105–108.

Thomas Davis

Thomas Davis was born before 1750 in Virginia, and he died there after 1815. He served as chaplain of the 1st Continental Dragoons from 1776–1777. The unit was formed from June 13, 1776, to September 10, 1776, in Williamsburg, Virginia. Thomas may have been present for the Battles of Brandywine and Germantown.

Thomas and George Washington became friends over the years. On July 4, 1798, George Washington joined in the city of Alexandria, Virginia celebration of the 4th. Washington attended a service at Christ Church where Thomas was pastor. Several months later on Washington's birthday, the pastor visited Washington at his home at Mt. Vernon and had dinner with him. Later in the day the pastor performed the wedding ceremony for Washington's nephew who married Martha Washington's granddaughter. Davis spent the night at Mt. Vernon. In 1793 Washington donated money to help buy an organ for Christ Church in honor of Pastor Davis.

On December 14, 1799, George Washington died at his home. Thomas Davis was asked to read the Episcopal funeral service. The service began at 3 in the afternoon. A procession, led by the mahogany coffin, passed through the gate at the left wing of the house. When the casket reached the crypt, Pastor Davis took his place and said, "I am the resurrection and the life, saith the Lord." When Davis had finished reading the Order of Burial he gave a brief eulogy of which no record exist.

Sources: 1. *From Its European Antecedents to 1791—The United States Army Chaplaincy* by Parker C. Thompson, 1978, page 216. 2. *Academic Journal Article in Anglican and Episcopal History*, article by Otto Lohrenz.

Samuel Doak

Samuel Doak was born in August 1749 in Augusta County, Virginia, and he died on December 12, 1830, in Bethel, North Carolina. His first wife Esther Montgomery died in 1807, and he married a widow, Margaretta McEwen. He graduated from the College of New Jersey, now called Princeton, in 1775 and became a tutor at Hampden-Sidney College. While there he studied theology and became licensed to preach in 1777.

In 1777 he moved to the Holston settlement, which was then a part of North Carolina and now a part of Tennessee. He was Tennessee's first Christian minister, and he preached in several areas. Living in the frontier was hard and dangerous for the Doak family. On one occasion Samuel left his wife Esther and their child at home to go to a nearby town for supplies.

Esther and the child were inside their cabin when the family dog began barking, which was warning Esther that a band of hostile Cherokee Indians was approaching. Esther took the sleeping baby in her arms, left the cabin, and hid in the woods. She watched the Indians rob their cabin and set fire to it. Once they left Esther walked through the forest, and even though there was no path she managed to locate her husband.

An interesting story about the founding of the Salem Presbyterian Church in 1780 by Samuel Doak may have some truth to it. Samuel was riding through the forest when he came upon some settlers clearing an area of trees. When they discovered that Samuel was a minister, they asked if he would preach them a sermon. Samuel preached using his horse as the pulpit, and the settlers were so impressed with the young minister that they asked him to stay. Samuel agreed and settled on the land that later would become the church, school, and cemetery.

By this time the fighting in the Revolutionary War had shifting to the south. A large group of Loyalist militiamen had been raised in the area led by British Major Patrick Ferguson. Much hatred had developed between the Loyalist militia and the patriot militia. Many of these militiamen were neighbors and in some cases members of the same family. The two groups converged on Kings Mountain in South Carolina near the border of North Carolina.

On the morning of September 26, 1780, patriot leader Colonel John Sevier had gathered his men and asked the Reverend Samuel Doak to speak to the men as they prepared to leave for battle. Doak began his sermon to them by saying, "My countrymen, you are about to set out on an expedition which is full of hardship and dangers, but one in which the Almighty will attend you. The Mother Country has her hands upon you, these American Colonies, and takes that for which our fathers planted their homes in the wilderness—OUR LIBERTY."

He then ended his sermon with a prayer that contained these final words: "O, God of Battle, arise in Thy might. Avenge the slaughter of Thy people. Confound those who plot for our destruction. Crown this mighty effort with victory, and smite those who exalt themselves against liberty and justice and truth. Help us as good soldiers to weild the SWORD OF THE LORD AND GIDEON."

Once the prayer ended Samuel grabbed his musket next to the pulpit and led his men to battle. Over 100 militiamen followed Samuel and Colonel Sevier to Kings Mountain. The men marched to battle with the battle cry "The Sword of the Lord and Gideon."

The Battle of Kings Mountain was fought on October 7, 1780, and lasted just 95 minutes. The men led by Colonel Sevier and Samuel Doak fought at the mountain's smallest area but its highest point. One of the bloodiest battles of the American Revolution was won by the patriots. This victory raised the morale of the Patriots and helped turn the tide of the war in the south in favor of the Americans.

After the war ended, Samuel for the next several years founded around 25 churches and several schools in the area. The schools included Washington Academy and Tusculum College. He became a pioneer in the movement to abolish slavery, and he freed his own slaves in 1818.

There is an interesting story concerning Samuel and the Revered Hezekiah Balch. They were both Scots-Irish and both Princeton graduates, and they lived in the same frontier area. Over the year they became friends, then enemies, and then old friends again. For a period of time they did not see eye-to-eye on religious thinking and they began to feud.

On one occasion they faced each other on a rainy street in Greenville. They were opposite each other on the same board over a puddle. Doak, the large, barrel-chested preacher said, "I never make way for the devil."

Balch, the smaller of the two men replied, "I do." He then stepped into the mud and water to let the embarrassed Doak pass by.

Sources: 1. *Touring the East Tennessee Backroads* by Carolyn Sakowski, page 110. 2. *Lineage Book National Society of the D.A.R.*, vols. 61–62, page 15. 3. *Encyclopedia of Virginia Biography*, Vol. II, page 143 4. Sons of the American Revolution Application. 5. *Marking Time: East Tennessee Historical Markers and the Stories Behind Them* by Fred Brown, pages 107–108. 6. *Pennsylvania Province and State History, 1609–1790*, Vol. II, page 417. 7., by Pat Alderman, pages 20–21.

Timothy Dwight

Timothy Dwight was born on May 14, 1752, in Northampton, Massachusetts, and he died on January 11, 1817, in Philadelphia, Connecticut. He married Mary Woolsey on March 3, 1777. He graduated from Yale at the age of 17 and he became a licensed minister in 1777. He was described as a man of very fine physique, large and strong, full of bodily proportions, and of a commanding mien. He stood about five feet, 11 inches high, perfectly straight, had a broad, open forehead, large, piercing black eyes, beautiful teeth, and a full chest and strong lungs.

Timothy served as an army chaplain from September 4, 1777, to March of 1778. His wife Mary applied for a window's pension after his death and received a yearly pension of $280. She stated in her application to the pension bureau: "My husband entered the Revolutionary Army in the autumn of the year 1777 not long after the Annual Commencement of Yale College. He served as chaplain during his connection with the army, and was attached to General Putnam. I believe he was stationed at West Chester County in the State of New York from the time of his joining the army until the winter or spring of 1778 when he was removed to West Point. In consequence of the death of his father he left the Army & returned home about November 1, 1778."

After General Putnam led his men to a key victory on October 7, 1777 [this was the Battle of Saratoga] Pastor Dwight preached a memorable sermon to the General and his main officers. His text was Joel 2:20, which states, "I will remove far off from you the northern army." The General believed that his chaplain had revised the text to make his point. An officer showed the General the passage in the Bible to prove that it was not altered. The General then remarked, "Well, there is every thing in that book, and Dwight knows just where to lay his finger on it."

After he returned home Timothy served as pastor of several churches in Massachusetts and Connecticut. In 1788 Dwight purchased a slave, a woman named Naomi, four years after Connecticut passed its gradual emancipation law. Because Naomi was born prior to 1784, she was not a "statutory slave" but a permanent slave, pending her master's decision to liberate her. Dwight's statement "I never intended her for a slave" means that he intended to allow her to buy her own freedom with her time of servitude. It is unknown whether she was successful in obtaining her freedom. It is also unknown whether he held her in slavery while serving as the President of Yale.

A manuscript in Yale's collection of the Dwight family papers, dated 1788 and signed Timothy Dwight, says: "This certifies that the conditions on which I bought Naomi, a negro woman formerly belonging to Deacon Daniel Andrews of Norfield, that she shall work for me and mine until she shall have refunded the money which I am to pay for her, at the rate of seven pounds sixteen shillings per year, and that she shall uniformly behave well, faithfully, and truly towards me and mine, and that she shall also be at the expense of the cloaths she wants during her service with me, and live with me and mine until she shall, at the same rate of hire, have discharged the expense arising from the same. In which case I voluntarily bind myself my heirs and my executors and my administrators, and I release her from all obligations to serve me (as I never intended her for a slave) any further time. In case she does not faithfully fulfill the above conditions, then this instrument is to be void and of none effect. Witness my hand this fourth of March 1788."

Timothy was elected president of Yale College in 1795 and later served two terms in the Massachusetts legislature.

Sources: 1. Pension Application W21025. 2. Sons of the American Revolution Application. 3. U.S. Pensioners 1818–1872. 4. *From Its European Antecedents to 1791—The United States Army Chaplaincy* by Parker C. Thompson, 1978, pages 171, 176, 205, 215, and 217. 5. Yale, Slavery & Abolition, June 23, 2016. 6. *The History of the Descendants of John Dwight of Dedham, Mass.* by Benjamin Woodbridge Dwight, page xxvi.

John Ellis

John Ellis was born on March 2, 1727, in Boston, and he died on October 9, 1805, in Franklin, Connecticut. He married Bethia Palmer on October 24, 1749. He was ordained on September 5, 1753. His ministry was not a very happy one, because many of the church members objected to his practice of infant baptism. Many joined the Baptist church to get out of paying taxes for his support. As a result, John's salary was in arrears, so when the war began he and his two sons enlisted on July 6, 1775. He was appointed chaplain of the 8th Connecticut at Roxbury.

Jazez Fitch, one of the men in his regiment, wrote in his diary, "Mr. Ellis took breakfast with us, and while we were waiting we had a little dispute concerning ecclesiastical establishments, which he spoke slightly about, on which the parson signified that if I was of such sentiments he wished I was in Rome or some other country, on which I told him I chose to be here and let those bigots who so much resembled the church of Rome go there, so as to enjoy their own opinions and have these Established by human or rather inhumane laws." The old fellow then replied, "You have given tit for tat."

John re-enlisted in the 17th Continentals, from which he later transferred to the 1st Connecticut under the command of Colonel Jedidiah Huntington. In May of 1777 he was appointed Brigade Chaplain and served in that capacity for the remainder of the war. Pastor Ellis was at Valley Forge and also with the troops at the Battle of Monmouth on June 28, 1778. At the Battle of Yorktown he and Israel Evans were the two chaplains with the longest continuous tenure of service that dated back to 1775. John

Ellis resigned October 31, 1783, and he accepted five years of pay instead of the half pay for life pension he was entitled.

Sources: 1. Sons of the American Revolution Application. 2. *From Its European Antecedents to 1791—The United States Army Chaplaincy* by Parker C. Thompson, 1978, pages 108, 143, 157, and 200. 3. *Yale and Her Honor-Roll in the American Revolution, 1775-1783* by Henry Phelps Johnson, page 275. 4. D.A.R. *Lineage Book*, Vol. 7, page 19. 5. *History of New London County, Connecticut* by Duane Hamilton Hurd, page 401.

William Emerson, Sr.

William Emerson was born on May 31, 1743, in Boston, and he died on October 20, 1776, in Rutland, Vermont. He married Phoebe Bliss on August 21, 1766. He served as chaplain of the Massachusetts Provincial Congress and chaplain of the Continental Army.

William recorded in his diary that in February of 1775 there was enough military equipment stashed in Concord to supply 15,000 men. The supplies included tents, lead balls, rum, salt, cloth, and medicine. This is the reason why Concord was such a tempting prize to British General Gage.

Before the battle Emerson preached to the men of Concord that he had months earlier encouraged to enlist. After the battle, he would tend to the wounded making him the first American army chaplain. Before the British arrived, Pastor Emerson was standing in the commons with musket in hand and his black robe flowing. The pastor urged the leaders of the militia to launch an immediate attack on the British instead of waiting for reinforcements. The leaders wisely chose to wait and not attack.

He urged and encouraged the men as the British approached by telling them, "Stand your ground! If we die, let us die here!" One young soldier in the group looked scared so Emerson slapped him on the back and said, "Stand your ground, Harry! Your cause is just and God will bless you!"

The militia pulled back and left the town to wait for reinforcements. As the British entered Concord they began searching for the American's hidden supplies and burning buildings. Fortunately, most of the supplies had been safely moved out and hidden out of town. One of the first homes the British came to was the home of Colonel James Barrett. They believed that there would be large amounts of supplies there since he was a rebel leader. Barrett's sons had recently plowed their crops and buried the supplies in the field. The British had marched right by the supplies.

When Colonel Barrett saw smoke coming from Concord he marched his men, now numbering 400, to the North Bridge. When they arrived at the bridge at about 11 o'clock they faced 100 regular British troops. The two sides stood their ground, each side not wanting to open fire. Suddenly, a shot rang out and probably by a nervous British private. This shot was made famous by Ralph Waldo Emerson, the grandson of Pastor William Emerson, in his "Concord Hymn" as the "shot heard around the world." William Emerson's wife Phoebe watched these events unfold through the northern window of her home. Men on both sides were killed during the first exchange of shots at the North Bridge.

The British, being outnumbered, fell back towards town to join with the main body of troops. Finding no supplies and the number of American militiamen growing by the minute, the British decided to leave Concord and retreat back to Lexington to await reinforcements.

Some of the rebels ran to the farm of Colonel Barrett to dig up their weapons and ammunition. As the British retreated the Americans hid behind trees, fences, and buildings and fired as the British marched in retreat. The numbers of militiamen continued to grow and shoot at the British. When the British finally made it back to Boston, they had 300 wounded and 73 killed. The militia surrounded Boston with 15,000 troops and laid siege to the British Army.

The following is an extract from the diary of William Emerson:

> 1775, 19 April. This morning, between one and two o'clock, we were alarmed by the ringing of the bell, and upon examination found that the troops, to the number of eight hundred, had stolen their march from Boston. This intelligence was brought us first by De. Samuel Prescott, who narrowly escaped the guard that were sent before on horses, purposely to prevent all posts and messengers from giving is timely information.

After the warning Emerson writes that the men formed and that some wanted to make a stand and face the British, but others thought it best to retreat until reinforcements arrived. They decided to retreat across the North Bridge. "The troops came into town, set fire to several carriages for the artillery, destroyed sixty barrels of flour, rifled through several houses, took possession of the town-house, destroyed five hundred pounds of balls, set a guard of a hundred men at the North Bridge, and sent a party to the house of Col. Barrett, where they were in expectation of finding a quantity of warlike stores. But these were happily secured, just before their arrival."

By now the militia had received many reinforcements and outnumbered the British. "In the mean time, the guard set by the enemy to secure the posts at the North Bridge were alarmed by the approach of our people, who had retreated, and were not advancing, with special orders not to fire upon the troops unless fired upon. These orders were so punctually observed, that we received the fire of the enemy in three several and separate discharges of their pieces before it was returned by our commanding officer. The firing then soon became general for several minutes, in which skirmish two men killed on each side, and several of the enemy wounded."

Emerson remarked that the Americans were very cautious about firing in the beginning, because they were not sure about what had happened at Lexington. The British at the bridge retreated and re-joined the main body of troops. The British now began their retreat back to Lexington. "For half an hour, the enemy, by their marches and counter-marches, discovered great fickleness and inconstancy of mind; sometimes advancing sometimes returning to their former posts, till at length they quitted the town, and retreated by the way they came. In the mean time a party of our men (one hundred and fifty) took the back way through the Great Fields, into the east quarter, and had placed themselves to advantage. Lying in ambush behind walls, fences, and buildings, ready to fire upon the enemy on their retreat."

Fort Ticonderoga contained cannons and supplies that the American Army would need. The fort also controlled the lakes George and Champlain. After the Lexington alarm plans were made to capture the fort, and on May 10, 1775, under the leadership of Benedict Arnold and Ethan Allen the fort was captured. In August of 1776 William Emerson left Concord to serve as chaplain of the American Army at Fort Ticonderoga.

Emerson wrote to his wife about camp life, "There are many things amiss in this camp, yet upon the whole, God is in the midst of us. I despair seeing a battle fought this time coming down." While at the fort Emerson came down with dysentery and became very ill.

He wrote to the commanding officer on September 10, 1776, "Sir, my Ill State of Health is such that I am not able to perform the Duty of a Chaplain and am advised by the Physicians to ask for a dismission from the Army." His dismissal was signed by General Gates and Emerson left for home. He traveled less than 50 miles before he died of fever in Rutland, Vermont and was buried in an unmarked grave. William was the first American army chaplain and may have also been the first chaplain to die while in the service.

Sources: 1. Sons of the American Revolution Application. 2. *The Concord Guide Book* by George B. Bartlett, pages 34–35 and 55. 3. *D.A.R. Lineage Book*, Vol. 12, page 224. 4. *Sword: The Battle of Bunker Hill and the Beginning of the American Revolution* by James L. Nelson, page 140. 5. *The Liberal Mob Is Endangering America* by Ann Coulter, page 139. 6. *Character Counts: Freemasonry Is a National Treasure and a Source of Our Founders Constitutional Original Intent*, page 358.

Philip Vickers Fithian

Philip Fithian was born on December 29, 1746, in Greenwich, New Jersey, and he died on October 8, 1776. He married Elizabeth Beatty on October 25, 1775. In 1770 he attended Princeton and after graduation he was ordained a Presbyterian minister.

He became chaplain in Colonel Silas Newcomb's battalion of militia from New Jersey in 1776. He left his bride for New York to serve a tour in which he never returned. Among his several duties, and that which he found most painful was taking care of the sick, wounded, and the dying in hospitals. He wrote in his journal: "After evening prayers I walked to the Hospitals of three Regiments; to ours & the two New England Battalions. A Sight that Forces Compassion. An unfeeling Heart here is brutal … & here I must daily visit…. My whole Frame revolts against it—! But I am not discouraged nor dispirited; I am willing to hazard and suffer equally with my Countrymen since I have a firm conviction that I am doing my Duty."

When the army was told to march from New Jersey to Long Island, Pastor Fithian marched with his men. He wrote in his journal, "I equipt myself for Action. With my Gun, Canteen, Knapsack, Blanket…" After a night of light firing, he left the fort to walk two and a half miles to where the major contest was going on. The Battle of Long Island on August 27 brought from him the comment "O doleful! Doleful!—Blood! Carnage! Fire!… Such a Din my Ears never before heard!—And the distressed wounded, came crying into the Lines!" After the battle the Americans began the retreat.

Pastor Fithian traveled near Fort Washington by sloop and discovered life there was very difficult. "Since Tuesday Evening we have had only Bread and raw Meat. Our men looked blue with the cold."

Due to the cold and the rain Fithian becomes ill, and yet sick he continues to fulfill his duties. He becomes to enjoy the army more: "There is something forcefully grand in the Sound of Drums & Fifes when they are calling such an Army as ours to contend with another of perhaps equal Force!"

After the Battle of Harlem Heights the dreaded dysentery enters the camp and strikes Fithian. On September 19, he wrote Betsy about his return to Greenwich and his hopes for their renewed life together. He ended the epistle with a prayer: "Peace & God's Blessing be with my Betsey, my dear Wife, forever may you be happy." It was the last letter Philip Vickers Fithian would ever write.

Chaplain William Hollingshead wrote of Fithian's final days, "visited Mr. Fithian who has been dangerously ill these some weeks. I found him lying upon a thin bed raised from the floor by a little straw covered with a blanket or two; with no other shelter from the inclemency of the season than a small Marque that with 3 other persons to lodge in it besides himself, 2 of whom was also sick. He had no physician to attend him but an unskilled quack of a Surgeons mate, & no nurse but an unknowing country lad."

Fithian died on October 8, 1776, and his friend Chaplain Hunter wrote of his burial the next day, "About 10 O'clock Mr. Fithian was buried—his funeral was attended by several Clergymen and Officers and Soldiers of Col. Newcomb's Regt. with as much decency as the nature of the case would allow…"

Source: 1. *From Its European Antecedents to 1791—The United States Army Chaplaincy* by Parker C. Thompson, 1978, pages 87, 97-98, and 138-142.

John Gano

John Gano was born on July 22, 1727, in Hopewell, New Jersey, and he died on August 10, 1804, in Kentucky. He married Sarah Stites who died in 1792 and he then married Sally Hunt in 1793. He was ordained on May 29, 1754, and became pastor of the Scotch Plains (New Jersey) Baptist Church. He left there in 2 years and preached at various places in the southern colonies.

Pastor Gano served as chaplain of the 19th Continental Infantry commanded by Charles Webb and later the 5th Regiment commanded by Colonel Louis Dubois. He also served as Brigade chaplain to General Clinton. He served at the battles of White Plains, Trenton, Princeton, Forts Clinton, and Montgomery.

At the Battle of White Plains on October 28, 1776, John Gano displayed calm and quiet courage while under constant fire at the Battle of Chatterton Hill. His regiment, the 19th Infantry, was part of the troops given the assignment to hold the hill against the advancing British and Hessian troops. The fighting was very intense, and both sides suffered many casualties before the Americans were forced to retreat.

Gano later wrote, perhaps with tongue in cheek, his role in the battle: "My station in time of action I knew to be among the surgeons; but in this battle I somehow got in front of the regiment, yet I durst not quit my place for fear of dampening the spirits of the soldiers, or of bringing on me an imputation of cowardice. Rather than do either, I chose to risk my fate."

After White Plains Gano spent time at home, and in December of 1776 he joined with General Lee. After Lee was captured on December 12, 1776, Gano joined under the command of General Glover whose men ferried Washington's army across the Delaware. John Gano crossed the Delaware River on Christmas night of 1776. The next morning he was in the battle line at Trenton with another chaplain, David Avery, also in this book.

Pastor Gano returned home in January of 1777 and late in the winter he received a letter from Colonel Dubois at Fort Montgomery requesting that he become the regiment's chaplain. Gano wrote in his memoirs: "On the receipt of this letter, I set off to the colonel's regiment, to refuse the invitation, therin contained. On my arrival there, I found General James Clinton, in company with the Colonel, both of whome, urged me to accept the office of Chaplain, in so forcible a manner, that I finally consented. I repaired to the fort, where I remained, till the British took it from us by storm."

The Battle of Fort Clinton and Fort Montgomery were fought on October 6, 1777. Gano wrote about the battle:

> We had been taught to believe, that we should be reinforced, in time of danger, from the neighboring militia; but they were, at this time, very inactive. We heard of the approach of the enemy, and that they were about a mile and a half from

Fort-Clinton. That fort sent out a small detachment, which was immediately driven back.

The British army surrounded both our forts, and commenced an universal firing. I was walking on the breast-work, viewing their approach, but was obliged to quit this station, as the musket balls frequently passed me. The enemy, kept up a heavy firing, till our men, gave them a well directed fire, which affected them very sensibly.

About sun-set, the enemy sent a couple of flags, into each of our forts, demanding an immediate surrender, or we should all be put to the sword. General George Clinton, who commanded in Fort-Montgomery, returned for answer, that the latter was preferable to the former, and that he should not surrender the fort. General James Clinton, who commanded in Fort Clinton, answered the demand in the same manner. The enemy commenced a very heavy firing.

Under the cover of night and the heavy smoke in the air, the Americans were able to escape from the fort and cross the river on some scows. John Gano escaped and returned home in time to be there for the birth of his daughter Susannah on November 8, 1777.

When the army spent the winter at Valley Forge, Gano had returned home. He did not join the army in winter quarters, because he believed that the men were not properly clothed to stand out in the harsh cold weather to hear him preach. When the winter had passed he returned to camp and asked how the men had made out. A solider replied, that they had "suffered all winter without hearing the Word of God." When Gano told the man that he was only thinking of their comfort, the man added, "True, but it would have been consoling to have had such a good man near us."

While at Valley Forge there is a legend that Washington came to Gano and asked to be baptized. John Gano's grandchildren signed affidavits in the 1870s and 1880s attesting to the event. They said that Gano's older daughter told them that it happened. In 1932 *Time* magazine published an article about the event and stated that 42 people witnessed the event. There is even a famous painting hanging in the Gano Chapel at William Jewell College depicting the event. It is a lovely story and a beautiful painting, but it probably never happened.

John Gano never served as chaplain under George Washington and the minister was not present at Valley Forge. Had this Baptism taken place, he surely would have written about it in his memoirs, which he did not do. Washington's church believed in infant Baptism, and his christening was recorded as having taken place on April 5, 1732, when he was six weeks old. Also, there is no written account by the 42 onlookers. The legend is popular, because it is used to prove that Washington has his religion in a fairly open and active fashion.

In the summer of 1779 Gano once again joined with General Clinton and became a chaplain on the expedition commanded by General Sullivan. The Americans were sent into upper New York to destroy the influence of the Tories and the Iroquois Indians that had been raiding Americans farms. Gano describes one event:

> In the morning, we heard the guns from the British garrison. We discovered amazing fields of corn, not yet gathered, which our army destroyed. It was supposed that the Indians were gone to the British garrison; and that they had concluded our intention was for the garrison. In the afternoon, our army wheeled about; and General Clinton, was ordered to encamp at the Genesee, and wait for our division to come up.
>
> The next day, we had a great feast in the garrison, and then arranged matters for our return to Easton. But here, I must not forget to mention a circumstance, peculiarly pleasing to me. Two or three young soldiers were under great distress of mind concerning their souls, and, frequently, came to see and converse with me. I mention a text to them when I thought of the Indians, and the devastations which were made in their country, "They shall walk through them, be an hungry, and curse their God and their King, and look upwards."

One morning as he was going to the regimental prayers, he passed by a group of officers, one of whom not seeing him approach was swearing in an excited manner. The other officers saluted the chaplain as usual, when the Lieutenant that was cursing turned quickly around and saw Gano and said, "Good morning doctor."

Gano returned the greeting and said to many, "I see you pray early." The embarrassed officer said, "I beg your pardon, sir." Pastor Gano quickly replied, "Oh! I cannot pardon you, you must carry your case to God."

On another occasion Gano was standing near some soldiers who had been ordered to cut some wood. An angry soldier shouted, "I be damned if I will do it." But he picked up the axe anyway and started to cut the wood. Gano stepped forward, took the axe, and told the man that he would cut the wood. The soldier said that a chaplain should not have to cut wood. Gano told him, "I just heard you say that you would be damned if you would cut it, and I had rather do it for you than that you should be made miserable forever."

One time when Gano was told that the army would be devastated if the six and nine months men did not reenlist, he told the men that "he could aver to the truth that our Lord and Savior approved of all those who has engaged him His service for the whole warfare." The men laughed how the pastor had stretched words of the Bible to get them to reenlist. Most of the men kidded each other into reenlisting.

When the British were surrounded at Yorktown, Gano was preparing to leave and join the Americans there. When he reached Baltimore with General Clinton's troops, Gano was ordered to stay behind and take care of the General's sick aid. By the time the man could travel and the aid and Gano reached Yorktown the surrender had taken place.

After the surrender John returned home and met his new son William, who had recently been born. He continued to serve as a chaplain until the final peace treaty was signed in 1783. On April 19, 1783, under orders from General George Washington, Gano was given the honor of announcing that the war was officially over and that the United States was free. He then assembled the officers and men and led them in a prayer of thanksgiving.

Sources: 1. *Biographical Memoirs of the Late Rev. John Gano of Frankfort*, 1806, pages 93–117. 2. *D.A.R. Lineage Book*, Vol. 8, page 265. 3. *From Its European Antecedents to 1791—The United States Army Chaplaincy* by Parker C. Thompson, 1978, pages 145, 148, and 208. 4. *New England Clergy & the American Revolution* by Alice Baldwin, 1928, pages 250–272.

Pierre Gibault

Pierre Gibault was born on April 7, 1737, in Montreal, Canada, and he died August 16, 1802, in Spain. He was ordained on March 19, 1768. He served in several parishes in the Northwest Territory which was considered a dangerous frontier, so the priest carried a gun and two pistols.

In 1778 Father Gibault met General George Rogers Clark of the American Army. The priest supported the Americans but worried about his Catholic congregation. Clark assured Gibault that under the laws of Virginia they would be free to worship as they pleased. Gibault was also informed that a treaty between France, a Catholic nation, and the U.S. had been signed. Gibault served as a chaplain, receiving no pay, for Clark on one of his expeditions.

Because of his support of the Americans Father Gibault fell out of favor with his superiors, and he was prevented from receiving land for his service to the American cause. Now in poverty Father Gibault moved to

New Madrid in 1793 and became a Spanish citizen. He died in 1802 and his body was returned to Canada, but his grave is unmarked.

Sources: 1. *Blackrobe in Blue: The Naval Chaplaincy of John P. Foley, S.J.* by Steve O'Brien, 1942, page 9. 2. *Catholic Military and Naval Chaplains, 1776–1917* by Aidan Henry Germain, 1929, page 15.

Spencer Grayson

Spencer Grayson was born in 1734 in Dumfries, Virginia, and he died there in December of 1798. He was an Episcopal clergyman and was ordained by the Lord Bishop of London on May 29, 1771. He married Mary Elizabeth Wagener in 1754, and after the war they lived on a plantation of 1,000 acres in Virginia. Spencer was described as a refined gentleman, a large man of distinguished being, and an eloquent speaker.

Spencer served as a chaplain with the rank of Captain in Colonel William Grayson's [Spencer's brother] Virginia Regiment, and he was known as a fighting as well as a preaching chaplain. He served from May 1777 until April 22, 1779.

He and his family were frequent guests of President George Washington and who was a personal friend. Washington had Pastor Grayson perform the marriage ceremony of Washington's nephew, Major George Augustine Washington. Spence was paid the large sum of $100 for performing the ceremony.

Sources: 1. *A Standard History of Georgia and Georgians* by Lucian Lamar Knight, Vol. 5, page 2339. 2. *The National Cyclopedia of American Biography, Vol. 1–Vol. 13* by George Derby and James Terry White, page 337. 3. Sons of the American Revolution Application.

David Griffith

David Griffith was born in 1742 in New York City, and he died on August 2, 1789, in Philadelphia. He married Hannah Colville on October 21, 1766. David received his degree in medicine in England and later was ordained in the Episcopal Church in London. He wrote in 1776 "that God did not require obedience to the king, whose acts were destructive to human happiness."

He served both as a chaplain and a surgeon in Lafayette's Division and Woodford's Brigade in the 3rd Virginia Regiment under the command of Colonel William Heth. Chaplains Andrew Hunter (also in this book) and David Griffith received honors from General Washington for their heroic conduct at the Battle of Monmouth.

The night before the Battle of Monmouth David Griffith paid a late night visit to the quarters of General Washington. The guard on duty was not going to allow him to see the General except Davis was very insistent. The guard took David to the General and the following was related to Washington's stepson by Colonel Nicolas of Virginia: "he warned him [George Washington] against trusting Lee with command in the next day's battle."

According to a David Jones' diary at Valley Forge, weeks before the battle the General had said to Griffith, "Doctor if you ever have anything private to communicate, never do it before my family." The term family was a reference to his staff. Washington may have been worried about disloyalty in his staff.

Whether or not this event took place we will never know because, it may just be hearsay only. There were officers disloyal to Washington during the early part of the war. Also, during the early part of the Battle of Monmouth, General Charles Lee did order a retreat while General Washington was advancing behind him. This angered Washington so much that he had heated words with Lee and relieved him of command on the spot.

Sources: 1. Valley Forge Muster Roll Project. 2. *For Liberty and Equality: The Life and Times of the Declaration of Independence.* 3. *Battle of Monmouth* by Chaplain Stanley W. Cuyler, 1986, page 11. 4. *From Its European Antecedents to 1791—The United States Army Chaplaincy* by Parker C. Thompson, 1978, page 182.

Daniel Grosvenor

Daniel Grosvenor was born on April 20, 1750, in Windham County, Connecticut and he died on July 22, 1834, in Petersham, Massachusetts. He married Deborah Hall on May 9, 1776, in Sulton, Massachusetts. He graduated from Yale in 1769 and was ordained on October 19, 1774. He gave up preaching in 1788 due to health problems.

When the Lexington alarm went out, he grabbed his musket and raised two companies of militia that totaled nearly 100 men. He was appointed their captain and marched them to Cambridge.

Sources: 1. Sons of the American Revolution Application. 2. D.A.R. *Lineage Book,* Vol. 63, page 26.

James Hall

James Hall was born on August 22, 1744, in Carlisle, Pennsylvania, and he died on July 25, 1826, in Iredell County, North Carolina. At the age of eight James and his family moved to North Carolina. He entered Princeton College in 1744 at the age of 31 to study the ministry and for the next 12 years became pastor of a church for three small communities, which covered nearly 600 square miles. He later served at Bethany church for 26 years.

When the British army under General Cornwallis moved into southern North Carolina in 1780–81 James raised a company of militia dragoons. The unit was mainly men from his own congregations and they would not march unless he took command.

He probably served at the Battle of Cowan's Ford on February 1, 1781, where his Commander William Lee Davidson was killed. When the General died General Greene appointed Captain James Hall to take his place. Hall turned down the promotion, because he did not want to leave his unit and also because he told Greene that he was a clergyman and that his military work was just temporary.

Dr. Robinson of Poplar Tent wrote, "When a boy at school at Charlotte, I saw James Hall pass through the town, with his three-cornered hat and long sword, the captain at the head of a company, and chaplain of the regiments."

Near the end of the war he returned to preaching and later did some missionary work. In his final years James became despondent and withdrawn. This depression took over his life, and he refused to preach for a year and a half. A neighbor finally "exercised a deaf-and-dumb demon" from him, and he became involved in the church again. There is no record of James having married.

Sources: 1. *This Day in Presbyterian History, Daily Devotional Readings in Scripture,* July 25, Rev. James Hall. 2. *Sketches of North Carolina, Historical and Biographical* by W. H. Foote, 1846, page 315-323. 3. *From Its European Antecedents to 1791—The United States Army Chaplaincy* by Parker C. Thompson, 1978, page 197. 4. *New England Clergy & the American Revolution* by Alice Baldwin, 1928, pages 245-249. 5. *Sketches of Western North Carolina* by C.L. Hunter, 1877, pages 90-19, 196-197, and 200-201.

John Heckewelder

John Heckewelder was born on March 12, 1743, in Bedford, England, and he died on January 31, 1823, in Pennsylvania. He arrived in New York in 1754 and in 1780 he married Sarah Ohneberg.

He was a Moravian missionary among Indians, and from 1778 until 1782 he acted as a spy for General Washington in Ohio. Colonel Daniel Brodhead, Washington's longtime commander at Fort Pitt, wrote on January 14, 1799: "I do certify that I have been acquainted with the Reverend John Heckewelder since the year 1778. That he resided on or near the Muskingum River as Missionary from the United Brethren to the Delawares & other tribes of Indians during my command in the Western Department and discovered a decided and firm attachment to the cause of the United States giving me every possible information or intelligence of the enemies parties approaching our Settlements or posts, by which many of them were defeated and destroyed."

General Edward Hand, who was a Colonel when he commanded at Ft. Pitt in 1778, confirmed Brodhead's statement on February 14, 1800, acknowledging that "in 1778 the United States were indebted to the active and patriotic zeal of Mr. John Heckewelder" in their western campaigns.

John kept the Americans informed of British activity and troop movements. In the fall of 1781 the British shut down Washington's spy ring in Ohio, and they arrested several missionaries in the area including the Rev. John Heckewelder. John and several others were taken to Detroit and put on trial for treason. He was later acquitted of the spy charges.

In the spring of 1782 John was again arrested for supplying Fort Pitt with intelligence about the British. He was taken back to Detroit, and he was considered too dangerous to release so he was held until the end of the war.

Sources: 1. *The Travels of John Heckewelder in Frontier America* by Paul A. Wallace, page 386. 2. *History and Customs of the Indian Nations Who Once Inhabited Penn-*

sylvania and the Neighboring States by the Rev. John Heckewelder, 1881, pages vii-xii. 3. *D.A.R. Lineage Book*, Vol. 34, page 104.

William Hill

William Hill was born in 1737 in Caroline County, Virginia, and he died on September 29, 1792, in Surry County, North Carolina. He married Elizabeth Halbert on January 13, 1758. He was a Baptist minister and a member of the Committee of Safety in the Salisbury District of North Carolina.

William served as a chaplain to the North Carolina militia at the Battle of Guilford Courthouse on March 15, 1781. The North Carolina militia formed the first line on the left and right flanks in the battle. The British defeated the Americans in the 90-minute battle, and in doing so they lost over one fourth of their men. One British Whig Party leader said, "Another such victory would ruin the British Army!" A few months later the British would surrender to the Americans at Yorktown.

William Hill, Jr., son of Pastor William Hill, stated in an article in *The Standard* of Raleigh dated November 4, 1857, "Before the battle a band of Tories Called at my father's house, where me and my mother were, and enquired about my father. On being told that he was not home they departed avowing their intention to hang him if they found him."

Sources: 1. *D.A.R. Lineage Book*, Vol. 117, page 147. 2. *Dictionary of North Carolina Biography: Vol. 3 H-K* edited by William S. Powell, page 139. 3. Sons of the American Revolution Application.

Enos Hitchcock

Enos Hitchcock was born on March 7, 1744, in Springfield, Massachusetts, and he died on February 27, 1803, in Providence, Rhode Island. He graduated from Harvard in 1767 and received his doctorate from Brown University in 1788.

When the war began he served as chaplain in the 3rd Continental Infantry and Patterson's Massachusetts' Brigade from March 1776 until 1780. He was at the Battles of Ticonderoga and Stillwater, and he was present for the surrender of General Burgoyne. He was stationed at West Point in 1780 and was there when Major Andre was captured and Benedict Arnold escaped.

Pastor Hitchcock noted the proceedings throughout the days of Andre's trial, and he witnessed the Major's execution. His account written on October 2, 1780, is as follows: "At twelve oClock this day was Executed Major Andre—He received his fate with greater apparent fortitude than others saw it—he appeared a most Genteel young fellow—handsomely dress in his regimentals—when he came to the Gallows, he said he well knew his fate but was disappointed in the mode—He ascended the wagon cheerfully fixed the halter round his own neck & bound his Eyes—said, smiling, a few moments would settle the whole—was asked if he had anything to offer—lifting up the handkerchief that covered his Eyes, said, Gentlemen, you will all bear witness that I met my fate like a brave man. Behold the end of humane greatness, by the hand of a common hangman."

After the war Pastor Hitchcock preached in several different communities until he finally settled in as pastor of the 1st Congregational Church in Providence, Rhode Island in 1783. He was a member of the Pennsylvania Society for promoting the abolition of slavery. At the time of his death in 1803 he was working to establish a public school system in Providence.

Sources: 1. *Harvard Alumni Veterans of the American Revolutionary War.* 2. *From Its European Antecedents to 1791—The United States Army Chaplaincy* by Parker C. Thompson, 1978, pages 191, 194, and 195. 3. *Sibley's Harvard Graduates,* Vol. 16, 1764–1767 by Clifford K. Shipton, Massachusetts Historical Society, 1972.

Andrew Hunter

Andrew Hunter was born c. 1752 in Virginia, and he died in 1823 in Washington, D.C. He moved to Princeton, New Jersey, and lived with his uncle. The uncle probably paid for his education at Princeton where Andrew graduated in 1772. A year after the Boston Tea Party, Andrew and 40 other patriots dressed as Indians and on December 22, 1774, they torched a load of tea destined for Philadelphia. This event became known as the Greenwich Tea Party.

In 1775 Andrew was commissioned a chaplain of the New Jersey

Brigade. Also around this time he married Ann Riddell. Ann died in 1793 and a year later Andrew married Mary Stockton the daughter of Richard Stockton who signed the Declaration of Independence.

Andrew kept a diary of his service in the Revolution. Below are two events that he took part in and wrote about. The diary gives a good account of battles and daily life of the soldiers. Part I of the diary covers the New York campaign from July 1776 until March 1777. Part II covers the Sullivan Expedition which took place in 1779.

Part I: The New York Campaign of 1776. The battle for New York took place primarily on Long Island and Manhattan Island and in Westchester County. This would be the first major battle of the Revolution after the signing of the Declaration of Independence.

Thursday August 22, 1776
> Very unwell in the morning—about 11 O'Clock an Express came from the Narrows that the Enemy were landing there and that Col. Hand the commanding Officer and his Regiment were retreating—our Drums beat *to Arms*—and every Regt. took its Alarm post—The Generals then viewed the Arrangement and detached two Rifle-Regts. and 3 Regts. of Muskettiers to meet the Enemy who then had advanced as far as Flatbush—Our Troops Marched near their Encampment and after placing proper guards lay down upon their arms.

Friday August 23, 1776
> A smart skirmish happened between our Men and an advanced Party of the Enemy—one of our Riflemen received a Musket Ball in his Thigh which broke the Bone. I was present at dressing the Wound a little distance from the place of Action—Oh the excruciating Pain! The Enemy's loss we are not yet able to ascertain tho' it is probable that it is not great—They however retreated to their main Body—We Detached 8 Regts. to relieve those who had been out the Day before. The Men upon our Lines all the Day engaged in making Piquets and Abbetiss, all in good Spirits and seem eager to fight.

Saturday August 24, 1776
> After visiting the Regt. I spent the former Part of the Day in Reading—A constant scattering Fire was kept up between the Enemy and our Men—little Damage was done on either Side—save that 7 of the Enemy were said to be killed—One of our men had his Leg shattered with a 6 Pound Ball—I was present when Dr. Warren amputated the Limb—the man fearcely distorted his Face, and never gave a groan. The operation was performed in about 3 minutes after the Tornequets were fixt—with very little Loss of Blood—Col. Martin on reconnoitring Party received a wound in his breast—Lieut. Thoms and four Privates taken Prisoners.

Tuesday August 27, 1776
> Early in the Morning the Enemy in the Woods attempted to surround our people in different Places which they in some degree effected—A warm engagement at different Quarters ensued—But the Enemy, being double in Number,

our Men were obliged to give Way. Many were killed, many wounded, some drowned, and others escaped by swimming—we make doubt but the Enemy's Loss was as great as ours, every Respect—we took about 30 of them Prisoners—We had about 300 Men lost—Two of our Brigadier Generals, Lord Sterling and Genl. Sullivan were taken Prisoners—Col. Johnson & Col. Terry were killed—The enemy appeared in open View in the afternoon in Large Columns—They began to cast up Works with about ¼ mile of Lines—a Lamentable Day.

Wednesday August 28, 1776

An incessant scattering Fire was kept up so that it was very dangerous to be out of a Fort—The Balls whizzed round our Ears from all Quarters—very little Damage Done on either Side—We were several Times alarmed with the Approach of the Enemy.

Thursday August 29, 1776

We remained in the same state—we threw several Shells at our Enemy, and they fired their Field-Pieces at us. In the Afternoon we received Orders to parade the different Regiments at 7 O'Clock to receive Orders. The Orders were to retreat to New York with all our Baggage, to carry off as much of our Artillery as possible—we were passing the River all Night in great hurry and confusion—This Retreat was wise determined and well executed—our People got safely over to N. York. We left the Tories of Long-Island in great Fear, and abandoned them to the Effects of their own cursed Devices.

During the retreat of the American army, Andrew and two others came close to walking into the enemy's hands. He wrote, "Colonel Brearly, Mr. Hollingshead, and myself, having missed the route of the troops, had nearly gone into the enemy's camp, had we not been prevented by some women whom we met running crying down the road."

Thursday September 5, 1776

Recd. Orders from Gen. Spencer to march immediately to Harlem—Col. Brearley went to Head Quarters to know what we should do for Tents—We were ordered by Gen. Washington to tarry in Town until Tents could be procured—The Flying Camp continued coming in all Day—There was a very smart Cannonading between our Batteries on the East River and the Rose on her Return to the Fleet—She received considerable Damage—An officer of our Train [i.e., artillery unit] had his right Toes shot off by a nine Pounder. Reports are spread abroad that we intend giving up the Town without Resistence, because all the Stores were moved out except what was thought requisite for carrying on an Engagement—We are determined to sell it at a high Price—much Blood and many Wounds.

The next day, on September 6, 1776, the first submersible, an underwater vessel, was used by the Americans. It was launched at 11 o'clock at night to sink the British flagship *HSM Eagle*. The lone crew member of the *Turtle* was Sergeant Ezra Lee, a volunteer. He made two attempts to attach a bomb to the hull of the British ship and both failed. Because of fatigue and the effects of breathing too much carbon dioxide, Lee abandoned his mission. It was the first recorded use of a submarine to attack a ship. In 1785 Washington wrote to Thomas Jefferson, "I then thought, and still think, that it was an effort of genius."

Monday September 9, 1776
    About 10 o'clock I marched with our Regt. from N. York towards Mount Washington and carried my Gun, Canteen and Ammunition, we arrived about 2 O'Clock P.M. where I met many of my old acquaintances of Col. Newcomb's Regt. and others—Lodged for the first Time in a Tent—Tents were procured for the Regt. but could not be pitched in season, so they were obliged to lye exposed to the Open Air—I thought then of many pleasant Nights I had spent without considering who had provided for me; or that I might be forced to live Harder—A Canonade was kept up all Day and as we came along the Road the Balls and Bombs were whizzing about us—we saw two large heaps of balls that had been picked up by our people wch. the Enemy had sent into the Camp. We are now got fairly into the spirit of a Soldier's Life.

Tuesday September 10, 1776
    About 9 O'Clock we had an Alarm that the Enemy had landed on a small Island called Blackwood's Island—The Drums beat and the Regt. paraded and were ordered to wait for Orders ready for Battle—An incessant Canonade all the forenoon near Hell-Gate—I find that York Island is formed by North River on the S. and W., by the Sound on the East and by Spikin Devil and Harlem on the North—those two small Streams flow together near Kings-bridge—We have an account that Genl. Lee is arrived in New York—Glad News to every Heart.

Monday September 16, 1776
    In the Morning about 9 O'Clock a smart Firing began between the advanced Parties of the Enemy and our people—They were reinforced on both Sides, so that a considerable number were engaged—The vollies were frequent from the Musketry—Some Field-pieces were introduced on both Sides—it continued for more than 2 hours, and ended much in our Favor—We lost about 50 killed, and had about 140 wounded. We took 3 or 4 prisoners and two of the Enemy's Field-pieces—Among our Dead was Col. Nolton [Knowlton] of the Rangers, a brave officer—We drove them more than a mile off the Ground—This small Engagement gave spirit to our Troops, and made some Retaliation for the shameful Scene of the Day before—I felt a great Degree of Composure thro' the whole, and desired to have an Opportunity of casting in my Mite, towards putting a Stop to the Ravages of a blood-thirsty Enemy. For 2 nights past I slept on the Lines w/the Regt.

Tuesday September 17, 1776
    The Drubbing which we gave the Enemy the day before produced an entire Cessation of every Thing hostile—we however lay upon the Line, 'til the Afternoon when we were relieved by other Troops and returned to our Camp much fatigued and having little to refresh us—Innumerable are the Fatigues of a Soldier's Life.

Hunter THE CHAPLAINS

Wednesday September 18, 1776
> Very little extraordinary happened—The Enemy made no Movement—A Captain of the Connecticut Troops was tried for forging a Pass from Gen. Wadsworth to carry him home—The Sentence of the Court Martial was that the Culprit should be dressed in Women's Cloths and having a wooden Sword by his Side, and a wooden Musket in his Hand, be placed on the Back of an old Horse to be carried thro the Camp in this ridiculous Manner and sent from Guard to Guard until he should get home. This Sentence was executed, with the addition of throwing Cow-dung and almost every Kind of excrement at the Rider—The insensible Scoundrel bore his fate with a good Deal of that resolution which every Rascal possesses—All this Effect of Cowardice—The basest of crimes in an Army.

Saturday September 21, 1776
> The Burning of the City of New York was this Morning confirmed by a Gentleman from Bergen Town who watched the Fire from 2 'til 4 O'Clock and saw the Steeple of the Old English Church where Dr. Auchmuty preached fall in, and the Enemy's Ships which were in the E. River move down towards Governor's Island.

In the early morning of September 21, 1776, the British destroyed nearly 25 percent of the buildings in New York City. An American prisoner, John Joseph Henry, aboard a prison ship was a witness to the fire and he claimed that it began in the Fighting Cocks Tavern, near Whitehall slip. Who started the fire remains a mystery.

British General Howe said the fire was deliberately set by a number of people that wanted to burn the town down. British governor William Tryon suspected that General Washington was behind it. Many Americans believed that Patriots started the fire. Some Americans accused the British troops of setting the fire, so that they could plunder the buildings.

Sunday September 22, 1776
> I preached to my Regiment in the Forenoon upon a small Hill out of the Noise of the Camp—The Soldiers seemed to give attention. After Service Majr. Livingston called at our Quarters and gave us a more particular Account of the Burning of New York—He informed that the West Side of Broad Way was burnt from opposite White Hall to Dean's Distillery above the College—In the Afternoon a Genl. Order came out for executing a Sergt. for Cowardice who had been convicted by Court Martial—and another [general order] for cashiering an Ensign for plundering—both N. England men. The Regiments of every Brigade were ordered to be paraded with all their Baggage—And the Field Officers to inspect their Knapsacks for plundered goods—Little or Nothing was found with our Brigade.

Monday September 23, 1776
> Attended in the forenoon on the Grand Parade where the Prisoner mentioned in yesterday's Orders was to be executed—The different Brigades between our

Lines and Kings Bridge were drawn up in two Columns with a large Interval between them—across this Interval was thrown up a Bank about 4 Feet high against which the prisoner was to stand that the Balls [i.e., firing squad's bullets] might not injure the Spectators—The Guard brought the reluctant malefactor and placed him near the Parapet—Dr. Leonard from the Eastwd. made a short Speech. The Prisoner was ordered to kneel down with his face towards the guard of 22 men who were to execute the Sentence of the Court—A white Handkerchief was bound over his Eyes—The Guard then advanced towards him with quick pace. The Provost Martial then read his Crime and his Sentence—In short all the Ceremony and Parade appeared as if the Man was immediately to be sent to the eternal World—But the clement and merciful Genl. Washington sent a written Pardon directed to the Adjutant General or other Commanding Officer. It was publicly read to the unspeakable Satisfaction of all present—But that he might not encourage such Base crimes by Clemency, he declared in the Reprieve that the next person guilty of the like conduct should suffer Death.—We hear that our People have evacuated Paulus Hook, but have got off all their ordinance and Stores—and have taken Possession of the Heights contiguous to it, which we trust they will be able to maintain.

Dysentery struck Chaplain Fithian, an old school mate of Andrew Hunter. Andrew visited him regularly and he later wrote to his young bride, "Were I in this situation should wish to see so near a Friend as a wife." Fithian died on October 9, 1776, before his wife could arrive.

Thursday October 31, 1776
> We had orders to march and join Lord Stirling's Brigade near North Castle. We marched accordingly about 4 O'Clock P.M., and encamped at a Tory's House with whom we supped and quartered that is the officers of Col. Cortlandt's Regt.—The Land Lord refused to take the Continental Money and we chose to give no other—About 9 O'Clock at night the Genl. gave orders to set Fire the House at the Plains—As much of our Baggage as we could we got off and burnt the remainder—The Ravages of War and the Destruction made by an Army's passing thro' a Country are unaccountable, not a living Creature, nor a Stick of Fence left, but what they kill and burn.

Monday November 4, 1776
> We heard from the Northern Department of our Army that upon the Enemy's attacking our Troops at Ticonderoga they were obliged to retreat with considerable loss. Two Deserters came in who inform that the Enemy in the New York Department intends making one more Stroke before they go into [winter] Quarters.—Genl. Heard came to Camp after having been at Home since the 27 of August—we had an officer shot by one of our own Sentries.

Wednesday November 6, 1776
> We are informed from good authority that the Enemy are retreating towards New York, via East Chester where a great Number of their Ships lie—We have a mouth Report that they are called Home on account of an expected Invasion

on Gt. Britain—Col. Martins and Newcombs Regiments are gone to Phillips' Mills near Dobb's Ferry. The Sick were all ordered up to Peck's Kiln to be safe in case of any sudden Movement.

Monday November 11, 1776

We marched early in the Morning upon a Letter from Ld. Stirling, and were ordered to halt at Slaughter's Landing—we passed in this Morning's Rout a place called Cases Landing, a place very convenient for Trade—We arrived about 11 O'Clock, and happily got lodging in a Whig's House on the Side of a Large Pond remarkable for Ducks and Fish called Cospeck or Snydicker's Pond—This place is opposite the [British] Men of War in the North River.

Tuesday November 12, 1776

Went with some Gentlemen to reconnoitre, we ascended a most prodigious Hill from whence we could discover that the Enemy's Ships were only about ½ mile from us—We heard that the Enemy had regularly besieged Fort Washington after having got Possession of the Heights contiguous to it—Genl Washington went down to enquire into the Circumstances of the Matter.

Wednesday November 20, 1776

In the Morning we had an Account of the Enemy's landing at Dobb's Ferry, and about 10 O'Clock we had orders to retreat taking what Baggage we could with us which was very little compared to what we left behind viz Tents, Cannons, Stores of every Kind. The Enemy soon took possession of Fort Lee, and had nearly taken a number of our Men—Col. Brearley, Mr. Hollingshead and Myself, having missed the Rout of our Troops, had nearly gone into the Enemy's Camp, had we not been prevented by some 200 men whom we met running crying in the Road—we halted at the New Bridge and encamped.

Andrew was with the 3rd New Jersey regiment at Valley Forge and at the Battles of Brandywine, Germantown, and Monmouth. After the battle of Monmouth he received a personal thanks from General Washington for his conduct during the battle.

Part II: The Sullivan Expedition of 1779. Andrew was one of five chaplains assigned to this expedition. The purpose of the expedition, ordered by George Washington, was to weaken the Tories and the four Amerindian nations of the Iroquois who had sided with the British.

Friday June 18, 1779

At 5 O'Clock A.M. the troops under the command of General Sullivan began their March from Easton for Wioming. We proceeded about five miles, halted and refreshed ourselves, after which we marched as far as Miller's Tavern where we arrived about 1 O'Clock in the Afternoon and formed our Encampment for the Night. According to the Order of March issued by the General, Maxwell's Brigade was in front, next Proctor's train of Artillery and last Poor's Brigade. The country we passed over this Day was hilly and stoney with scarcely any Timber fit for improvement. The ground is covered over with a thick brush called ground-oake. The inhabitants very few, and very ignorant of every thing except what passes in their native mountains. Our course this day was westwardly. Our distance 12 miles.

Wednesday June 23, 1779

In the morning the General ordered that the troops should clean and dress themselves. About 8 o'clock we marched for Wyoming—In about 3 miles we came to the place where Capt. Davies and Lt. Jones with a corporal and four privates were murdered by a party of the savages consisting of about twenty in April last. Two boards are set up at the very spots where Davies and Jones were killed with their names on them, and that where Jones was killed is besmeared with own blood. At this melancholy sight all without distinction appeared affected and many paid the universal indication of sorrow. Col. Proctor out of respect to the deceased caused his Band to play Roslin Castle. In about 2 miles farther we had a view of the River Susquehanna. We halted and made the necessary arrangement for an orderly march into town. Genl. Hand and many other Officers met us and welcomed us in. What we generally call Wyoming is called by the people of Connecticut who at present claim it Westmoreland County. It is laid out in 6 Townships Willsbury, Lackawaney & Nanticoke on the East, Exeter, Shawaney & Kingston on the West. The land is extremely good for about a mile in breadth on each side the River, the lots running from that to the mountain containing about 500 Acres each. They had a church & court house with many decent dwelling houses all which the enemy burnt after the memorable battle fought between the Butlers, in which about 250 of our men were killed, 100 of whom had wives and children. The widows and orphans having lost all their property have scarcely food to eat or clothe to wear. Near the Town is an excellent coal mine, said to contain a vast quantity of coal. After we had marched to our encamping ground, a number of us dined with Genl. Hand and some with other Officers. Went in the afternoon to visit the fort, and redoubts, which we judged not to be very defensible.

Sunday June 27, 1779

Agreeably to General Sullivan's orders I preached to the Jersey Brigade in the forenoon, and in the latter part of the day spent my time in reading the Bible.

Monday June 28, 1779

Began a sermon in the forenoon and after Dinner visited Col. Proctor of the Artillery.

Tuesday June 29, 1779

Visited two men in the provost, who were under sentence of death—one of whom I found to be a little tender [i.e., of spirit?], the other more stupid than usual. I endeavoured to array before them the sinfulness of their nature, the heinousness of their crimes and particularly that of which they had been convicted by a court martial, seducing several of our soldiers to desert. This day arrived about 35 boats from Sunbury loaded with stores and provisions for the Expedition up the river under convoy of the First Jersey Regiment which had been sent to Fort Jenkins, 30 miles from Wyoming & the same distance from the forks of Susquehanna, for that purpose. The boats, which the inhabitants call Batteaux, carry between two and three tons.

Saturday July 17, 1779

Studied the forenoon—Informed that the Indians had been committing some outrages on the west branch of Susquehanna, by killing 9 or 10 men who were making hay at Lacommon.

Wednesday July 21, 1779

This morning an express arrived with the following intelligence from the main Army. That on the night of the 15 inst. General Wayne with a part of his Light Infantry surprized and took the whole garison at Stoney-point, with all their cannon and stores, tents and baggage of every kind with the loss of 4 or 5 men. The garison consisted of British, Scots, and New-levies—with 2 or 3 companies of grenadiers and matrosses—in all about 500.—We had also information of a party of Indians being at Minisink and burning and plundering as they went.

Wednesday July 28, 1779

News arrived of a large body of Indians having drawn about 140 of our Militia stationed on the Delaware above the Minisink into an ambuscade. 18 or 20 only of the party made their escape. All the rest fell a prey to savage barbarity. This unfortunate affair happend 22d Inst.

Friday August 13, 1779

The army after marching all night arrived at Chemung, 15 miles from Tioga, about 5 o'Clock in the morning—The advanced party entered the town which they found evacuated, and after searching the houses, etc., were ordered to advance some distance beyond the town along the river. On their advance they found where the Indians had lain the night before and proceeding in pursuit of them were fired on from the top of a little hill where they had formed an ambuscade. Genl. Hand ordered his men to advance upon them, upon which they ran into an almost impervious front. The party returned towards the town and the whole had orders to cross the river and march about 2 miles up on the west side to destroy some large fields of Corn. When they were cutting down the corn, the Indians fired again across the river from the same place without effect. We had 6 men killed and 7 or 8 wounded. Among the latter were Capt. Carbury & Lt. Houston both of the 11th Pennsylvania Regt.—while the advanced party was pursuing the Indians the other Troops set fire to the town, which consisted of about 30 houses, and carefully attended it 'till consumed. The troops then returned to Tioga much fatigued, having been marching the whole night and day almost without intermission.

Monday August 16, 1779

The party to meet Genl. Clinton under command of Genl. Poor & Genl. Hand marched about 10 o'Clock A.M. An Express arrived from Wyoming by whom Genl. Sullivan received a Letter from Genl. Clinton informing that he intended to leave Ononguage the 16 instant—Recd. a letter from Mrs. Hunter of the 26 ultimo. informing of her ill state of health. The letter had been broke open, but as it contained no secrets nor did any discredit to the writer, it gave me no uneasiness. The practice of breaking letters always excites in one a sufficient degree of contempt abstracting from the meanness of the agent.

Tuesday August 17, 1779

Began to read Burlamaqui on the principles and law of Nature—A party of Indians said to be ten or twelve waylaid six men belonging to the German Battalion who had been out hunting horses—The parties fired on each other and both endeavoured to escape—We had one man killed whom the savages scalped before they went off, and one wounded who got in—Detachmts. were immediately sent out, but could not overtake them.

Thursday August 16, 1779

About half after twelve o'Clock the army, except about 500 men, lame, sick and cowardly under command of Col. Shreve, & all the women, marched about 4 miles up the Caiuga branch, where we encamped about 3 o'Clock—along the river side for this distance we had exceeding good wild meadow, which bears a luxuriant burden of grass nutritious and agreeable to both horses and black Cattle. I took leave of several of my friends who tarried behind with some scruples about the time and manner of my seeing them again. About 20 boats accompanied us to carry some supernumery articles of provision.

Friday August 27, 1779

Marched about 7 o'Clock A.M. and reached the lower Chemung flats about 10 o'Clock at night—The road this day generally pretty good except a long defile formed by a mountain and the river, at the end of which we were detained about 6 hours before we could make it passable and after every thing we could do it took 100 men with drag ropes to assist the waggons and artillery—notwithstanding the former were not half loaded—At these flats we found large quantities of Indian Corn cultivated probably by the Tories for the Indian expeditions against our frontiers, which after taking as much as we could use, we destroyed—Many of the soldiery found other plunder taken from our distressed friends at different places. We crossed two clever streams of water between the defile and this camp—our distance 6 miles & our course N W.

Saturday August 28, 1779

On account of our late arrival last night we did not move till 3 o'Clock P.M.— and arived at Chemung about 6 o'Clock—on this days march we crossed the Caiuga branch to the west side and after marching about two miles we recrossed it. The stream was not more than middle deep; but so rapid that many of our men and horses were swept down and would have been drowned had it not been for the timely assistance of those who were stronger—I myself dragged one and carried another across. At Chemung there are fine flats on both sides of the river—This day Genl. Sullivan ordered the troops to live upon corn and beans to lengthen out our provision assuring us that we should not be credited by that day's rations.—Our distance about 4 miles and our course N. W.

Sunday August 29, 1779

Marched from Chemung about 11 o'Clock—after marching about three miles our advanced party was fired on by a few Indians—The Army was halted and reconnoitring parties sent out who discovered that the enemy had thrown up extensive works of wood and bushes on the farther side of a small creek and swamp, the right of which extended almost to the confluence of this creek with the Caiuga branch—The General after giving the necessary orders to every department detached Genl. Poor's brigade to turn their right flank and at the same time began a canonade in their front with two pieces of artillery which soon occasioned them to leave their works with great disorder. Genl. Poor however fell in with them in their way to take post on a high hill to the left of their lines, and had a severe scattering engagement and caused them to retreat in great confusion—We had during the whole action only three men killed and about 30 wounded—We took 11 scalps and two prisoners both Tories—The engagement began about 2 o'Clock and continued 'till 5 in the afternoon after which we marched on about 2 miles and encamped at a small town, on the ground where the enemy had lain about 8 days. We found large quantities of corn growing on the flats on both sides of the river, which we effectually destroyed—We took a great deal of plunder at different places and secreted in different ways—It appeared upon the examination of the prisoners that the famous Butler and Brant were both of the party—and that their number was 220 whites called Butler's rangers and 400 Indians—I attended the amputation of an officer's leg the same night which was a scene more distressing than that in the day.

Wednesday September 1, 1779

Began our march about 10 o'Clock. The country continued open about 5 miles except one bad defile, we then entered a thick woody swamp, covered with pine, Hemlock, etc., which continued near 5 miles and cost us much difficulty to pass. In this swamp we came upon a large stream which runs northerly and empties into the Senekaa Lake. This is the first turn of the waters. After we crossed the swamp we turned down the east side of it thro a large tract of bottom land and in three miles came to French-Catarine's Town, consisting of about 15 houses, etc., within 3 miles of the south end of the Senekaa-lake. Here we found two very old squaws who had been left by the Indians to suffer the calamities of war. They informed us that the families and the warriors had considerable altercation about leaving the Town, the former were for staying and submitting to their fate, the latter urged that they should be obliged to give up prisoners to redeem them—The families left the place about the middle of the day and the warriors not 'till near sun-set—The Genl. left the old squaw that was brought into Camp a small bark house and provision enough to subsist her several Days—She was exceedingly Thankful that the *Great-Spirit* had put it into his heart to spare her life—Before we arrived at Cathrine's town the most distressing scene took place—Before the rear of the army got thro' the swamp mentioned above, night came on, the troops got separated from their own corps and the pack-horses and Artillery intermixed—In a word the whole army was a perfect chaos, without order or distinction, and to complete all the enemy were in our front—In this State the front of the Army marched near three miles, the rear however lay in the swamp 'till next morning. In this confused scene we had two or three horses drowned in the creek runing thro the swamp which the army forded near twenty times—Our distance this day 13 miles and our course nearly North.

Tuesday September 14, 1779

After destroying the corn and seting fire to the houses we left Kossawauloughary about 12 o'Clock. This Town's name signifies, the spear laid up—After crossing a creek about 20 yards wide and passing thro' a small tract of bottom land we got into one of the largest and most beautiful planes I ever saw, called Chenesey Flats—It is supposed to contain upward of 10,000 acres of land, and is covered with grass from 4 to 8 feet high—Here the whole army and its apparatus could be seen at one view, which exhibited a most lovely prospect especially to one acquainted with their virtue and bravery—In about two miles we came to the great Seneca river which we forded, being not more than 40 yards wide; we then left the Flats, ascended the hill, and stood down the river for Chenesee which we reached in about 4 miles. Chenesee was the Capitol of the 6 nations and especially of the Senecas, consisting of near 50 houses. The quantities of corn were unaccountable, field upon field, and that the most luxuriant—Here we found two of the prisoners taken the day before, supposed to be Lt. Boyd & a private, most barbarously murdered—Lt. Boyd's head was cut off, skinned, both eyes taken out, and his tongue cut out by the root—his body was speared in 7 places and his private parts cut off—The soldier's head was cut off and skinned, the flesh was cut in steakes off his shoulder, and back—Barbarity and cruelty itself instigated by the Devil could not shew a more shocking spectacle. Here we encamped for the night. Our Whole distance about 6 miles this day and our course about No. West.

Wednesday September 15, 1779

The forenoon continued at Chenesee to destroy the corn, and about 2 o'Clock after seting fire to every thing combustible we marched agreeably to general orders towards Cossawaulougharey on our way to Tioga. No symptoms of joy ever appeared more strongly painted in the countenances of a set of men, than those discovered at the order for our return, and no obedience was ever paid with greater alacrity. Before we left Chenesee a white woman with her child about 2 years old who had made her escape from the Savages came to us. Her history was truly lamentable. Her husband, herself and three children were made prisoners at Wyoming in the spring of 78 and brought into the Indian country—Her husband was murdered after they arrived at Cossawaulougharey, where she has been kept ever since, her two elder children who were little Girls about 8 or 10 years old were torn from her and taken to a distant town where she supposes they have continued ever since—This tragical story she related pathetically—her dress was much in the Indian taste, but her appearance was delicate—Chenesee is said to be between 70 and 80 miles from Niagara and about 30 from lake Ontario. This evening we returned as far as the creek at the east end of the Chenesee plains.

Wednesday September 29, 1779

The whole army began their march for Tioga about 11 o'Clock and arrived at the plains of lower Chemung about 3 in the Afternoon, where we encamped. After night the parties under Dayton & Cortland returned and reported that they had destroyed several cornfields.

Thursday September 30, 1779

The army began their march about 9 o'Clock and arrived at Tioga about 3 in the afternoon—on our way we were met by many of the Officers from Tioga who gave us a very hearty welcome—Col. Shreve gave an invitation to all the principal Officers of the Army to dine with him—accordingly all the General Officers, etc., partook of his dinner with great Festivity—Upon our arrival we were saluted by the firing of 13 pieces of cannon from the fort and returned the salute with 13 rounds from our grass hoppers [small cannons].

Friday October 1, 1779
> About 3 o'Clock in the afternoon Col. Dayton, Major Ogden, and myself took leave of our friends, embarked with our baggage on board of a boat for Wyoming—where we arrived the next day after sunset, after rowing the whole night.

After the war ended Andrew taught and became active in local politics. One of his sons, David, later became a leading Union general in the Civil War. He entered the United States Navy as a chaplain in 1811. He was assigned to prepare a curriculum for the young midshipmen stationed at the Washington Naval Yard, and he became the organizer and for a time the entire faculty of what was to be the Naval Academy at Annapolis.

Sources: 1. *Hunter Family Records* by William M. Clemens, 1914. 2. *From Its European Antecedents to 1791—The United States Army Chaplaincy* by Parker C. Thompson, 1978, pages 87, 142–143, 182, 186, and 188. 3. Diary of Andrew Hunter. 4. *Encyclopedia of New Jersey*, page 396. 5. *The Chaplains and Clergy at the Battle of Monmouth* by Chaplain Stanley Cuyler, 1986, page 10. 6. *The Campaign of 1776 around New York and Brooklyn* by Henry Phelps Johnston, 1878.

David Jones

David Jones was born on May 12, 1736, in Delaware, and he died on February 5, 1820, in Chester County, Pennsylvania. He married Anne Stillwell on February 15, 1762. He became a Baptist preacher, after he completed his training at Hopewell Academy in New Jersey and went to the wilderness of Ohio to convert Indians to Christianity in 1772. While navigating the Ohio River in a canoe, one of his companions was the famous George Rogers Clark.

Because he preached in favor of the patriot cause he felt his life was in danger from the Tories, so he moved from New Jersey to Chester County, Pennsylvania. In 1776 he was appointed by General Anthony Wayne as chaplain and doctor to a Pennsylvania regiment under the command of Colonel St. Clair. Pastor Jones held the rank equal to that of a Major.

He was also a scout and courier carrying messages between General Wayne, George Washington, and Benjamin Franklin. In a letter written to Benjamin Franklin by General Wayne from Fort Ticonderoga on July

29, 1776, Wayne wrote, "We are so removed from the seat of Government of the free and independent states of America, and such an Insurmountable Barrier, Albany, between us that not one letter, or the least intelligence of anything that's doing with you can reach us. Through the medium of my Chaplain [David Jones] I hope this will reach you as he has promised to blow out any man's brains who will attempt to take it from him."

While serving under Colonel St. Clair he was stationed at Fort Ticonderoga and the enemy was expected to attack at any time. Before the battle he preached a sermon trying to steady the nerves of his men. He told them that the individual soldier is, *"the ultimate weapon."* He then delivered a rousing sermon of blessings and curses.

The fort was under the command of Generals Schuyler and St. Clair. The two men decided to give up the fort to the British with almost no resistance. Both men were criticized for their decision. John Adams wrote, "I think we shall never be able to defend a post until we shoot a general." Both generals were relieved of their commands.

Pastor Jones became the Brigade Chaplain under General Wayne, and on September 11, 1777, he was at the battle of Brandywine. Jones knew the area quite well having lived in the area as a young boy. Armed with two pistols he led a detachment of cavalrymen to do a recon of the area. He led a failed attempt to capture a mounted Hessian patrol, but he did manage to personally capture a British dragoon at pistol point.

News of the pastor's exploits spread through the ranks and it was said that General Wayne, upon hearing of the event, laughed "immoderately." Later, when Jones rode by a group of British prisoners of war the man he had captured recognized the minister. The prisoner tipped his hat and bowed. During the Battle at Brandywine Jones had a horse shot out from under him. The British were also aware of his heroism on the battlefield, because British General Howe offered a reward for his capture.

Pastor Jones also served in the Battles of Germantown, Monmouth, Paoli, and Greenville. He was also with Washington at Valley Forge. Because Valley Forge was near the home of Jones, he was sent on several scouting assignments to discover the enemy's movement. On one mission he stopped at a tavern to spend the night. While he was eating his supper, he noticed a stranger that made him suspicious. He walked over to the man, drew his pistol, and placed him under arrest. The man later confessed to being a British officer.

At the Battle of Paoli on September 20, 1777, an American force under the command of General Anthony was left behind, as the main body of Washington's army was retreating from Brandywine. Anthony was given the assignment to harass the British army as it marched to Philadelphia.

At 10 p.m. the British launched a surprise attack on the Americans near the Paoli Tavern. Over 1,200 British troops charged in three waves against the sleeping Americans. To keep the attack a surprise British General Grey ordered the men to remove the flints from their muskets. The General was later given the nickname "No Flint" Grey. The British, using their musket butts and bayonets, killed, wounded, and captured over 200 Americans. Some of the wounded were bayonetted as they tried to surrender. When the Americans later recovered the butchered bodies of their friends they swore revenge.

Pastor Jones wrote in his diary that he had a feeling that something was going to happen that night. Jones slept in his clothing, had his horse saddled and ready to ride in a moment's notice. This action may have saved his life.

Jones was also with Washington at the surrender of Cornwallis at Yorktown in October of 1781. Most chaplains wore their black robes, and a few would wear something other than black. At Yorktown Jones wore "a coat of a dark color, mixed black and white, trimmed with a cord—and he wore an officer's hat."

After the war Pastor Jones returned home and resumed being a country preacher. In 1794 General Wayne took command of the army in the Northwest Territory to fight Indians. Once again 58-year-old David Jones was appointed chaplain. He became the second chaplain ever of the Regular United States Army, and he continued to serve until 1800.

When the War of 1812 began President Madison asked Jones, now 76, to again serve his country as a chaplain. Once again the old man served with the troops at battles in Ohio, Fort Detroit, Forts Erie, and Fort Ontario. In 1815 he was discharged and returned home. Had Jones been alive in 1845 during the war with Mexico, he would have probably served again.

Jones died at his home on February 5, 1820. It was said of him, "In danger he knew no fear, in fervent patriotism he had no superiors and few equals, in the Revolutionary struggle he was a tower of strength … and in piety he was a Christian without reproach."

Sources: 1. *Pictorial Field Book of the Revolution* by Benson J. Lossing, Vol. II, 1850. 2. *From Its European Antecedents to 1791—The United States Army Chaplaincy* by Parker C. Thompson, 1978, pages 146, 173–174, 180, 182, 185, and 277. 3. Pennsylvania Veterans Burial Cards 1777–2012. 4. *D.A.R. Lineage Book*, Vol. 1, page 272. 5. *The Chaplains and Clergy at the Battle of Monmouth* by Chaplain Stanley Cuyler, 1986, pages 9 and 16.

Thomas Kendall

Thomas Kendall was born on April 15, 1745, in Hopkington, Massachusetts, and he died on December 5, 1836, in New Lebanon, New York. He married Ruth Walters on July 8, 1784. He graduated from Dartmouth College in 1774 and preformed missionary work with the Caghuawaga Indians of Canada.

Thomas enlisted January 1, 1776, in Colonel Parson's Regiment and served around Lake Champlain. He later served as chaplain in General Knox's Continental Artillery Regiment at Forts Ticonderoga and Mount Independence. He might had been at the Battle of Trenton, because he served under Knox until January 1, 1777. He received a yearly pension of $240 for his service.

Sources: 1. *Historic Homes & Institutions and Personal Memoirs of Worcester County, Massachusetts*, published in 1907. 2. Pension Application S10935. 3. Sons of the American Revolution Application. 4. *D.A.R. Lineage Book*, Vol. 22, page 20.

Samuel Kirkland

Samuel Kirkland was born on December 1, 1741, in Norwich, Connecticut, and he died on February 28, 1808, in Clinton, New York. He married Jerusha Bingham on September 18, 1769. In 1762 he entered Princeton College and received his degree in 1765.

Like many of his classmates Samuel became a missionary among the Indians. He spent a year and a half among the Senecas, a powerful and warlike member of the Six Nations. He hoped to enlist the Indians on the side of the Americans, or at least convince them to remain neutral. In 1777 each member of the Six Nations decided who they would support in the war. Four of the nations supported the British and two, the Oneidas and Tuscaroras, supported the American cause. Samuel then went to live among the Oneidas.

Samuel knew many of the hunters and trappers who roamed through the New York wilderness. Because these men had information about the British and the Indians tribes that supported them, Samuel would gather information that could be useful to the American Army. In addition to gathering intelligence, he also became a chaplain on the staff of American General Sullivan. Congress paid Samuel $300 for this double duty.

He was assigned to Fort Stanwick deep in the New York wilderness. He saw the importance of personal contact with the troops when he wrote, "I am to be faithful in improving opportunities of personal intercourse with the troops, to enliven their love of God and of liberty, and their readiness to do and to suffer for the cause of the country."

After the war Samuel continued to work and live among the Oneidas. The state of New York together with the Oneida Indians gave Samuel 4,700 acres of land so that he could live among the Indians. In 1793 he established the Hamilton Oneida Academy (later Hamilton College) for educating Indian and white children. In 1796 Samuel was thrown from a horse and was seriously injured. He never recovered from the accident and was an invalid until he died in 1808. The Oneida Chief, Skenando, who became a loyal and close friend of Samuel, later requested that he be buried next to his white friend.

Sources: 1. *From Its European Antecedents to 1791—The United States Army Chaplaincy* by Parker C. Thompson, 1978, pages 183, and 186-187. 2. *The Chaplains and Clergy of the Revolution* by Joel Tyler Headly, 1864, pages 239-244. 3. *A History of Wilkes-Barre* by Oscar Jewell Harvey, 1909, pages 1190-1191. 4. *Samuel Kirkland's Mission to the Iroquois* by Herbert John Lennox, 1935, pages 8-9. 5. *With Musket and Tomahawk: The Saratoga Campaign and the Wilderness War of 1777* by Michael O. Lopez, pages 141-143. 6. *Reminiscences and Memorials of Men of the Revolution and Their Families* by A.B. Muzzey, 1883, pages 144-146.

Abiel Leonard

Abiel Leonard was born in 1740, and he died on August 14, 1777. He served as chaplain in the 3rd Connecticut Infantry from May 1775 until January of 1776, when he was transferred to Colonel Knox's 20th Artillery Regiment under the command of Lt. Colonel Durkee. He served in the 20th Regiment until the summer of 1777.

The Chaplains — Leonard

On December 15, 1775, George Washington wrote to Jonathan Trumbull, the governor of Connecticut: "Having heard that it is doubtful whether the Reverend Mr. Leonard from your Colony, from the circumstances of his affairs, will have it in his power to continue here as a Chaplain, I cannot but express some concern, as I think his departure will be a loss—His general conduct has been exemplary and praiseworthy—In discharging the duties of his office, active and industrious—He has discovered himself a warm and steady friend to his Country, and taken great pains to animate the Soldiery and impress them with a knowledge of the important Rights we are contending for—Upon the late desertion of the Troops he delivered a sensible and judicious discourse, holding forth the necessity of courage and bravery, and at the same time of perfect obedience and subordination to those in Command."

On February 7, 1776, Abiel Leonard was appointed to the 20th Regiment. In March of 1776 George Washington valued Leonard's service so much, that he wrote the pastor's congregation asking that Leonard be allowed to extend his army tour.

In 1777 army life began taking a toll, both physically and mentally. The inoculation Leonard received for protection against smallpox left him in a weakened and troubled state. Abiel had a history of mental illness which began to resurface by the summer of 1777. He attempted suicide by cutting his throat. In a letter from a "Camp 5 Miles North of Peeks Kills" on August 2, 1777, Chaplain Ebenezer David wrote": I suppose you have heard the shocking news of Parson Leonard's making an attack upon his own Life with a Razon the Gash was deep & his life despaired of some time but hopes are now entertained of his recovery— What are men when left to themselves—this awful accident gives me great concern not only as it respects himself & his immediate connections but on account of the use which the Enemies of our Religion & Country will make of it—People here are generally satisfied what disappointments lead him to so dreadful an act...." Leonard died 12 days after this letter was written.

Sources: 1. *From Its European Antecedents to 1791—The United States Army Chaplaincy* by Parker C. Thompson, 1978, pages 108, 117–119, and 272. 2. *Sacred Scripture, Sacred War: The Bible & the American Revolution* by James P. Byrd, page 43. 3. *God of Liberty: A Religious History of the American Revolution*, pages 120–121. 4. archives.gov/documents/Washington. 5. *D.A.R. Lineage Book*, Vol. 12, page 45.

Isaac Lewis

Isaac Lewis was born on January 21, 1746, in Stratford, Connecticut, and he died on August 27, 1840, in Greenwich, Connecticut. He married Hannah Beak in 1768. He was commissioned chaplain from May to December 1776 in Colonel Philip Bradley's Connecticut state Militia.

When the British attempted to land at Norwalk, Lewis gathered his people to repel them. The attack began on Sunday, July 11, 1779, although some of the monuments commemorating the battle have it beginning on the 12th. The mistake is probably due to people not believing that the British would attack a town on a Sunday.

Norwalk was attacked because it was a Patriot base for espionage, for munitions' manufacturing and a supply depot. Twenty-six hundred British and Hessian troops landed and faced 800 American troops. British Commander Tyron sat in a rocking chair atop a hill and watched the town being burned. During the attack Pastor Lewis had a cannon ball strike the ground three feet away from where he was standing. Much of the town was destroyed by the time the British retreated.

Lewis gathered his people together after the battle and preached to them from Isaiah. "Our holy and beautiful house, where our fathers praised thee, is burned with fire, and all our pleasant things are laid to waste. Wilt thou refrain thyself for these things, O Lord, wilt thou hold thy peace, and afflict is very sore."

Sources: 1. *The Minute Man*, Vol. 11–20. 2. *Yale and Her Honor-Roll in the American Revolution* by Henry Phelps Johnston, page 244. 3. *The Chaplains and Clergy of the Revolution* by Joel Tyler Headley, 1864, pages 71–72. 4. Sons of the American Revolution Application. 5. *D.A.R. Lineage Book*, Vol. 51, page 104. 6. Tombstone.

Louis Eustace Lotbiniere

During the Revolutionary War a handful of Catholic priests served as chaplains for the Americans. Louis Lotbiniere, a French Canadian, is considered the first Catholic chaplain in the American Army. He served with "Congress' Own" 1st and 2nd Canadian Regiments.

In 1775–76 two regiments of French Canadians were recruited for the army, because the Canadian soldiers were predominately Catholic. He was appointed on January 26, 1776, by Benedict Arnold, and when the siege of Quebec ended he accompanied the troops back to U.S. soil and remained with the army the remainder of the war serving mainly in the Philadelphia area.

Bishop Jean-Olivier Briand of Quebec had told Canadian Catholic troops not to join the American Army. Louis, who joined the army when he was over 60 years old, was excommunicated and his possessions were taken away. Louis died in poverty in 1786 at the age of 71.

Sources: 1. *Blackrobe in Blue: The Naval Chaplaincy of John P. Foley, S.J.* by Steve O'Brien, 1942, pages 8–9. *Chronology of the American Revolution: Military and Political Actions Day by Day* by Bud Hannings, page 49. 3. *From Its European Antecedents to 1791—The United States Army Chaplaincy* by Parker C. Thompson, 1978, pages 181 and 200.

Daniel McCalla

Daniel McCalla was born on July 23, 1748, in Neshaminy, Pennsylvania, and he died in May of 1809 in Charleston County, South Carolina. He married Elizabeth Todd on April 7, 1778. He was licensed to preach, by the First Presbytery of Philadelphia, on July 20, 1772. Daniel was appointed by Congress to be the chaplain of General William Thompson's 2nd Pennsylvania Battalion. He was the only chaplain that Congress ever appointed.

General Thompson was sent to reinforce American troops in Canada. The Americans learned that a force of only 300 British troops were at Trois-Rivieres. General Thompson was not aware that a major force of British reinforcements had arrived. The General was not familiar with the geography, so consequently he led his force of 2,000 of Americans into a swamp. The American force arrived late in the morning, losing the element of surprise, and they were entangled in the swamp when they attacked the British. Chaplain McCalla charged the enemy alongside General Thompson, and the two of them plus 234 other American soldiers were captured.

Daniel was declared a "rebel parson" and was confined for several months on a British prison ship. He was subjected to harsh treatment and near starvation. He was eventually paroled, not exchanged, so he could not reenter military service. Daniel returned to his congregation, and as a result of his captivity he suffered from a "protracted disease" for the rest of his life.

Pastor McCalla was later charged with having violated his parole by praying for his country. Fearing arrest he left and escaped to Virginia. He was soon released from his parole by an exchange of prisoners. In 1788 he moved to South Carolina and became minister of a Congregational Church near Charleston. He died in May of 1809, and in his funereal sermon the Rev. De. Hollingshead of Charleston described Daniel: Dr. McCalla was in person a graceful figure; polite, easy and engaging in his manners; entertaining and improving in conservation; of a lively fancy and a generous heart; of unfettered liberality and undissembled candour."

Sources: 1. *From Its European Antecedents to 1791—The United States Army Chaplaincy* by Parker C. Thompson, 1978, pages 123–124. 2. *Annals of the American Pulpit* by William Sprague, Vol. 3, pages 320–322. 3. *By the Hand of Providence: How Faith Shaped the American Revolution* by Rod Gragg, page 81. 4. *Pennsylvania in the War of the Revolution: Battalions and Line*, 1775–1783, page 51.

Samuel McClintock

Samuel McClintock was born on May 1, 1732, in Medford, Massachusetts, and he died on August 27, 1804, in Greenland, New Hampshire. His first wife was Mary Montgomery and they had 15 children. They had four sons that fought in the Revolution and three of them were killed. Samuel graduated from the College of New Jersey in 1751 and was ordained in 1756. He was pastor of the Congregational Church in Greenland from 1756 until his death in 1804. He served as a chaplain in the French and Indian Wars.

On June 17, 1775, he was at the Battle of Bunker Hill serving as chaplain in Colonel Stark's 1st New Hampshire Regiment. He later served with Colonel Reed and Colonel Poor. When Stark's regiment arrived at the scene, he was ordered to deploy his men where he thought they would do the most good. Colonel Stark believed that the British would try and flank the rebels by landing on the beach of the Mystic River about 1,000 feet north of Breeds Hill. Stark took his 400 men and had them "fortify a two-rail fence" in the area.

He had his men three deep behind the fence, and when the British troops were almost on them he ordered them to stand and all fire at once.

Ninety of the enemy were at once killed and the rest fled in a panic. A second and third charge by the British was met with the same result. The remaining British troops decided to attack somewhere else. Colonel Stark's men were later ordered to help provide cover for the retreating American troops.

In the painting by Trumbull of the Battle of Bunker Hill, representing the fall of General Warren, Samuel may be seen in a group of clergy men grouped together and carrying a flag. He is standing behind rebel Thomas Knowlton who is holding a musket.

Sources: 1. *The Twentieth Century Biographical Dictionary of Notable Americans* by Eli McClish, Vol. VII. 2. *D.A.R. Lineage Book*, Vol. 39, page 64. 3. *Princeton Alumni Weekly*, Vol. 9, page 313. 4. Sons of the American Revolution Application. 5. U.S. Revolutionary War Rolls 1775–1783. 6. *The Soldiers' Memorial 1893–1921 Storer Post*, No. 1, page 46 and 47. 7. *From Its European Antecedents to 1791—The United States Army Chaplaincy* by Parker C. Thompson, 1978, page 113.

Charles McKnight

Charles McKnight was born c. 1710 in Northern Ireland, and he died on January 1, 1778, in Middletown, New Jersey. He married Elizabeth Stevens on August 19, 1746. He arrived in America c. 1740 and was ordained as a Presbyterian minister in 1742.

He preached loud and often against the British rule in the colonies. He once told his congregation, "God will take care of your liberty if you will take care of the redcoats." He served as a chaplain at the Battle of Princeton on January 3, 1777, and was wounded by a British saber.

On April 13, 1777, the British attacked the town of Matawan from several directions with the main objective to burn the Mount Pleasant Church and capture its preacher Charles McKnight. Men on both sides were killed and the pastor was captured. McKnight was taken to the prison ship *New Jersey* and held there until the end of the year. Due to his harsh treatment in captivity his health began to fail. He developed pneumonia and died on January 1, 1778, shortly after his release.

Sources: 1. *This Old Monmouth of Ours* by William S. Homor, page 155–56. 2. Sons of the American Revolution application. 3. *New Jersey Marriage Records 1683–1802*, page 258. 3. *By the Hand of Providence: How Faith Shaped the American Revolution* by Rod Gragg, page 81. 4. *Matawan and Aberdeen: Of Town and Field* by Helen Henderson, page 42–43. 5. *Cranbury: A New Jersey Town from the Colonial Era to the Present* by John Whiteclay Chambers, page 34.

Robert McMordie

Robert McMordie was born in Ireland in 1722, and he died on May 22, 1796, in Gettysburg, Pennsylvania. He married Janet Boyd on December 12, 1754.

Robert became chaplain of the 11th Pennsylvania Line on May 17, 1777, and he was promoted to Chaplain of the 1st Pennsylvania Brigade on July 15, 1780, by General St. Clair. He was at Valley Forge and he served until 1782. He received 400 acres of land in Jefferson County, Pennsylvania, for his service. The census of 1790 records him owning one slave.

His obituary in the *Pennsylvania Herald & York General Advertiser*, June 8, 1796, stated, "Died a few days ago, the Rev Robert M'Murdie, aged above 70 years. He enjoyed an uncommon state of good health during his whole life, even a few moments before his death he was reading in his chair, from which he fell, & expired without a groan. He was a Chaplain during the greater part of the War & marched at the head of the Regiment with his sword always ready for action. He was a loving husband & affectionate parent, a sincere friend & an outgoing neighbor."

Sources: 1. Tombstone. 2. *The Centennial Memorial of the Presbytery of Carlisle*, Vol. 2, 1889, page 38. 3. The State Society of the Cincinnati of Pennsylvania.

Alexander McWhorter

Alexander McWhorter was born on July 15, 1734, in Newcastle, Delaware, and he died on July 20, 1807, in New Jersey. He was licensed to preach in 1758. When the Revolution began he was so outspoken for the American cause that Congress sent him to North Carolina to win people of loyalist sympathies to the side of the patriots. The Tories hated him so much that he was forced to flee North Carolina and return to New Jersey. In June of 1775 he met George Washington, who was in Newark on his way north to take command of the Continental army in Massachusetts. In 1776 he joined the army and became a personal chaplain of George Washington. Alexander was present at the Council of War on the Pennsylvania side of the Delaware River when Washington prepared his attack on Trenton. He crossed the Delaware and fought with Washington at Trenton on December 26, 1776.

In the winter of 1777–78 he suffered the hardships at Valley Forge. In the summer of 1778 General Knox made an urgent request that Alexander become his chaplain of his brigade that was encamped at White Plains. He agreed, and he was with the army at the Battle of Monmouth on June 28, 1778. Knox's artillery provided cover for the American troops. Alexander was present when Mary Hayes (Molly Pitcher) manned the gun, which her husband operated after he was killed. During the battle Alexander helped move the heavy cannons up and down hills many times under intense fire.

During the battle Mary Hays attended to the soldiers by giving them water. It was well over 100 degrees during the battle, and many men on both sides suffered from heat exhaustion. When her husband William was severely wounded and carried off the battlefield, she took his place at the cannon. She continued to "swab and load" the cannon with a ramrod. During the battle a British cannon ball passed between her legs and tore her skirt. She was reported to have said, "Well, that could have been worse," and she continued loading the cannon.

Later that summer Alexander's wife, Mary, was injured by lightning, and although not killed he was needed at home to take care of her. In the spring of 1779 he moved to North Carolina to become the minister of a church there and president of a local academy. When the British invaded North Carolina in 1780 Alexander returned north. In April of 1781 Alexander became pastor of his old church in Newark and remained there for the rest of his life.

George Washington wrote to him on October 12, 1778, and requested his assistance. Washington wrote: "There are now under sentence of death, in the provost, a Farnsworth and Blair, convicted of being spies from the enemy, and of publishing Continental currency. It is hardly to be doubted but that these unfortunate men are acquainted with many facts respecting the enemies affairs, and their intentions which we have not been able to bring them to acknowledge. Besides the humanity of affording them the benefit of your profession, it may in the conduct of a man of sense answer another valuable purpose—And Whole it serves to prepare them for the other world, it will naturally lead to the intelligence we want in your inquiries into the condition of their spiritual concerns. You will therefore be pleased to take the charge of this matter upon yourself, and when you have collected in the course of your attendance such information as they can give you will transmit the whole to me. I am Sir &c."

John Blair and David Farnsworth were convicted for spying and possessing a large sum of counterfeit money and were sentenced to death. The use of counterfeit money was a form of strategy used in warfare for centuries. The purpose was to flood the enemy's economy with the fake money, which would drive down the worth of the real money resulting in economic collapse. The two men were captured with over $10,000 of fake currency. Washington declined to spare either man and they were executed on Rocky Hill at Hartford on November 3, 1778. A distant relative of David's, John Farnsworth, was convicted of spying for Japan during the 1930's. John, a naval officer, served 11 years in prison.

Sources: 1. National Archives. 2. *From Its European Antecedents to 1791—The United States Army Chaplaincy* by Parker C. Thompson, 1978, page 147. 3. *The Chaplains and Clergy at the Battle of Monmouth* by Chaplain Stanley Cuyler, 1986, pages 13 and 17. 4. *The Chaplains and Clergy of the Revolution* by Joel Tyler Headley, 1864, pages 327–330. 5. *Appleton's Cyclopaedia of American Biography*, Vol. 8, page 269. 6. *D.A.R. Lineage Book*, Vol. 2, page 131.

John Mudge

John Mudge was born on November 21, 1755, in Sharon, Connecticut, and he died June 5, 1839, in Highland, Michigan. He was a farmer and at the age of 21 he became a Baptist minister and settled in New York. He had no formal education and was not educated in the ministry. He preached in several small towns in the area of Genesee County, New York. Since he was not a recognized preacher, he joined the army as a common soldier. He gave the following information in his pension application: "In the month of April 1775 I entered the service of the United States as a volunteer, in a Regiment of Militia of the State of Massachusetts commanded by Col. Patterson in the company commanded by Capt. Porter and Lieut. Ashley for eight months. During that period I resided at West Stockbridge in Massachusetts. From that place I marched to Cambridge, when I joined my Regiment. From thence to a place called Lechmeres Point between Cambridge & Boston where I, with the Regiment was stationed, under General Putman to guard against the British until I was discharged from service. At Lechmeres Point I saw General Washington."

In the month of June 1776 he volunteered again in the militia for four months and marched to Fort Ticonderoga. A year later he again volunteered for the militia for two months. "I marched to Granville in the State of New York. Thence to Fort Ann. From this place I together with the rest of the American troops stationed there to guard it were compelled by the British forces to retreat to Fort Edwards. From Fort Edward I with others of the American troops were ordered back to a place then called Halfway Brook between Fort Edward and Fort Ann. I remained there until I was discharged."

John served in the militia for a total of 14 months from 1775 until 1777. He received a yearly pension of $46.66 for his service.

His granddaughter, Miss Henrietta Nelson, wrote this about John:

> I remember his as a tall, large, dark complexion man,—my ideal of all that was grand, noble and good. My grandfather was, as I have told you a Baptist minister, very zealous, and somewhat superstitious, and always deemed it a sacred duty to overrule my parents in what to them were honest and likewise sacred convictions of right.
>
> My grandfather, Rev. John Mudge, was not educated for the ministry at any earthly institution of learning, save inspirational, if I may so speak, and I would not be irreverent. He had scarcely a common school education, judging him by this our day, yet he was deemed a "powerful preacher." When he was speaking, silence reigned profound, and tears of sympathy and approbation often bedewed the cheeks of his attentive and appreciative hearers.

John Mudge was married three times. His third wife, Widow Lucy Jones, drowned in the Tonawanda which was a stream in Genesce County. John and Lucy were riding together along the banks of the stream when the horse took fright. The horse rushed onto the ice of the stream, which broke throwing the two riders into the stream. John was saved by a boy named Francis Loomis, but his wife could not be saved.

Most sources show John as serving as a chaplain in the army from 1775 to 1781. He was not recognized as an army chaplain, and his pension record indicates that he served from 1775 to 1777.

Sources: 1. *D.A.R. Lineage Book*, Vol. 9, page 241. 2. *Memorials: A Genealogical Account of the Name of Mudge in America* by Alfred Mudge, pages 85–87. 3. Pension Application S29341.

John Peter Gabriel Muhlenberg

Peter Muhlenberg was born on October 1, 1746, in Trappe, Pennsylvania, and he died on October 1, 1807, in Grays Ferry, Pennsylvania. He married Anna Barbara Meyer on November 6, 1770, and they had six children. His father Henry came to America from Germany and started the Lutheran Church in America. For his service in the Revolution Peter received 850 acres of bounty land.

On April 27, 1763, Peter, along with his two brothers, sailed for London to attend school in Halle, Germany. Although Peter liked to read he was a poor student and he became angry at a professor and Peter gave him a thrashing. It was decided that he should learn a trade and Peter was expelled from school. Peter was sent to work for a man named Leonhard Niemeyer who promised to teach Peter about running a business and teach his about medicine. Niemeyer worked Peter hard every day in his shop, and he was taught nothing else.

Peter, being very unhappy, joined a German cavalry unit. He later contacted a man named Captain Fiser, a friend of the family, who was recruiting men for the British Army. Peter joined a regiment of British Dragoons, and with his fiery attitude he was given the nickname "Devil Pete." He became known by this name in British and German circles. The regiment was shipped to America, and the nickname for Peter followed him there. Peter's father paid for his trip home and secured Peter's release from the army.

Peter felt a calling to religion, so in 1767 he entered college in Pennsylvania and studied for the ministry. He was ordinated in 1768, and in 1772 he returned to London to receive ordination from an English bishop. He returned to America in 1772 and settled in Virginia and the duties of a country pastor.

In 1774 the people of his county elected him the chairman of the Committee of safety, whose duty was to organize troops from Virginia in case of war with England. His brother Frederick, also a minister, believed that Peter should stay out of politics and war. Peter replied that being a minister did not relieve him from the duty to fight for his country. When the news of Bunker Hill reached Peter, he knew that, was going to become a soldier.

This is part of Peter's response to his brother: "Do you think, if America should be conquered, I should be safe? Far from it. And would you not sooner fight like a man than die like a dog? I am called by my country to its defense. The cause is just and noble. Were I a bishop, even a Lutheran one, I should obey without hesitation, and so far am I from thinking that I am wrong, I am convinced it is my duty so to do, a duty I owe to my

The Chaplains   **Muhlenberg**

God and to my country." Two or three years later Peter's brother Frederick left the church for the state, and he entered Congress under the Federal Constitution.

On January 21, 1776, Pastor Muhlenberg preached a rousing sermon on Ecclesiastes 3:1, "To everything there is a season, a time for purpose under heaven." When he finished his sermon he said, "There is a time to preach and a time to fight. And now is the time to fight." He removed his black robe to reveal the uniform of a Revolutionary Army officer. He marched down the center aisle of the congregation, while looking forward the whole time. Once outside he ordered the drum to beat for recruits.

The men swarmed around their pastor, the drum kept beating, and soon others not in church began running up to see what was happening. In the first 30 minutes 162 men joined the army. That evening Colonel Muhlenberg and almost 300 men marched off to war as the 8th Virginia Regiment. No one had suspected that weeks earlier General George Washington had urged Peter to command the 8th Virginia Regiment.

On June 28, 1776, the 8th Virginia was at the Battle of Sullivan's Island, but it was not in action. Because of his leadership skill Peter was promoted to the rank of Brigadier General on February 21, 1777. At Valley Forge Peter commanded the 1st Virginia Brigade which was made of the 1st, 5th, 9th, and 13th Virginia Regiments, which also included the German Battalion. Peter was under the command of Major Nathanael Greene's Division.

General Muhlenberg and the Virginia Brigade was in some of the heaviest fighting and some hand to hand at Brandywine, Germantown and Monmouth. At the Battle of Germantown his men faced the Hessians, who recognized Peter mounted on his horse. In a terrified voice they passed the word down the line, "Hier kommt teufel Pete" ("Here comes Devil Pete!").

Peter known for his coolness, courage, and determination, was selected by General Wayne to command the reserves at the victorious assault on Stony Point on July 16, 1779. In 1780 Peter was sent back to Virginia to rebuild the state's decimated defenses. He was given the task to recruit men with almost no provisions.

On April 25, 1781, Peter and his troops joined with Baron von Stebuen and fought the British at Petersburg. The Americans were defeated, but they were able to slow the advance of the British in the south.

At the Battle of Yorktown the British had two fortified positions called redoubt 9 and redoubt 10 that needed to be taken. The French were assigned to take number 9 and the Americans number 10. Peter led the attack at 6:30 on the evening of October 14, and the Americans with fixed bayonets marched toward redoubt 10. Under heavy fire they stormed the fortification and captured it after hand to hand fighting. Washington reported on the assault saying the men "advanced under fire of the enemy without returning a shot and effected the business with bayonet only."

The commander of the attacking Americans, Colonel Alexander Hamilton, wrote the report of the attack and took all the credit for the results. Peter being humble said nothing. He was wounded in the attack and later contracted camp fever and was sent home to recuperate. Once back home he felt that his actions in the war no longer qualified him to resume as a minister. He then began to serve in various political jobs until his death in 1807.

Sources: 1. *The Chaplains and Clergy of the Revolution* by Joel Tyler Headley, 1864, pages 121–126. 2. Warrant No. 1495 for bounty land issued 18 May 1799. 3. *The Imperial Origins of the King's Church in Early America 1607–1783* by J. Bell, page 192. 4. *Armsbearing and the Clergy in the History and Cannon Law of Western Christianity* by Lawrence G. Duggan, page 45. 5. *One Nation Under God: A Factual History of America's Religious Heritage* by Leon G. Stevens, page 13. 6. *The Crisis in the Early Life of General Peter Muhlenberg* by Rev. William Germann, 1849, pages 298–329. 7. *The Chaplains and Clergy at the Battle of Monmouth* by Chaplain Stanley Cuyler, 1986, pages 14–15. 8. *From Its European Antecedents to 1791—The United States Army Chaplaincy* by Parker C. Thompson, 1978, pages 127–129.

John Murray

John Murray was born on December 10, 1741, in Alton, England, and he died on September 3, 1815, in Boston. He married Judith Sargent on July 5, 1788. He came from a strict Calvinists upbringing, and in 1760 he embraced the Universalistic teaching of the Rev. James Relly. John was excommunicated from his church for these beliefs, and in 1770 he came to America.

The Universalist believed that the God of love would not create a person if that person was destined for damnation in Hell. Some Universalists even denied that Hell existed. The belief was that all people are destined to receive salvation. John Murry founded the Universalism movement in America.

On September 10, 1775, John had dinner with his friend General Nathanael Greene and George Washington. Soon after John was appointed by Washington as the chaplain of the Rhode Island Militia commanded by Greene. Because of John's radical beliefs he was not welcomed by other chaplains and they objected to his commission as chaplain. Their main objection was John's belief that there was no Hell. Near the end of 1775 Murray retired as chaplain due to health problems. In 1809 John suffered a stroke which forced him to give up preaching. He died in Boston six years later.

Source: 1. *From Its European Antecedents to 1791—The United States Army Chaplaincy* by Parker C. Thompson, 1978, pages 116–117.

Samuel Phillips Payson

Samuel Payson was born on January 18, 1736, in Walpoe, Massachusetts, and he died on January 11, 1801, in Chelsea, Massachusetts. He married Elizabeth Stone. He graduated from Harvard in 1757 and was ordained pastor of the church in Chelsea.

He was openly friendly to the Royal government, which led to him being condemned by several of his patriotic minister friends. One of them, the Reverend Treadwell, even refused to exchange pulpits with him which was the custom. When Samuel witnessed the destruction and death done to his countrymen at Lexington, he became a supporter of the patriot cause.

As the British left Lexington and Concord they marched back to Boston. Hundreds of militiamen waited along the road to Boston and began firing at the British behind trees, fences, and buildings. Pastor Payson took up his musket and led the men in his congregation in attacking the British along the road. Pastor Payson and his men attacked a party of 12 of the enemy who were carrying supplies they had looted. The rebels killed one British soldier and captured the rest. An account in the August 2, 1775, Pennsylvania Journal stated: "The Rev. Mr. Payson, of Chelsea, in Massachusetts Bay, a mild, thoughtful, sensible man, at the head of a party of his own parish, attacked a party of regulars, killed some and took the rest prisoners. This gentleman has been hitherto on the side of government, but oppression having got to that pitch beyond which even a wise man cannot bear, he has taken up arms in defense of those rights, civil and religious, which cost their forefathers so dearly."

Sources: 1. *Diary of the American Revolution: From Newspapers and Original Documents* by Frank Moore, 1860, page 66. 2. *From Its European Antecedents to 1791— The United States Army Chaplaincy* by Parker C. Thompson, 1978, page 92. 3. *The Chaplains and Clergy of the Revolution* by Joel Tyler Headley, 1864, page 60.

William Plumbe

William Plumbe was born on December 26, 1748, in Middletown, Connecticut, and he died there on June 2, 1843. He graduated from Yale in 1769. He served in the army as a chaplain for four years and received a yearly pension of $480 for his service.

He joined Colonel Thomas Marshall's Massachusetts State Regiment on September 7, 1776, and was stationed at Castle William in Boston harbor. In the spring the regiment marched to Fort Ticonderoga, where it was assigned to General DeFermoy's Brigade and William was later appointed Brigade Chaplain.

After the retreat of the Americans from Fort Ticonderoga in early July 1777, General Gates appointed William Chaplain of the Hospitals in the Northern Department. He served in this capacity from August 20, 1777, until January 1, 1781.

The work of the hospital chaplains was mainly to take care of patients who were separated from their units over a long period of time. Because hospital chaplains had much greater job-related expenses, they were paid $60 a month which was much more than the chaplains in the field.

The following is from the pension application filed in 1835 by William: "In the summer of 1776 I engaged to serve in the office of a Chaplain in a regiment commanded by Col. Marshall for that year till the close of that campaign. In the beginning of the year 1777 I again engaged to serve in the same office. In the spring I went with the regiment to Ticonderoga. I was appointed to the office of Brigade Chaplain. I received an appointment to the office of Chaplain to the General Hospital of the Northern Department about the same time. The paymaster in the Brigade drew pay for me also for my service in the Brigade & offered it to me but I refused to take it & requested him to replace it in the public chest."

After the war William returned to Middletown, and although still known as a clergyman he studied and practiced the law. He died at the age of 94 and was at that time the oldest graduate of Yale.

Sources: 1. *From Its European Antecedents to 1791—The United States Army Chaplaincy* by Parker C. Thompson, 1978, page 172. 2. *Massachusetts Soldiers and Sailors of the Revolutionary War*, Vol. 12, page 472. 3. *Yale and Her Honor-Roll in the American Revolution* by Henry Phelps Johnston, pages 261–262.

Benjamin Pomeroy

Benjamin Pomeroy was born on November 11, 1704, in Suffield, Connecticut, and he died on December 21, 1784, in Hebron, Connecticut. He graduated from Yale in 1733 with the highest honors of his class. He married Abigail Wheelock in 1734. He served as a minister in Hebron from 1734 to 1784. Benjamin was a chaplain in the army during the French and Indian War which took place from 1754 to 1762.

He wrote a letter to his wife on July 23, 1759, during the French and Indian War which gives a glimpse into the life of a chaplain in war: "My Dear, Saturday last, at break of day, our troops to the number of twelve thousand, embarked for Cabrillons, all in health and high spirits. Mr. Beebe and I, by the advice of our Colonel, stay behind, but expect soon to follow. A considerable number of sick are left here in the hospitals. Five died last night. A poor, wretched criminal, Thomas Bailey, was executed. Mr. Brainard and myself chiefly discoursed with him, but almost all his care was to have a life prolonged—he pleaded with us to intercede with the general for him, but there was no prospect of succeeding. His crime was stealing or robbing whereof he had frequently been guilty. Once received one hundred lashes, and once reprieved from the gallows, but being often reproved, he hardened his heart, and was suddenly destroyed. Several prayers were made at the place of his execution—the poor creature was terrified, even to amazement and distraction, at the approach of the King of Terrors. He struggled with his executioners, I believe, more than an hour ere they could put him in any proper position to receive the shot. The captain of the guard told me since, that he verily believed that the Devil helped him."

At age 71 he fought as a soldier at the Battle of Bunker Hill in 1775, and later he served as a chaplain in Colonel Wylly's Regiment in the Connecticut line from January 1, 1777, to July 1, 1777. His son Ralph served in the same regiment as a Lieutenant. He was once pursued and fired upon by a party of the enemy near the lines at New York as he was riding to visit the hospital, and he narrowly escaped death.

Sources: 1. *D.A.R. Lineage Book*, Vol. 4, page 224. 2. *Massachusetts Soldiers and Sailors of the Revolutionary War*, page 196. 3. *Yale and Her Honor-Roll in the American Revolution* by Henry Phelps Johnston, pages 182–183. 4. *The Chaplains and Clergy of the Revolution* by Joel Tyler Headley, 1864, page 341–346.

Nehemiah Porter

Nehemiah Porter was born on March 22, 1720, in Ipswich, Massachusetts, and he died of a liver complaint on February 29, 1820, in Ashfield, Massachusetts. He married Rebecca Chipman on February 14, 1749. He entered Harvard at the "foot" of his class because his father, a weaver, had a low status. He graduated from Harvard College in 1745 and was ordained in 1750.

During the Revolution Nehemiah served as a chaplain under General Gates. He joined about mid–August 1777 and stayed until after the surrender of British General Burgoyne in the fall of 1777. One time when the army assembled for prayer a profane soldier said, "I don't want to leave until that man gets done praying." This took place just before General Gates marched north to meet Burgoyne. Pastor Porter also told the men to expect the help of Heaven in the upcoming battle. Porter died just before his 100th birthday, and it was said that he had over 230 descendants at the time of his death.

Sources: 1. *History of Ipswich, Essex, and Hamilton* by Joseph B. Felt, 1966, page 262. 2. *Boston Recorder*, No. 33. Vol. V. 3. *D.A.R. Lineage Book*, Vol. 51, page 202. 4. *Historical Sketches of the Times and Men in Ashfield, Mass. During the Revolutionary War*, page 4.

Joseph Rhea

Joseph Rhea was born in 1715 in Ireland, and he died in 1777 in Piney Creek, Maryland. He married Elizabeth McIlwaine in Ireland. He graduated from the University of Glasgow, Scotland and became pastor of a church in Ireland. He came to America and landed at Philadelphia in 1769 and then moved to Maryland.

He was described as large in stature, six foot tall, with a cheerful disposition, full of Irish jokes, and charitable to a fault. He had been known to take his shirt off and give it to the needy. As pastor of his new church in Piney Creek, Maryland he received a yearly salary of 112 pounds, which then was equal to about $560.

In 1776 he became chaplain for the troops under Colonel Christian's Cherokee Company and joined him on the Cherokee Expedition, which was a four week engagement in 1776. The following is from an orderly book that belonged to Captain Joseph Martin: "Six Mile Camp, October 5, 1776. Parole William Burge. General Orders: Mr. Ray [Rhae] will preach on the Augusta Line at one o'clock, and Mr. Cummins on the Fincastle Line. All other who choose to attend may do it. The church will be at the time to give warning, the men to attend with their arms by companies, and to observe as much decency and regularity as the ground will admit of."

After Pastor returned home to Maryland, he became ill with pneumonia and died. Two of his sons fought for the patriots at the Battles of Brandywine and Kings Mountain.

Sources: 1. *Notable Southern Families Vol. II* by Zella Armstrong, 1922, page 294. 2. Sons of the American Revolution Application.

Hezekiah Ripley

Hezekiah Ripley was born on February 14, 1743, in Windham, Connecticut, and he died on November 29, 1831, Fairfield, Connecticut. He married Dorothy Britnail on January 9, 1765. Hezekiah was a graduate of Yale in 1763, and he was pastor at Green's Farm, Connecticut where his house and church were burned by the British during the invasion of July 1779. As his wife and children escaped the British, they were fired upon by British soldiers.

His voice for the patriot cause made him especially obnoxious to the British, who hated all "pulpit drummers." And open they swore their intention "to make Dr. Ripley's head a button for a halter." There were several British attempts to capture Ripley. Usually, friends learned of the plot and gave the pastor a warning. On one occasion he was captured, but fortunately his guards fell asleep and he escaped.

Soon after Washington was appointed commander of the American army he passed by Hezekiah's house on the way to Boston. The pastor mounted his horse and rode along with the general and stopped at Bulkley's Inn to have dinner. After dinner the men were waiting for their horses to be brought to them, and Washington began talking to Hezekiah about the war. Washington told the pastor that if the Americans could prolong the war for one year, that they would ultimately win. He said by that time arms and ammunition could be obtained, and the Americans would be invincible.

In 1776 Hezekiah became chaplain of Colonel Silliman's brigade during a part of the campaign around New York in 1776. When the army retreated from the British in New York on September 15, 1776, Hezekiah narrowly escaped being captured. The following statement from the pastor appeared in the book *Life of Burr* about Colonel Aaron Burr.

> I was the officiating chaplain of the brigade then commanded by Gen Gold S. Silliman. From mismanagement of the commanding officer, that brigade was unfortunately left in the city of New York, and at the time before mentioned. While the brigade was in front, and myself considerably in the rear, I was meant by the late General Putnman, deceased, who then informed me of the landing of the enemy above us, and that I must make my escape on the west side of the island. Whereupon I on foot crossed the lots to the west side of the island, unmolested excepting by the fire from the ships of the British, which at that time lay in the North river. How the brigade escaped, I was not an eyewitness; but well recollect, from the information I then had from General Chandler (now deceased), then acting as a colonel in said brigade, that Mr. Burr's exertions, bravery, and good conduct, was the principal means of saving the whole of that brigade from falling into the hands of the enemy, and whose conduct was then by all considered judicious and meritorious.
>
> But, however, I well recollect, before I had the information alluded to from General Chandler, I had seen Mr. Burr, and inquired of him how the brigade had made their escape, who then told me the particulars, which were afterwards confirmed by all the officers; who were all of opinion that, had it not been for him, they would not have effected their retreat and escape.
>
> As to my own opinion of the management of the troops on leaving New York, I then, and still suppose, as did General Chandler, that Colonel Burr's merits there as a young officer ought, and did, claim much attention, and whose official duties as an aid-de-camp on that memorable day justly claimed the thanks of the army and his country.

The following incident was from William A. Ripley a great-grandson of Pastor Ripley as told to him by his grandmother. "During the exceptionally severe winter of 1779–1780, Gen. Washington's headquarters were at sorts of destitution. Rev. Hezekiah Ripley was put in charge of an expedition consisting of several men and two wagons, and sent through the neighboring country to collect clothing and general supplies—shoes being especially needed. He came as far east as his own parish of Green's Farms, with comforting success."

One time the pastor was faced with a problem of officiating two weddings at nearly the same time in his church. The custom, which the pastor followed, was for the pastor to kiss the bride at the end of the service. One girl, Miss J., was a young lady from a good family and of lovely character. The other girl neither deserved nor received the respect of the community. Miss J had her wedding first.

The first wedding ended with no kiss from the pastor and nothing was said. At the end of the second wedding, the mother of the bride called out, "Dr. Ripley, there is one thing you have not done. You haven't kissed the bride." The pastor replied, "Oh well, kissing has gone out of fashion. I married Miss J. earlier and did not kiss her." After that he never again kissed a bride at the end of the service.

In August of 1831 Hezekiah was present at the death of his wife. After she died he said with tears rolling down his cheeks, "She was the light of my eyes." Three months later he was re-united with his wife.

Sources: 1. *Chapter Sketches, Connecticut Daughters of the American Revolution* by the Connecticut D.A.R., pages 331–337. 2. *Memoirs of Aaron Burr* by Matthew Davis, Vol. 1, 1837, pages 102–103. 3. *Yale and Her Honor-Roll in the American Revolution* by Henry Phelps Johnston, page 236. 4. *D.A.R. Lineage Book*, Vol. 42, page 342.

Ammi Ruhamah Robbins

Ammi Robbins was born in 1740 in Bradford, Connecticut, and he died in 1813 in Norfolk, Connecticut. He graduated from Yale in 1760 and was ordained in 1761. Ammi served as a chaplain in Colonel Burrell's Regiment in 1776. He enlisted in March of 1776 and was with the army as it retreated from Canada. During his service he kept a diary of his service.

On March 28, 1776, he recorded in his diary, "After prayers, attended the execution of a sentence of court martial upon three poor Pennsylvania soldiers, who received thirty-nine lashes each. The whole army drawn up."

During much of his service, Ammi was sick with various ailments. He wrote in his diary:

> July 26—Conversed with Doctor Potts who informed me I must instantly take ipecac; the bile was collecting so fast, it would throw me into the inflammatory camp disorder. I took a solution of manna, cream of tartar, senna and anise seed; had a sick day.
>
> July 29—I am peculiarly unfitted to do the duties of a chaplain, on account of my bilious constitution. I envy brother Avery [Rev. David Avery, also in this book] his health. He will go through the hospital when pestiferous as disease and death can make it with a face as smooth as a baby's and afterward an appetite as healthy as a woodpecker. I would not shrink from the work. Our war is a righteous war; our men are called to defend the country. I hope to return to my work.
>
> August 23—Doctor Potts told me it was at the risk of my life to go into the hospitals. But if the physician goes, why not a minister of the great Physician.

Ammi regained his health and continued visiting sick and wound men in the hospitals. On October 31, 1776, Ammi left the army and returned to his home.

Sources: 1. *Yale and Her Honor-Roll in the American Revolution* by Henry Phelps Johnston, pages 225-226. 2. *Journal of Rev. Ammi R. Robbins in the Northern Campaign of 1776*, 1850, pages 5, 33, and 34. 3. *From Its European Antecedents to 1791—The United States Army Chaplaincy* by Parker C. Thompson, 1978, page 153. 4. *D.A.R. Lineage Book*, Vol. 116, page 284.

Azel Roe

Azel Roe was born on March 20, 1738, in Setauket, New York, and he died on December 2, 1815, in Woodbridge New Jersey. He married Rebecca Foot who died in 1794, and then he married Hannah Boswick. He became the pastor of the First Presbyterian Church in Woodbridge from 1763 until 1815.

A group of Tories had encamped near Blazing Star Ferry in New Jersey, and a patriot captain had tried to raise a group of men to attack the enemy. The local men would not join the captain, so the young officer appealed to the Reverend Roe to encourage the men who just happen to belong to the pastor's congregation. Roe addressed the men and encouraged them to follow him and the captain into battle with the Tories. The men agreed telling the pastor that if bullets started to fly, then the pastor would need to get out of harm's way. As a result, the encamped Tories were chased off.

The pastor became so active in stirring up men to fight against the Tories, that the enemy sought help from British troops to capture the pastor.

They seized the pastor one night while he was with his family, they and carried him off to the Sugar House prison in New York City. Sugar Houses in New York City were converted into prisons by the British troops. Thousands of American patriots were said to have died in Sugar House prisons during the war. The pastor was soon released in an exchange of prisoners.

In November his second wife, Hannah, died. The Reverend Roe was so grief stricken that he developed a throat problem caused by excessive grief, and he died four days later.

Source: 1. *Annals of the American Pulpit of Distinguished American Clergymen* by William B. Sprague, D.D., Vol. III, 1858, pages 232–234.

John Rosebrugh

John Rosebrugh was born in 1714 in Ireland, and he died on January 2, 1777, in Trenton, New Jersey. He came to America with his older brother William c. 1730. His first wife, Sarah, he married c. 1733, and both Sarah and her baby died in childbirth. John decided to become a minister, and he graduated from Princeton in 1761 and he was ordained on December 11, 1764. He began preaching in Warren, New Jersey and married Jane Ralston in the spring of 1766.

In 1769 he became pastor of a church in Allen Pennsylvania and became outspoken for American independence. In December of 1776 British General Howe's army was marching toward Philadelphia, while prompting General Washington to issue a call to the Pennsylvania militia to join his army in the defense of the city.

Pastor Rosebrugh assembled his congregation and read to them Washington's appeal for help. He offered to go with them at the age of 63, if they would march to the country's rescue. They agreed to go, but only if John was their chaplain and their commander. He asked to be allowed to consult with his wife about the decision to lead them into battle.

John talked to his wife that night knowing that it was a difficult decision for her to make, because she felt her husband had a responsibility to the congregation. She also was well aware of the dangers her husband faced, since her sister's husband was in the army and was a prisoner of war. Her reply to her husband was to go. That night before bed, John made out his will.

The next morning John rode to the church with his oldest son to meet with the men assembled in front of the church. He told them that he would lead them and told the men that if they felt it was their duty to go and fight then join him and if they felt it was not their duty to fight then they should go home to their families.

John took his musket and marched off with the men and his son by his side. When they had reached the top of a hill, John stopped and kissed the boy good-by. He told the boy to return home to his mother and be a good boy until he returned home. The boy would never see his father alive again. The men marched on and joined the army of General Washington.

Pastor Rosebrugh and his men were part of a unit that guarded Philadelphia while Washington led the rest of the army to Trenton. On December 25 John wrote his first letter to his wife and in it he said, "The important crisis seems to draw near, which I trust may decide the query whether Americans shall be slaves or free men. An engagement is expected in a few days. All our company are in Philadelphia in good health and I good spirits. We will be ordered to New Jersey tomorrow or next day."

In Trenton on December 26, 1776, Washington defeated the Hessians. After the victory Washington ordered the troops defending Philadelphia to re-join the main army. At this time Rosebrugh was relieved of his command and told to remain with the army as chaplain of the Northampton County Militia.

On December 27, 1776, Pastor Rosebrugh was with the troops from Philadelphia at Bristol Ferry preparing to enter into New Jersey to join Washington's army. John wrote the following, probably on horseback, brackets in the letter show where the paper or parts of it are gone. The letter is yellow and much broken. "[Friday] morning 10 o'clock at Bristol Ferry, December 27th, 1776 I am still yours [but] I haven't a minute to tell yo[u] that by God's grace [our company] are all well. We are going over to New Jersey. You would think strange to see your Husband, an old man, riding with a French fuse slung at his back. This may be ye la[st letter] ye shall receive from your Husband. I have counted myself you [several missing words] larged of our mutual love to God. As I am out of doors [I cannot at present] write more. I send my compliments to you, my dear, and children. Friends pray for us. From your loving Husband, Jno. Rosbrugh." On the back of the letter is written "the last letter." The words were written in the handwriting of his wife, no doubt this was the last letter she received from John.

On January 2, 1777, Cornwallis attacked Washington at the 2nd battle of Trenton. That night after the battle Washington withdrew his army to Princeton. He led behind about 500 men with the camp fires burning bright to convince the British soldiers that the Americans were still there. The next morning the remaining Americans withdrew.

It was a miracle that Washington had any troops there to fight Cornwallis. Most of Washington's men's terms of enlistment had expired on December 31, 1776. On the 30th Washington appealed for the men to stay with him for one more month for a bounty of $10. He appealed to their patriotism, and that they were fighting for their families and homes. The majority of the men agreed to stay and money to pay them arrived on January 1st.

It was during the battle on the 2nd that Rosbrugh had lost his life. After the battle Captain John Hayes, the commander of Rosbrugh's company, found the body of the pastor and buried him. There were several accounts of what happen to John. The most trustworthy account is given by Captain Hayes.

During the battle Rosbrugh was trapped on the Trenton side of the river. He spent the day evading capture by the British. That night when most of the fighting was over John rode to a nearby tavern to get something to eat. He tied his horse outside and went in to eat. Soon an alarm went out that the Hessians were approaching. The pastor ran out of the tavern to discover that his horse had been stolen, so he began to walk along the river to find a spot that he could cross over to the American side. He soon became surrounded by Hessians commanded by a British officer. Seeing that escape was not possible, he surrendered himself as a prisoner of war.

He offered his captors his gold watch and money, if they would spare his life for his family's sake. Knowing that they were going to kill him, he knelt down in front of a tree and began to pray for his enemies. Before he could finish, 17 bayonet thrusts were made on his body, and one bayonet was even broken off in his body. His killers then slashed his head with their sabers and they then robbed his body of anything of value.

The British officer that was in command left and went into the tavern where the pastor and visited earlier. He displayed the pastor's watch and boasted that he had killed a rebel pastor. The woman of the tavern knew Rosbrugh and recognized the watch. She told the officer, "You have killed that good man, and what a wretched thing you have done for his helpless family this day." The officer threatened to kill her, if she continued talking, and he then ran away as if afraid of being pursued.

When Captain Hayes found out what had happened he found the body, wrapped it in a cloak, and buried the pastor. Later, another army chaplain, Mr. Duffield, took the body and reburied it. No one knows for sure where the body of Pastor Rosbrugh is buried. Most of his descendants believe that the body was buried in Philadelphia.

Sources: 1. *Rosbrugh: Tale of the Revolution or Life, Labors and Death of Rev. John Rosbrugh* by Rev. John C. Clyde, 1880, pages 42–60. 2. Sons of the American Revolution Application. 3. *From Its European Antecedents to 1791—The United States Army Chaplaincy* by Parker C. Thompson, 1978, pages 150–154. 4. Tombstone.

David Sanford

David Sanford was born on December 11, 1737, in New Milford, Connecticut, and he died on April 7, 1810, in Medway, Massachusetts. He married Bathsheba Ingersoll on August 14, 1757. He graduated from Yale in 1737 and became pastor of the Second Church of Christ in Medway, Massachusetts.

The following is the letter that assigned Pastor Sanford his commission as a chaplain in the army.

> The Committee of the Council of Massachusetts Bay, To David Sanford. Greeting:
>
> We being informed exemplary life and manners, and reposing especial trust in your abilities and good conduct, Do by these presents constitute and appoint you the said David Sanford to be Chaplain of the Regiment whereof Lemuel Robinson is Colonel, raised by this Colony to reinforce the American army, until the first day of April next. You are therefore carefully and diligently to inculcate on the minds of the soldiers of said Regiment, as well by example as precept, the duties of Religion and morality, and a fervent love to their country in all other respects, and to discharge the duty of a Chaplain in said Regiment, observing from time to time such Orders and Instructions as you shall receive from your superior officers, according to military Rules and discipline established by the American Congress,— in pursuance of the trust reposed in you, for which this shall be a sufficient Warrant.

David Sanford had a commanding personal appearance, an impulsive fearless spirit, and he had the power of expression in merely a look. An example of the powerful look is demonstrated once while he was preaching to the troops in a run-down church.

During his sermon a board that had been placed in one of the shattered windows blew down. The soldiers made so much noise trying to put the board back up, that David had to stop his sermon. Soon the board again blew in, and again the soldiers made a racket trying to put the board back up. When the board fell down a third time, and the soldiers rushed to it to put it back up, Pastor Sanford had enough of the noise. He thundered out, "let that board alone!" Immediately the startled men returned to their seats.

After the service a local citizen asked the commanding officer how he liked the preacher. He replied, "Very well, but I should have liked him better if he hadn't sworn so." "Sworn Captain?" said the citizen, "I didn't hear any oath." The captain replied yes he did, he said, "let that board alone." The citizen told the Captain that that was not an oath. "Well," said the captain, "if he did not say those very words he looked them." This later became a bye-word so whenever a preacher saw another preacher give a strong frown of displeasure, they would say good-naturedly, "don't swear so."

The troops loved Davis for his strong patriotic belief and his stern manner. On one occasion a young preacher told Davis that he had refused a call to a certain place on account of an extensive pine swamp. Pastor Sanford turned to the man and said, "Young man, it is none of your business where God had put his pine swamp." In 1807 the old pastor was struck with paralysis and after suffering for three years he died.

Sources: 1. *The Chaplains and Clergy of the Revolution* by Joel Tyler Headley, 1864, pages 361–364. 2. *Yale and Her Honor-Roll in the American Revolution* by Henry Phelps Johnston, page 208. 3. *D.A.R. Lineage Book*, Vol. 16, page 103. 4. Sons of the American Revolution Application.

John Simpson

John Simpson was born in 1740 and died in 1807 in Pendleton, South Carolina. He married Mary Remer in 1765, and he graduated from Princeton in 1768. John served as Chaplain in Colonel Francis Marion's Regiment and Colonel John Moffatt's South Carolina Militia.

When Charleston, South Carolina was captured by the British on May 12, 1780, and many Americans were killed at Abraham Burford's defeat at Waxhaws, the patriots were anxious to get revenge. Patriot Captain John McClure and his men promised to keep on fighting regardless of the odds against them. Captain McClure gathered his men who were dressed in their hunting shirt and armed with a knife and a rifle. They were joined by Pastor John Simpson, who was promoted to captain the next day. The men joined up with the newly formed Turkey Creek Regiment under Colonel Edward Lacey.

The Patriot Militia engaged the Tories at Alexander's Old Field on June 6, 1780, and defeated the Tories with little loss of life on both sides. Two days later the patriots again defeated the Tories at the Battle of Mobley's Meeting House. After the battle, some of the patriot militiamen left to join the army in North Carolina and the rest returned home. The Tory commander Christian Huck and his men decided to go after Pastor John Simpson, because they regarded him as one of the major leaders in the area.

On June 11, 1780, the Tories did not find him at his church so they burned the church, Simpson's home and the library. They missed Pastor Simpson, because a few days earlier he took his musket and marched off under the command of Captain McClure. The Tories also missed his wife, because she had heard gunfire when the church was attacked. Negroes near the church had heard the Tories say they were going to burn the pastor's house, so they ran to the Simpson home and warned the pastor's wife.

Mary Simpson took her four children and hid in the orchard. She threw the silverware into the wood pile and the family ran for the orchard. She watched as the soldiers took the rest of the family's valuables and began to torch the house. After the Tories left she was able to save some of the pastor's library, and in doing so was burned and nearly died. She and her children were taken in by a neighbor and four weeks later she gave birth to her fifth child.

Later, Mary began to make clothes for her children since they had lost their cloths in the fire. Tories returned again and robbed her of the clothes and took the cattle that she had. She did recover some of the clothes, when she complained to the Tory leader. The cattle were taken two miles down the road and were put into a pen. That night two of the large steers broke through the pen and by morning all the cattle had returned back home. This may have been the only time in the war that patriot cows that had been taken prisoner escaped and returned home safely.

During the summer of 1780 Pastor Simpson was with the troops commanded by General Sumter. On August 15 the patriots under Sumter defeated the British at the Battle of Wateree Ferry. The Americans captured much needed supplies during this short battle. Due to the defeat of the Americans at Camden on August 16, 1780, Sumter and his men began to retreat to the south on a very hot day.

When the Americans reached the Catawba Ford Sumter, believing they were safe it allowed his men to rest during the heat of the day. He was not aware that British Lt. Col. Banastare Tarleton had been following him. The British, when finding many of the Americans asleep, horses unsaddled, and totally unprepared attacked them. This became known as the Battle of Fishing Creek. During this battle 150 of Sumter's men were killed, about 350 captured, and all the supplies they had previously captured was lost. General Sumter, without his boots and half dressed, jumped on an unsaddled horse, rode off, and did not stop for many miles.

At the start of the battle Pastor Simpson was standing next to his horse repairing a bridle with his gun beside him against a tree. He barely escaped being taken a prisoner. He jumped on his horse without the bridle or saddle and he had to direct the horse by striking her on the side of the head. The horse leapt several brush fences, and it crossed a public road in front of two British soldiers.

John soon met up with two other soldiers who had also escaped. The men agreed that further fighting would be useless, so they agreed that they should all return home. John was in the most danger, because the pastor was still wanted by the British and Tories. He did not remain home long because he left with some troops for North Carolina. After the British surrender at Yorktown, he finally returned home for good.

His house and church were rebuilt, after giving his last sermon in October 1807. The next day he fell ill, and after lingering for three months he died at the age of 68.

Sources: 1. *The American Revolution in South Carolina.* 2. *D.A.R. Lineage Book*, Vol. 34, page 208. 3. *The Day It Rained Militia: Huck's Defeat and the Revolution in the South Carolina Backcountry, May–July 1780* by Michael Scoggins. 4. *Princeton College During the Eighteenth Century* by Samuel Davies Alexander, 1872. 5. *The Descendants of Simpson-Roach Families of South Carolina* by Max Perry, 1974.

Cotton Mather Smith

Cotton Mather Smith was born on October 16, 1731, in Suffield, Connecticut, and he died on November 27, 1806, in Sharon, Connecticut. He married Temperance Worthington around 1757. Cotton graduated from Yale in 1751 and was ordained in 1755.

He encouraged his congregation to fight against the British after he learned of the Battles of Lexington and Concord. The pastor's wife gave this description, "Before the close of the last hymn a messenger, with jingling spurs, strode down the aisle and set up the high pulpit stairs and spoke to my husband, who proclaimed, in clear, ringing tones the 'die has been cast; blood has been shed, and there is no longer any choice between war and slavery.'"

The pastor led his men in their initial training and marched with them in 1775 to Fort Ticonderoga. He served nearly a year under General Philip Schuyler in Colonel Benjamin Hinman's 4th Regiment. General Schuyler helped to plan the invasion of Canada, but due to illness he was replaced by Richard Montgomery. Besides preaching he was in constant attendance to the sick and wounded. Toward the end of 1775 Pastor Smith developed camp fever and became very ill. Unable to continue his duties he had to leave the army and return home.

Sources: 1. *Colonial Families of America, Volume 1* by Frances M. Smith, pages 287–288. 2. *Voices of Revolutionary America: Contemporary Accounts of Daily Life* by Carol Sue Humphrey, page 23. 3. *Yale and Her Honor-Roll in the American Revolution* by Henry Phelps Johnston, page 203. 4. *The Memorial History of Hartford County, Connecticut, 1633–1884: Town Histories*, page 411. 5. *The Chaplains and Clergy of the Revolution* by Joel Tyler Headley, 1864, pages 305–317.

Hezekiah Smith

Hezekiah Smith was born on April 21, 1737, on Long Island, New York, and he died on January 24, 1806, in Haverhill, Massachusetts. He married Hephzabah Kimball on June 22, 1770. Hezekiah graduated from Princeton in 1762 and became pastor of the Baptist church in Haverhill. He served as chaplain in Nixon's 4th Massachusetts Regiment from July 1775 until October 1780.

When Hezekiah joined the army, he soon became an intimate friend of George Washington and received the confidence and esteem of the officers and men he served with. He repeatedly exposed his life, trusting implicitly in God, to use his frequent favorite expression that "every bullet had a commission." He encouraged the soldiers and took care of the wounded and the dying.

The Chaplains — Hezekiah Smith

In the records of the church at Haverhill, under the date of July 12, 1775, it is written, "Voted, that our Pastor shall comply with the request of Col. Nixon, and supply as Chaplain the quarter part of the time for the future in his regiment." Hezekiah and men from his church left to join the army of Brig. General Sullivan at Winter Hill, Massachusetts about 33 miles away. Much of Hezekiah's military journal has been lost.

The following records are letters that he wrote to his wife. This author has selected parts of some of the letters to give a reader a sense of what Pastor Hezekiah experienced. Some of the large gaps in the dates of the letters occur when the pastor took time off to return home and tend to his congregation.

> Camp Winter Hill on July 31, 1775, My Dear and Loving Wife: Last night and this morning we had several skirmishes with the regulars. Near the common, before you come to Charlestown New York, was one, in which our people killed one regular, and got four or five of their guns, without losing a man, or having one wounded, though this day we lost one or two men by a cannon ball.
>
> On August 1, 1775, I understand by Mr. Eliphalet Smith, that my dear wife has been somewhat unwell and also our little son. I hope by this time you are both getting better. Our kind God can easily heal you both.
>
> Camp Winter Hill on December 18, 1775, My Dear: This day I expected to see another battle with the regulars, but hitherto am disappointed. Perhaps it will be brought on before night, though I do not expect it. The reason why I expected an engagement with the enemy this day was, because they fired a number of cannon and sent several bombs at our people yesterday and last night on Lechmere's Point.
>
> On December 25, 1775, Yesterday at General Sullivan's I saw a regular deserter, who left Bunker Hill the night before. He says it is sickly amongst the regular troops, and many of them die. That they have no fresh provisions for the soldiers. They are in difficulty on account of fire-wood, having none but what they pick up, being obliged to burn the floors of marquees, tents, etc.
>
> There are about 500 men on Bunker Hill, commanded by Col. Agnew.

Before the barracks were ready on Bunker Hill for the winter garrison, the troops encountered cutting winds and driving snow. The troops had to live in their tents.

> Camp Winter Hill on March 11, 1776, My Dear Hephzibah: Since my last, the movements of the ministerial army give us reason to think they are about leaving Boston. But in what direction, they will go from thence is uncertain. We expect they will aim for the Southern colonies. If so our army will soon move, and be ready to attack them when they land.
>
> As I shall want to send my linen with the baggage, should be glad if you would send me my fine shirts, with my cotton to Haverhill before my departure.
>
> Camp Winter Hill, on March 20, 1776, My Dear Hephzibah: This day I was in

Hezekiah Smith   THE CHAPLAINS

Boston, where I saw a number of houses destroyed by the regulars; but the damage in that town is not so great as I expected; and what they left amounts to a large sum, which is a proof that they left the town in great fear and with much precipitation.

This day Col. Nixon told me that if he was going into battle, he would choose to leave me behind to pray for him, for he says it is not my place to be in danger; and I have concluded to act in my own department and not expose myself to danger.

Pastor Smith had taken leave and returned home to tend to the duties on his church. He returned to his regiment in New York on September 18, 1776, having been away for one month. On the 27th of August the disastrous Battle of Long Island was fought and ended, when General Washington retreated across the East River. Hezekiah's Regiment moved near Fort Washington and the pastor spent the next several months preaching and tending to the sick and wounded. He returned home when the army took winter quarters. In June of 1777 he rejoined his regiment in Sudbury. The men later marched to Fort Anne, and Pastor Smith preformed his usual duties the remainder of the summer.

Hezekiah gives an account of events in his diary from Tuesday July 22 to Thursday August 14, 1777:

After an engagement with the enemy on Tues, 23rd at Kingsbury, our baggage was removed with all the tents, etc., to Fort Edward. Our brigade left their ground, after repulsing the enemy, about dusk; and were ordered to march to a height about one-half or three quarters of a mile from where our tents were carried. So that the brigade could not have the benefit of them that night; but after the fatigue of fighting and marching, were obligated to lie in the open air under a heavy dew. The brave Gen Nixon, who scorned to shrink from danger or screen himself from hardship, took his lot in the open field with his brigade, without a cloak or great coat to cover him, and many of the soldiers without a tight bodied coat on.

From this miserable situation, we were removed the 27th to Moses's Creek, where we encamped in the woods. The Indians around would fire on our sentinels. From this place we were ordered to Fort Miller, the 30th. The enemy was in our rear, and drove in our rear guards; upon which I was sent by Gen. Nixon to Gen Schuyler, to inform him of a large body of the enemy near; but he neither sent his Aid-de-camp, nor went himself, nor sent any troops to cover their retreat, supposing our brigade should have been worsted with a superior number or strength. After our arrival at Fort Miller, which was about 10 o'clock at night, our brigade was ordered about half a mile as an advanced picket, directly from the river and the tents, etc., having nothing but the heavens to cover them. Some of the men had been without victuals 24 hours. We were ordered from thence to Saratoga on the 31st where we remained till the 3rd of August which was a very awful day on account of Gen. Schuyler's conduct who acted more like a mad man than the Commander-in-Chief.

General Schuyler was not popular in the New England States, and he was not particularly fond of the troops from New England. It might have been traced back to jealousies between the colonies of New York (the General's home) and New England over territorial limits. The General allowed the militia to go home, and then he asked Washington to send replacements from the South of the Hudson River while saying to his friends, "One Southern soldier was worth two from New England."

The New England troops were brave, devout, and God fearing. They were fighting from a sense of religious duty. They believed that Schuyler was lacking courage, and he "cursed, damned, and swore." They believed he was not the one to lead and inspire with love and confidence for the troops. Smith went on to write in his diary: "He [Schuyler] beat some of the soldiers who were preforming their duty. He cursed, damned, swore, profaned the name of God in a most horrible manner, and swore by his Maker, that if he could light on the Major of our brigade, he would split his head open and scatter his brains upon the ground. He attempted to thrust an officer through, and afterwards made his brags of it, that it was happy for the officer and unlucky for the service that he had not killed him. Many particulars of like conduct."

The following is an account in Smith's diary of the first of the two great battles fought on Bemis' Heights in Stillwater, which resulted in the surrender of British General Burgoyne. Pastor Smith was with the main body of troops making up the right wing.

> Friday, September 10, 1777, A warm battle was fought between Gen. Burgoyne's army and one division of our army commanded by Gen. Arnold. The action began early in the afternoon between Gen. Fraser's flying camo and Col. Morgan's Corps, consisting of the rifle men and our light infantry. At first we drove them back, and the firing ceased. The enemy being reinforced, they renewed the attack about half after three, which continued almost three hours, the firing being heavy and incessant. The evening closed the action. We lost sixty-four killed, two hundred and seventeen wounded, and thirty-eight missing.
>
> Saturday 20, Sunday 21. We expected another engagement and were so alarmed and preparing to meet the enemy, that I did not preach.
>
> Monday 22–Saturday 27. Often alarmed and preparing for battle. Frequently taking prisoners and receiving deserters.
>
> Camp Stillwater on October 3, 1777, My Dear Hephzabah: Since the battle mentioned in a former letter, we have either taken prisoners or had deserters come in from the enemy almost every day. I have expected a general engagement before now, but when it will take place I know not. By the best information the enemy's provisions grow short. This day we had eight deserters come in from Gen. Bur-

goyne's army. One day last week, we had upwards of forty prisoners. Our army is in high spirits.

During the last of September and the first week of October, it became clear to British General Burgoyne that he was not going to receive any reinforcements or supplies. During this time there were small skirmishes between the two sides. By October 7th Burgoyne's troops faced about 12,000 American troops. The British had more troops, but they had only about 5,000 effective battle ready troops. Loses and desertions from the battle on September 19 had reduced the strength of his army. On October 7, 1777, the British attacked the Americans in the early afternoon. A little more than 8,000 Americans took the field that day.

> Tuesday, October 7, The troops under General Burgoyne: twenty-four out of each company of each regiment of grenadiers, and twenty-four out of each company of each regiment of their light troops, with others, fifteen hundred in all, advanced towards our lines, when we gave them battle, took the ground, and drove the enemy into their works. We took possession of part of their works, with considerable ammunition, several ammunition wagons, eight pieces of artillery, a number of horses and carts, army tents, and much baggage.
> Wednesday 8, Our army marched to give them battle, but they declined coming out to meet them. That night Gen. Burgoyne began his retreat and left 340 sick and wounded behind.
> Thursday 9, It was very rainy, which prevented our pursuing them.
> Friday 10, We passed and overtook them at Saratoga. Great numbers of deserters have come in from the battle, and are daily coming in.
> Saturday 11, We took fifty prisoners in the morning.
> Monday 13, Thirty odd prisoners brought in; and in the evening Gen. Burgoyne sent in a flag of truce, and proposed to Gen. Gates for one of his field officers to have a conference with him. Ge. Gates conceded to the proposal, and appointed 10 o'clock next day for it.
> Tuesday 14, In the evening, Gen. Burgoyne sent a flag to Gen. Gates with a letter acknowledging the superiority of our numbers and strength, also the good disposition of our army, etc. Cessation of arms ensued till Fri., 17, when the articles of capitulation were signed in the morning. Before noon I saw Gen. Burgoyne, Gen. Phillips, Gen. Gates, Gen. Hamilton, with their attendants, come into our lines at the meeting of Gen. Burgoyne and Gen Gates. Gen. Burgoyne addressed his self thus: "The fate of war has put me into your hands." Gen. Gates replied: "If enterprise, courage, and perseverance could have given you success, the victory would have been yours," or words to that effect. Gen. Gates addressed himself to this effect to Gen. Phillips: "Gen. Phillips, I did not expect to see you here, but I am glad to see you as well." They were all invited to dine with Gen. Gates. In the afternoon, Gen. Burgoyne's army, who were paraded before he came into our lines, left their arms and marched off from their parade, etc. Gen. Burgoyne's army at the time of capitulation consisted of British troops 2,442;

THE CHAPLAINS   **Hezekiah Smith**

Foreigners 2, 198; Canadians and Tories 1,100. Gen. Nixon's brigade marched down the river the same direction about five or six miles.

When the defeat of General Burgoyne at Saratoga reached the King of France the French realized that the Americans could win the war. This British defeat led to the French aiding the Americans with money, supplies, and troops. In response to the British surrender, the Congress declared December 18, 1777, as a national day for Thanksgiving and praise. This became the nation's first official observance of a holiday with the name "Thanksgiving."

After the victory at Saratoga, most of the army went with General Washington to Valley Forge for the winter. Hezekiah Smith returned home on December 12, 1777, until April 28, 1778. Some researchers claim that Smith was at Valley Forge for the winter. However, Smith's diary disproves this. The pastor rejoined General Nixon's troops stationed in New York around the West Point area. For the next six months the troops marched around the New York area and Pastor Smith spent the time preaching and preforming other chaplain duties. In mid–October of 1778 he returned home again for six months.

It was not uncommon for chaplains to return home for extended periods of time. Unlike regular soldiers they did not sign up for a specific number of months or years. They were still responsible for their congregations back home and tried to get back as often as possible. Many chaplains returned home after a battle had ended, or before the army settled in at their winter quarters.

Pastor Smith rejoined the troops under General Nixon on April 16, 1779. By this time much of the large scale fighting was shifting toward the southern colonies. Smith wrote in his diary about an unusual event that occurred on July 6, 1779. "We had a very heavy shower of rain, attended with lightning and thunder, in the midst of which the lighting killed one of Capt. Whipple's soldiers and shocked many more in Col. Putnam's regiment, 31 of whom were considerably affected, some being deprived of their reason, some not able to walk, only to crawl out of their huts or tents, or others much scorched with the lighting, so as to be exceeding sore."

On April 24, 1780, the Haverhill Baptist Society meet and voted that "Rev. Mr. Smith be requested to return from ye army to his charge as soon as he can with honor." In the latter part of October 1780 Pastor Smith returned home to the delight of his congregation. The pastor continued to correspond with George Washington after the war, and Washington visited Hezekiah in Haverhill in 1789.

Sources: 1. *Chaplain Smith and the Baptist* by Reuben Aldridge Guild, 1885, pages 162–282. 2. Sons of the American Revolution Application. 3. *Massachusetts Soldiers and Sailors*, Vol. XIV, page 412. 3. *From Its European Antecedents to 1791—The United States Army Chaplaincy* by Parker C. Thompson, 1978, pages 157, 163, 164, and 283. 4. *D.A.R. Lineage Book*, Vol. 3, page 154. 5. *Massachusetts Soldiers and Sailors*, Vol. XIV, page 412.

Robert Smith

After preaching a sermon praising the defenders of Fort Sullivan, he enlisted as a private to successfully defend the fort from the British in June of 1778. One writer later wrote, "The late Bishop Smith shouldered his musket, and amidst scenes of the greatest danger, both by precept and by example stimulated to intrepid resistance."

He was soon made chaplain of the 1st South Carolina Regiment, and later he served as chaplain of the Continental hospital in Charlestown. In 1779 Robert was promoted Chaplain-General of the Southern Department of the Continental Army.

In 1780 Charleston was captured by the British, and Pastor Smith was taken prisoner and his property confiscated. He was watched closely and was soon offered his freedom, his pulpit, and property if he would take an oath of loyalty to the crown. He refused, saying, "Rather would I be hanged by the King of England than go off and hang myself in shame and despair like Judas." In June of 1781 he and other prisoners were transferred to Philadelphia, and in 1782 Smith was released. In 1795 he was elected the first Bishop of the Diocese of South Carolina.

Sources: 1. *Anecdotes of the Revolutionary War* by Alexander Garden, page 199. 2. *The American Revolution and Righteous Community* by Robert Smith, pages 22–26. 3 *From Its European Antecedents to 1791—The United States Army Chaplaincy* by Parker C. Thompson, 1978, page 171. 4. *Dictionary of American Biography*, 1936, 9:336.

Elihu Spencer

Elihu Spencer was born on February 12, 1721, in East Haddam, Connecticut, and he died on December 27, 1784, in Trenton, New Jersey. He graduated from Yale in 1746 and served as a chaplain in the French and Indian War.

In 1775 he was appointed by the Continental Congress as one of the chaplains to tour North Carolina to win people of loyalist sympathies to the revolutionary cause. In 1777 he became hospital chaplain and he was paid $60 a month, three rations, and forage for one horse. When the Hessians occupied Trenton, his house was burned down by them because of Elihu's support of the patriots.

Sources: 1. *D.A.R. Lineage Book*, Vol. 10, page 124. 2. *Yale and Her Honor-Roll in the American Revolution* by Henry Phelps Johnston, pages 193–194.

Samuel Spring

Samuel Spring was born on February 27, 1746, in Uxbridge, Massachusetts, and he died on March 4, 1819, in Newburyport, Massachusetts. He married Hannah Hopkins on November 4, 1779. He graduated from Princeton in 1771, and at the outbreak of the war he served as a chaplain under the command of Colonel John Fellows during the siege of Boston.

When Colonel Benedict Arnold invaded Canada in the summer of 1775, Pastor Spring agreed to serve as a chaplain of the expedition. When most of the troops left Boston on September 13, 1775, Samuel Spring was wearing his heavy woolen clerical suit in the sweltering summer heat. The troops sailed to Newburyport and from there sailed to Maine.

While at Fort Wester near present-day Augusta, Maine, the pastor was called on to counsel Private James McCormick, who had been sentenced to death for firing his musket at an officer and killing a sergeant when he missed. The private was marched to the gallows and then given a reprieve and sent back to Cambridge. The journey through Maine was difficult and left many of the men tired and ill. Some of the men elected to turn back.

The troops became devoted to Samuel, who cheerfully shared all their privations and hardships. When Sunday came the men would pile their knapsacks tier upon tier for a pulpit, on which an orderly would help him mount, while they gathered around to listen.

Food became very scarce, and the men began to eat anything they could find. One day Pastor Spring came upon a company of men gathered around a fire, while boiling some dog's claws they had saved to make a soup with. They urged the pastor to sit with them and share the disgusting meal. When the dog gave out, the men took off their moose skin moccasins and boiled them to extract a little nourishment. They felt their feet could withstand the cold November mornings more than their stomachs could endure the hunger pangs.

In November the starving men reached a French Canadian settlement who gave the Americans food and clothing. The troops finally reached Quebec, which was the only walled city in North America, and they began a siege of the city. Pastor Spring converted a hotel outside of the city into a hospital and a chapel.

Samuel went with General Montgomery and Colonel Arnold on a raid during a snowstorm on New Year's Eve. They tried to by-pass the cities stone walls by attacking the wood palisade that protected the lower town along the banks of the St. Lawrence River. The Americans were not aware that the area was well defended and after running into heavy cannon and musket fire they were forced to retreat. Unfortunately, General Montgomery and several officers were killed, and Colonel Arnold's leg was shattered by a musket ball. Arnold was dragged to safety, and the pastor examined the leg and tried to stop the bleeding the best he could. Arnold did not want to leave the battlefield and he insisted on standing so his men would not become discouraged by having their commander ineffective. Pastor Spring supported Arnold so he could stand and when the Americans retreated the pastor was one of the men that carried the wounded Colonel from the battlefield back to the hospital.

The invasion of Canada became a disaster, and the troops finally left the area in June of 1776. Many of the troops, including Pastor Spring, were ill. The pastor arrived at a new encampment built on the eastern shore of Lake Champlain in October 1776. On Sunday, November 3 Samuel held a service there and preached to the troops.

Toward the end of 1776 Samuel left the army and returned to Newburyport to become a pastor of a church there. The next year he married Hannah Hopkins. In his later years Samuel became very influential in a fundamentalist wing of the Congregational Church. John Quincy Adams disagreed with the teachings of Samuel, and he wrote that Samuel's views were "extremely contracted and illiberal" and that he had the enthusiasm of a bigot.

When Samuel died on March 4, 1819, some of his last words were "Oh, let me be gone—do let me be gone—I long to be home."

Sources: 1. Sons of the American Revolution Application. 2. *From Its European Antecedents to 1791—The United States Army Chaplaincy* by Parker C. Thompson,

1978, pages, 122-124. 3. *Blackstone Valley Tribune*, Vol. II, no, 10, 5 December 2008, article by Michael Potaski, page 5. 4. *Genealogies of the Families and Descendants of the Early Settlers of Watertown, Massachusetts, 1885*, Vol. 1, page 446. 5. *The Chaplains and Clergy of the Revolution* by Joel Tyler Headly, 1864, pages 89-106.

James Sproat

James Sproat was born on April 11, 1722, in Scituate, Massachusetts, and he died on October 18, 1793, in Philadelphia. He graduated from Yale in 1741. He was pastor of a Presbyterian Church in Guilford, Connecticut for almost 25 years, and then he moved to Philadelphia in 1769 as pastor of the Second Presbyterian Church.

On February 10, 1778, Congress elected him as a Chaplain for the Hospitals in the Middle Department located in the surrounding counties around Philadelphia. He served in this capacity until the end of the war in 1781. He kept a journal between 1779 and 1781 recording his visits to the hospitals in his district. This is an example of one of his entries: "April 28, 1778—Rode to the camp at Valley Forge—was a good deal pleased with the situation of the camp. Met my son [Captain William Sproat, 4th Pennsylvania Line] in health. Heard from my family at Egg Harbor. Dined with my nephew Col. [Ebenezer] Sproat [12th Massachusetts Line], my son, and several gentlemen. Went over the Schuylkill to get lodgings. Lodged at Gen, Reed's where I met good Mrs. De Bert. Called on Hugh Hodge. Nighted at W. Henry's."

After the war he returned to the Second Presbyterian Church in Philadelphia. During the yellow fever epidemic of 1793 Pastor Sproat remained in the city to serve his congregation while many people fled the city. He later became infected as did his wife Mary, oldest son, and youngest daughter. They all perished from the fever. It was very difficult to have the usual funeral and many times the dead were just placed on a cart and taken out and buried. In the case of James Sproat some colored men of various religious beliefs offered to carry his casket. The procession included about 50 people who followed the remains of the preacher to the cemetery on Arch Street.

Sources: 1. Sons of the American Revolution Application. 2. *From Its European Antecedents to 1791—The United States Army Chaplaincy* by Parker C. Thompson, 1978, pages, 172-173. 3. *Pennsylvania Magazine of History and Biography*, Vol. XXVII, 1903, number 1, pages 441-443. 4. *Philadelphia History 1609-1884*, pages 1270-1271.

John Steel

John Steel was born in Ireland in 1715 and came to America in 1742. He died on August 17, 1779, in Carlisle, Pennsylvania. He married Margaret Hutchinson, who was the sister of the mother of Andrew Jackson. John was appointed pastor of the church in New London Pennsylvania in 1745.

The frontier was overrun by Indians, so John carried his rifle with him to his church and kept it by his side for use at a moment's notice during the service. If an Indian attack threatened he would gather a company of riflemen together and prepare to defend the settlement. John served as a chaplain and Captain of the Provincial troops during the French and Indian War.

He served in the Armstrong expedition that marched to destroy the Indian town of Kittanning on account of atrocities the Indians committed against the English. They destroyed the settlement on September 8, 1756. On the morning of the attack Colonel Armstrong had his men leave all unnecessary equipment, including bedrolls, behind to be guarded by eight men. When Armstrong and Captain Steel returned from Kittanning, they found that the men left behind had been killed by Indians. This site became known as "Blanket Hill." The Indians counterattacked Armstrong's men, so they retreated back to their fort leaving all their supplies at Blanket Hill.

It was during this time that Pastor Steel first met George Washington, who was a surveyor at Fort Ligonier. They remained friends for the rest of their lives. During the Revolutionary War Pastor Steel became known as the Reverend Captain Steel, when he commanded the Carlisle Militia in 1777 under the command of Colonel Ephraim Blaine.

Sources: 1. Sons of the American Revolution Application. 2. *D.A.R. Lineage Book*, Vol. 9, page 4. 3. Historical Marker at Blanket Hill. 4. *History of the Middle Spring Presbyterian Church, Middle Spring, Pa. 1738–1900* by Belle McKinney Hays Swope, 1900, page 208.

James Tate

James Tate was born in Ireland and came to America in 1760. He studied under Presbyterian influence, but he never affiliated himself with one congregation. He preached anywhere the people wanted to hear the gospel.

James became chaplain of the 1st North Carolina Regiment on October 13, 1775, and later served in the 3rd Regiment. On June 1, 1778, he was made North Carolina Brigade Chaplain and served until the end of the war. He was at the Battles of Germantown in 1777 and Monmouth in 1778. He was also with the troops at Valley Forge. He received 1,553 acres of land on October 21, 1783, for his service. He died a bachelor in 1795.

Sources: 1. *Dictionary of North Carolina Biography*. 2. *Roster of Soldiers from North Carolina in the American Revolution*, page 48. 3. *The Chaplains and Clergy at the Battle of Monmouth* by Chaplain Stanley Cuyler, 1986, pages 13 and 17.

Joseph Thaxter

Joseph Thaxter was born on April 23, 1742, in Hingham, Massachusetts, and he died on July 18, 1827, in Edgartown, Massachusetts. He graduated from Harvard in 1768 and he married Mary Allen in 1781. He also served as a surgeon, and he was considered the last surviving chaplain of the Revolutionary War.

Pastor Joseph Thaxter was at the Battle of Concord on April 19, 1775. He and Pastor William Emerson (also in this book) were under the command of Major Buttrick. Joseph, who had been preaching at Westford, was in the front line armed with a brace of pistols. On November 30, 1824, Joseph Thaxter wrote in a letter the following account of the Battles of Concord and Bunker Hill:

> I was an eyewitness to the following facts. The people of Westford and Acton, some few of Concord, were the first who faced the British at Concord Bridge. The British had placed about ninety men as a guard at the North Bridge; we had then no certain information that any had been killed at Lexington, we saw the British making destruction in the town of Concord; it was proposed to advance to the bridge; on this Colonel Robinson, of Westford, together with Major Buttrick, took the lead; strict orders were given not to fire, unless the British fired first; when they advanced about halfway on the causeway the British fired one gun, a second, a third, and then the whole body; they killed Colonel Davis, of Acton, and a Mr. Hosmer. Our people then fired over one another's heads, being in a long column, two and two; they killed two and wounded eleven. Lieutenant Hawkstone, said to be the greatest beauty of the British army, had his cheeks so badly wounded that it disfigured him much, of which he bitterly complained. On this, the British fled, and assembled on the hill, the north side of Concord, and dressed their wounded, and then began

their retreat. As they descended the hill near the road that comes out from Bedford they were pursued; Colonel Bridge, with a few men from Bedford and Chelmsford, came up, and killed several men. We pursued them and killed some; when they got to Lexington, they were so close pursued and fatigued, that they must have soon surrendered, had not Lord Percy met with them with a large reinforcement and two field-pieces. They fired them, but the balls went high over our heads. But no cannon ever did more execution, such stories of their effects had been spread by the tories through our troops, that from this time more wont back than pursed. We pursued to Charlestown Common, and then retired to Cambridge.

When the army collected at Cambridge, Colonel Prescott with his regiment of minute men, and John Robinson, his Lieutenant Colonel, were prompt at being at their post. On this 16th of June, Colonel Prescott and Colonel Bridge were ordered upon Breed's Hill to heave up a breast work; they laboured all night, and were left to fight the British. Reinforcements were ordered, but not one company went in order. Many went to Bunker's Hill; some went from there as volunteers, part of which belonged to General Starks' regiment. Among the volunteers was the ever-to-be lamented General Warren. When he was introduced to Colonel Prescott, the Colonel said, "General Warren, I have not the pleasure of a personal acquaintance with you, but from your known character, I shall fight with cheerfulness under you." General Warren replied, "Colonel Prescott, I have not come to take command, but to learn to fight under you." This I had from Colonel Robinson, and believe as much as if I had heard with my ears; a braver and more upright man I never knew. Such men as Prescott and Robinson, ought not to be forgotten by those who write the history of the commencement and prosecution of our glorious revolution. The vile slander, cast upon old General Putnam are totally without foundation. He did all that man could do to reinforce Prescott on Breed's Hill. A braver men never lived. At that time our army was little better than a mob, without discipline and under little command, till General Washington came and Gates, and gave to it some regularity. Whole regiments were ordered on perilous duty at once, and the loss of men was from a small circle. The Breed's Hill loss fell upon the county of Middlesex, about one half of the loss was in Prescott's regiment, viz, forty-nine killed and forty-five wounded. This evil was remedied by Washington and Gates, and in '76 victory delivered Boston, &c. A decent monument at Concord Bridge, where the first spark was struck, and quite as glorious as Breed's Hill, considering the circumstances, would be doing no more honour to Robinson and Buttrick than they richly deserve. I have lived in obscurity on this island, and never thought myself of importance enough, and capable of doing justice to a historical account of the transactions of the memorable 19th of April 1775, or of the 17th of June. Many anecdotes, of those days, that would do honour to individuals, it is most probable will be forgotten. The following is one. The Rev. Edward Brooks, who lived at Medford, got intelligence of a small party going with relief to meet the British; they had a wagon-load; Mr. Brooks mustered a few men, waylaid them near West Cambridge meetinghouse, and shot the horses, and wounded the lieutenant who commanded them, took several prisoners before the British came up, and retired.

At the Battle of Bunker Hill Pastor Thaxton, who was the chaplain of Colonel William Prescott's Regiment, was severely wounded during the fight and walked with a limp for the rest of his life. Colonel Prescott and his men were among the last to retreat from the battle. Thaxton was discharged because of his injury but he later rejoined the army. He wrote the following to General Lincoln: "I find that I cannot enjoy myself in Retirement, so well as camp. I therefore should be glad of an Appointment as I have not the Happiness to be acquainted with the Brigadiers who are to act in the Jersies or that part of the Country. Should esteem it a Favour, should you think it consistent, that I might have an Appointment Should such a Thing take Place, it would be with greatest Cheerfulness that I should obey the call."

On the 23rd of January 1776 he was appointed Chaplain of Colonel John Robertson's Regiment of Westford. Thaxton returned to the army in time to fight in the Battles of White Plains, Trenton, and Princeton in 1776. While at Westford he addressed a detachment of 12 of Westford's soldiers, as they were about to march to Fort Ticonderoga. A story was told that one of the men, Thomas Rogers, refused to stand when Pastor Thaxter spoke to them. It was reported that all the men, except for Thomas Rogers, returned from the fort alive.

After the war Joseph became pastor of a church in Edgartown, Massachusetts. On the 50th anniversary of the Battle at Bunker Hill he was invited to officiate as chaplain at the laying of the Bunker Hill Monument cornerstone.

Sources: 1. *Massachusetts Soldiers and Sailors of the Revolutionary War, 1775-1783*, page 514. 2. *Harvard Alumni Veterans of the American Revolution.* 3. *From Its European Antecedents to 1791—The United States Army Chaplaincy* by Parker C. Thompson, 1978, page 92, 112, 113, and 158-159. 4. *The American Monthly Magazine*, Vol. 37, page 238. 4. *History of the Town of Westford 1659-1883* by Rev. Edwin Hodgman, 1883. 5. *A History of the Fight at Concord of the 19th of April 1775* by Rev. Ezra Ripley, 1832, pages 29-30. 6. Sons of the American Revolution Application.

Charles Thompson

Charles Thompson was born in 1748 in Amwell, New Jersey, and he died on May 1, 1803, in Charlton, Massachusetts. He married Sarah Child on November 26, 1770. He was appointed Chaplain of Colonel Christopher Green's Battalion of the 1st Rhode Island in May of 1777.

Pastor Thompson was probably at the Battle of Red Bank when the regiment successfully defended Fort Mercer against an attack by 2,000 Hessians. The pastor was with the American troops during the winter at Valley Forge. He was at his home visiting on the morning of May 25, 1778, when the British came to his town and burned the meeting house, Thompson's house, and they took him prisoner. They took him to Newport and released him about a month later.

Sources: 1. *A History of New England: Containing Historical and Descriptive Sketches* edited by R.H. Howard and Henry E. Crooker, 1880, page 418. 2. *D.A.R. Lineage Book*, Vol. 33, page 147. 3. U.S. Revolutionary War Rolls 1775–1783, Folder 12. 4. Sons of the American Revolution Application. 5. *Manual of the Rhode Island Society of the Sons of the American Revolution*, page 118.

Charles Mynn Thruston

Charles Thruston was born in 1738 in Gloucester County, Virginia, and he died on March 21, 1812, in Louisiana. He served under the command of George Washington in the French and Indian War. He was educated at the College of William & Mary in 1765, he went to London for the purpose of examination and ordination by the bishop of that diocese. When he returned home he became a pastor of a parish in Gloucester County, Virginia.

As war with England approached, he used his pulpit as a planform to speak out against the British rule. He even gathered weapons and supplies in case war broke out. In the winter of 1776–77 he raised a company of volunteers, which were composed of the elite of the young men of the county. His company appointed him Captain, and they marched to join General Washington who was in New Jersey.

After a short time at headquarters Pastor Thruston became impatient and was anxious for a fight with the British. General Washington gave him 500 men with the option to use them as the Pastor saw fit. Very soon the Pastor and his men engaged the Hessians near Perth Amboy, New Jersey. He led his 500 men in an attack against a fortified position of 1,500 troops. During the fight Thruston was shot by a musket ball in his arm just above the elbow.

The Pastor fainted from the pain and loss of blood from the shattered arm. He was carried from the field with his 12-year-old son, Charles, by his side. Thruston said to his son, "Were you to run Charles, I would shoot you." The wounded man was taken back to Washington's headquarters, and had him attended by his own surgeon.

The surgeon recommended that the arm be removed and Thruston replied, "Doctor, I am a bad hand to have an arm cut off," and he also remarked that he preferred death to mutilation. The doctor bandaged the arm, and it healed in about 12 months. During the healing several pieces of bone worked their way down through the muscles and came out in his hand. Washington later promoted the Pastor to a Colonel.

Unfortunately, men could not be raised for the new Colonel's regiment. With no men to command Thruston retired from the service, returned home, and chose to also retire from the clergy. He took up farming and entered local politics. His first wife, Mary, died in 1765 and he was left with a large land inheritance from her. Over the years he sold off the land and had invested it in land in parts of Kentucky and Western Virginia. Toward the end of the 1700's that investment became very valuable.

Charles remarried and began another family with Ann Alexander. The children from his first wife felt that the land owned by their mother should go to them and not the new family. This resulted in a family quarrel which lasted until 1787. That year Thruston gave the three sons from the first marriage 41,000 acres of land, and he kept 1,000 acres for himself. The three sons soon left Virginia for their new land in Kentucky.

Before Charles Thruston died in 1812 he purchased and moved to a plantation below New Orleans, which became the very battleground on which General Andrew Jackson defeated the British in January of 1815. Charles applied for a pension and received $20 a month due to his disability. His pension papers were destroyed in a War Office fire in 1800.

Sources: 1. Sons of the American Revolution Application. 2. *D.A.R. Lineage Book*, Vol. 5, page 327. 3. *Cecelia and Fanny: The Remarkable Friendship Between an Escaped Slave and Her Former Mistress* by Brad Asher, pages 33–36. 4. *The Southern Literary Messenger: Devoted to Every Department of Literature and the Fine Arts*, Vol. VI, 1835, pages 164–167.

Benjamin Trumbull

Benjamin Trumbull was born on December 19, 1735, in Hebron, Connecticut, and he died on February 2, 1820, in North Haven, Connecticut. He married Martha Phelps on December 4, 1760.

He was appointed chaplain of the 1st Connecticut Regiment in April 1775. He served in the Canada Expedition. It was first under Schuyler, then under Montgomery, with Wooster leading the Connecticut troops. Benjamin was at the siege of Fort John and nearby Fort Chambly on September 17 to November 3, 1775. He wrote in his diary about the opening attack on September 25, 1775.

> September 25th. This Day about 3 O'clock in the Afternoon the Bomb Battery and two Gun Batters were opened and began to play on the Forts. A very hot fire continued on both Sides until the night.
> Tuesday and Wednesday 26 & 27. Were very cold, wet and stormy. About 3 o'clock on Wednesday the storm abated and a heavy Fire began on both Sides and continued till night. We had one man killed with a Shell, and another wounded.

Fort Chambly surrendered to the Americans on 18 October, which was followed by the surrender of Fort John on 3 November. The surrender of Fort John was noted in Benjamin's diary.

> November 2 the Garrison sent Captain Williams and Captain _____ with a truce.
> November 3 the Fort stores and shipping ordnance &c. were delivered up and the Americans took possession of them.

After the capture of the forts Benjamin marched with the army to Montreal and captured that city. He later returned to Fort John on 18 November.

> November Monday 6th General Wooster's Troops were ordered to march for Mountreal. Colonel Waterbury with his Regiment marched about 11 o'Clock. General Woosters marched a Part of them about 1 o'Clock, and the Rest were detained for want of Carts and Carriages to Carry our Baggage. The Day was cloudy and heavy and towards night it rained hard. The Roads ever Since Friday have been mud and mire and Scarce a Spot of dry Ground for miles together. The Land is all Flat in this Country and a great Part of it drowned Lands for 50 or an 100 miles on End. Our People have lived in mud and mire most of the Time since they began the Siege. There is but little Settled weather in these Parts this Season of ye year, our men Sometimes have been Wet near Twenty Days together. The Fatigues and hardships of the Men During a Siege of Fifty Days have been unusually hard, they lay in a Swamp, and traveled a great Part of the Time in mud & Water had an obstinate Enemy to Encounter, well Skilled in Defence, well Secured by strong Works, well Supplied with Military Stores, and had a fine Artilery as well as a large Number of men to defend their Forts.
> Lords Day November 12 was a cold Blustering Day, wind at Northwest, cloudy and Sower, difficult Passing the River on account of the Wind and Current which is rapid and Strong. Colonel Ward comes in to Day with his Party, and the Troops wc had crossed the River, with the Generals. Marched into the Subarbs of Mon-

treal and Encamped just without the City. Monday November 13. The Generals marched into the City just at Evening. The Citizens before their Entrance Proposed Terms of Capitulation, but the Generals observed that they had no Right to any Capitulation. That they had no men to defend them no Artilery or any means of Defence; that the Troops came not as Enemies but as Friends to prated them, and as they pretended to be affraid that the Troops would Plunder them they Assured them that they should not be plundered but should be Safe in their Persons and Estates.

Saturday Novr 18th. A clear cold morning. I am not so Well as I was yesterday. I am Sick at my Stomach and distressed in my Bowels with some Fever, but I trust and believe in God y* he will direct all yl concerns me in the best manner. To him I commit myself and Family and all that Concerns me. At 20 Minutes after 10 having Luckily got a man to carry my Baggage to St. John's I marched from Le Praire for that Post.

Benjamin was part of the New York campaign, which was a series of battles between British forces under General Howe and American troops under General Washington for the control of New York City. In late August the British landed about 22,000 troops on Long Island, and by August 27, 1776, they had driven the Americans back to their fortifications in Brooklyn Heights.

Thursday August 15th. One Dickinson Died out of Colonel Douglasses Regiment. He was of Capl Higgins Company, and belonged to Hadam. The Enemy this Day were discovered to be very Busy in getting men on board their Ships. 40 Transports were moored and lay off receiving men on board down towards the Narrows. Boats were seen so thick on the Waters and there was so much passing & repassing that it seemed almost as though there had been a Bridge of Boats a forming across the Waters. Deserters which come from the Enemy represent that they despise the American Army, and expect to make an easy Conquest of them at once. They the report that they Care neither for our Numbers, nor our Preparations. They boast themselves on conquering us as though they had put off the Harness.

August 22. There is this morning a great Motion of the Enemy. Many Transports and Some Heavy Ships fall down through the Narrows and before noon begin to Land on Long Island. The out Posts of the Continental Army Set Fire to the Corn buildings &c before the Enemy which make a great Smoke and Show. The Account this Day is that four or five Thousands are landed on the Island. It is probable to me that more than double that Number have or will soon Land there.

August 27 Tuesday Morning as early as three o'Clock Our Out Posts were some of them attacked, and it Soon appeared that the Enemy by a Strategem, had passed a road on our Left and brought on their Light Horse and Light Infantry, so as to surround our Men, and Lord Sterling with a considerable party of Men, who went out to his Assistance, were flanked and in a manner Surround them so that many of them were killed and taken, Lord Sterling is missing, and General Sul-

> livan [he was captured], Colonel Was Killed, Colonel Clark is missing and many other officers. Colonel Huntingtons Regiment a great Part of them are missing. All our out Posts were Lost, and the Enemy advanced near the Lines.

On September 15, 1776, General Howe landed about 12,000 troops on lower Manhattan and he began to take control of New York City. Washington withdrew his troops to Harlem and they held their ground there in a skirmish the next day. Benjamin wrote of the skirmish in his diary.

> Monday Septr 16. A large body of the Enemy advanced towards our Lines, Supposed to be three or four Thousand, and a little before Twelve o'clock a very Smart and Heavy Fire Commenced between them and our Rangers and riflemen on the Advanced posts. This was sustained by the Rangers Bravely till they were reinforced from the Lines, when the fire grew more sharp and Heavy on both Sides, and continued in the whole for 2 or three Hours, in which Time the Enemy were several Times considerably broken and formed anew, and finally were driven by the Americans about 2 miles, though they were often reinforced. Our men by this Time were much Fatigued, and had some of them almost Spent their Ammunition, and the General Thought best to order them to retreat. But few men were Killed and wounded on the Side of the Provincials considering the Heat and duration of the A6tion. It was Supposed after the Action that not more than 20, or 25 men were killed and about 50 Wounded, but by the Returns afterwards, as far as I could learn about were killed, and about wounded. It appeared by the blood and trails of the Enemy where they retreated that their Loss was considerable. Our Troops had the honour of behaving well, and the issue of the Battle gave Spirit to them.

Once Washington was chased out of New York City he marched his army north to White Plains about 30 miles away on 21 October. The British army followed and on 28 October they attacked the Americans and defeated them. On 31 October Washington began to retreat farther north. Benjamin Trumbull was with the American army and wrote of the battle in his diary

> Monday the 21st Oct. Marched about 10 o'Clock at Night for the White Plains, Carried our Tents on our Backs Packs Pots Kettles and provisions &c. The Army Marched all Night excepting Some small Halts, almost fainted under their Burdens and were greatly fatigued. Arrived early next morning at the Plains.
> Tuesday 22nd. lay on our Arms in the high Way till after 12 o'Clock as no Place was determined upon for an Encampment. The Men slept on the ground in the Streets had nothing to coock with or to cover them, and many of them, were exceeding hungry as well as Sleepy and Weary. In the afternoon were ordered to a Place of Encampment back on the Road towards a mile and had to tread back with Weary Steps the ground we had before in vain with so much labour travelled over. Our ground was marked out for the Encampment and the men

got up their Tents just as it began to be night, & in the Evening built Fires for cooking, &c. The men are worried in a manner to Death and are treated with great hardship and Severity, and in my Opinion are put to much unnecessary Hardship and Fatigue. On the Night of the 22nd, 36 of the Enemy Rogers's Rangers were taken by one of our Scouts, and this Morning were brought in to Lord Stirling at the White Plains. This Day Commedant Chesters Brigade marched from the Lines for the White Plains, continued their March the most of the Night ; a very considerable Part of the Army marched from Kings bridge and that Way for the White Plains and Canon Baggage and Troops were passing the most of the Night. Commedant Chesters Brigade and a great Number of Troops arrived at the White Plains the Latter Part of the Night and early in the Morning, and Wagons and Troops are constantly coming on.

October 28th. The Enemy this Day advanced early towards the Lines, and Part of General Wadsworth's Brigade were sent out to Skirmish with their Advanced Parties; about nine o'Clock our Scouts and Guards to push in towards the Camp, and the Enemy Soon made their Appearance on the Road, and on the high grounds opposite to them, and soon came on briskly, and their Field Pieces and Hobits began to play upon us soon almost as they made their Appearance. They were extremely Numerous, and they most cautiously avoided meeting us in Front; when they came upon us in Front and received our fire they would break and retreat immediately out of the Reach of Musket shots and would wait all in order till their Field Pieces came up and their bits and mortars, from which they threw Shot and Shells very teribly, and they would throw them so as to kill and wound our men on the Hill where yy could see them, and when they layover the hills beyond them; at the Same Time they would keep out Parties to flank and Surround us, and so they drove on till they reached the Heights opposite our Lines ; Where they halted and thew Shot and Shells. The number out to Skirmish with this numerous body were not more than 800, or 1000 men. Numbers were killed and wounded on both sides, but I believe there was nothing very Bloody on either Side. This Day I understand General Washington had an Express from Fort Washington acquainting him that the Enemy attacked our Lines on Sunday below fort Washington and that the Shiping drew up in a Line below the Fort; and that the Enemy were repulsed at the Lines and the Shiping was much Damaged, obliged to Ship their Cables and to fall down the River. We were obliged to strike all our Tents and lay so till 8 or nine o'Clock, when they had liberty to set ym up again. Tuesday Octr 29th at 2 o'Clock the Troops in General Spencers Division had orders to Strike their Tents and Carry them out about one mile and an half by hand and then to return to the Lines. The men went out and carried on their Tents, and then returned and brought on their Cooking Utensils, and then went back again to the Lines. Many of the Men though they had been engaged almost all Day with the Enemy and had been obliged to Wade through a River and were very wet had no sleep at all. I was afraid I should be sick for I had been in the River almost all over, and could not change me, was much fatigued with the Action of the Day preceeding; but I am to Day well and vigorous.

During the Battle of White Plains on 28 October the American militia controlled Chatterton Hill. The British were repelled the first time they tried to capture the hill. Soon Hessian artillery opened fire on the hill and a larger British force attacked. The attack led to a rout of the American militia commanded by Colonel Brooks. It was later recorded "they fled in confusion, without more than a random, scattering fire." This exposed the flank of the Marylanders and New Yorkers and left them alone and unsupported.

Aroused by the shameful flight of the militia, Pastor Trumbull seized a musket and joined the ranks and fought like a common soldier. Cannon balls were exploding around him, and yet he loaded and fired with uncanny coolness. When the men were ordered to retreat and join the main army he began to cross the river with the rest of the men. The deep water made crossing difficult for Benjamin. Colonel Tallmadge was on his horse and was next to Benjamin. The pastor jumped on the back of the horse, which startled the animal. The animal fell in the water, dunking the Colonel and Trumbull. Both men swam to the shore and continued retreating with the soldiers.

> Thursday Octr. 31st. Rainy this Morning, but warm for the Season of the Year. Several Deserters come to us this Day and a Sergeant, a very Intelligible Fellow was taken. He had a Plan of the Enemies Lines and Camp; and by Accounts which seem to agree General howe had given orders for a General attack upon us this Morning but the Rain prevented. Nothing Special Happened. The Enemy appeared to be erecting five Batteries to play upon the Hill where we lay."
>
> Friday November 1st. This Morning Our Guards come off and leave the Lines in the Centre of the Town called White Plains, and to destress the Enemy burn all the Barns of Hay and Grain and Houses, where the Inhabitants had Stores of Wheat and Corn and also Stacks and Barracks of Hay and Grain. The Enemy advanced on to the Hills we left in the Fore Part of the Day, and came on about mile in Pursuit but were soon Stoped by our Canonade from the Hills. The Wind comes round in the North West, and the afternoon is Sower and blustering, and the Night is much the coldest we have had this Year. Things feel and look as though Winter was at Hand.

After the Battle of White Plains Washington's army retreated toward New Jersey and Benjamin returned home. "Thursday November 28th a pleasant Day for the Season. Just about 8 o'Clock in the Evening I arrived at my own House in Safety, found all my Family alive and in usual Health."

On January 15, 1777, Benjamin joined a company of local volunteers that numbered about 100 men. That summer Governor Tryon, who was also a British General began raiding towns along the Connecticut coast, which included New Haven where Pastor Trumbull lived. These raids were mainly against the civilians in the area. Benjamin and the local company of militiamen went out to stop the advance of Tyron. During one skirmish the pastor was mounted on a horse that was use to the sound of battle. While the other militiamen were firing behind trees and fences, the pastor sat in the saddle in open view firing and reloading. When he was shot at he would duck behind the horse's head, and then raise up and take careful aim and fire.

When the war ended Benjamin Trumbull returned to his duties of being a country pastor. In the winter of 1879 he came down with a lung fever and died in February of 1780. His last words were "Come quickly, amen. Even so come, Lord Jesus."

Sources: 1. Collections of the Connecticut Historical Society, 1898, Vol. VII, *Journal of Benjamin Trumbull*, pages 136–215. 2. Service of Connecticut Men in the War of the Revolution. 3. *Records of the Revolutionary War* by William T. Saffell, page 152. 4. *Special Operations in the American Revolution* by Robert L. Tonsetic, pages 88–89. 5. *The Chaplains and Clergy of the Revolution* by Joel Tyler Headley, 1864, pages 233–238. 6. *Westchester County, New York, During the American Revolution* by Henry Barton Dawson, pages 280–288.

Abner Waugh

Abner Waugh was born on January 17, 1746, in Orange County, Virginia, and he died on September 13, 1806, in Caroline County, Virginia. He married Philadelphia Claiborne around 1774. Abner studied at William and Mary in 1765 to 1768 and traveled to London to be ordained by the Bishop of London. When he returned to Virginia he was made pastor of St. Mary's Church in Caroline County, Virginia. St. Mary's was one of the largest and most beautiful churches in Virginia during that time.

Pastor Waugh's job at St. Mary's was to officiate at baptisms, marriages, and funerals. His annual salary was 16,000 pounds of tobacco, plus the percentages for cask and shrinkage. He was also to have the use of a farm or plantation of at least 200 acres, with a suitable rectory and appropriate outbuildings for agriculture production.

During the war Pastor Waugh served as chaplain of the 2nd Virginia Regiment from October 24, 1775, until March 2, 1776. The Colonel of the regiment was William Woodford who also had a plantation in St. Mary's Parish. The two men were well acquainted with each other and good friends. Abner was in the Field with the soldiers during fighting in the Norfolk area and twice was the courier of messages from the colonel to the Fourth Convention in Virginia.

The battle that Pastor Waugh was engaged in was called the Battle of Great Bridge fought on December 9, 1775. The militia forces under Colonel Woodford forced Loyalist Governor Lord Dunmore and the last of the British power from Virginia. The two sides met at Great Bridge and began fighting early in the morning. After exchanging fire the Tory forces of Lord Dunmore retreated with 62 men killed or wounded. The only causalities on the American side were one man shot in the hand and one shot in the thigh. One Virginian later wrote of the battle, "I then saw the horrors of war in perfection, worse than can be imagined; 10 and 12 bullets thro' many; limbs broke in 2 or 3 places; brains turned out. Good God, what a sight!"

When Lord Dunmore learned of the defeat of his troops he "raved like a madman" and even threatened to hang the boy who brought him the bad news. Many loyalists in the area, learning of the defeat, began to leave the area.

Colonial Virginians were very fond of dancing and it was important for them to be proficient in the various dances. The upper classes gave balls, often lasting for several days. Abner Waugh's superior dancing brought admiration from many of the society ladies. Presbyterians and Baptists looked upon dancing as sinful, while the Anglican ministers saw it as an innocent way of socializing and having fun.

For years after the war Pastor Waugh became wealthy and purchased thousands of acres of land. In 1782 he paid taxes for 28 slaves that he owned. In his final years he was definitely in the upper echelon of the social class in Virginia.

Sources: 1. "The Reverend Abner Waugh: The Best Dancer of the Minuet in the State of Virginia" by Otto Lohrenz, from the *Kentucky Review*, Vol. 15, no. 2, article 3, pages 28–37. 2. *The American Revolution in the Southern Colonies* by David Lee Russell, page 72.

Samuel West

Samuel West was born on March 3, 1730, in Yarmouth, Massachusetts, and he died on September 24, 1807, in Tiverton, Rhode Island. The Reverend Joseph Green prepared him to enter Harvard while Samuel worked as a farmhand. During Samuel's interview at Harvard in 1750 he got into a dispute about a Greek text with one of the examiners, but Samuel won his point. He graduated first in his class in 1754. He preached at several churches, and in 1760 he became pastor of the First Congregational in Dartmouth. He was paid 66 pounds a year, and members of the church fed and housed his horse and two cows.

Samuel was a large man over six feet tall and over 200 pounds. Since he cared little for his appearance, his clothes were usually well worn and dirty. By 1768 he had enough money to marry, and he married Experience Howland and they had six children. After the death of Experience he married the widow Lovice Hathaway Jenne. They had no children, and Samuel also outlived his second wife.

He was extremely absent-minded, he often forgot where he was going or why. Sometimes he was not even aware to events going on around him. Friends would sometimes find him sitting on his horse as the horse was grazing on the side of the road. The bridle was loose, and Samuel would be sitting on the horse with his hands folded on his breast totally absorbed in his own thoughts.

One time he met a friend, and he said to the man that he and his wife were on their way to visit him. The friend asked him, "Where is your wife?" Samuel replied, "Why, I thought she was on the seat behind me." His wife was getting ready to join him and Samuel had ridden off without her.

On another occasion he left for the mill, and was leading his horse and carrying the grist on his own shoulder. Once, before his second marriage, Samuel was going to the town clerk to publish the wedding bans. He walked the whole distance leading his horse, passed by the house of the town clerk, and did not stop until he reached the end of a wharf.

After the Battle of Bunker Hill Samuel volunteered as a chaplain. When General Washington had his headquarters at Cambridge, he learned that the British Admiral at Newport, Rhode Island had received secrets of American civil and military affairs. Finally a cypher letter was found by Washington, which indicated that it was written by someone on his own staff. Washington's trusted men could find no one to decipher the letter, until someone said there was a chaplain with troops at Dorchester who might be able to read it. They summoned Chaplain Samuel to crack the code in the letter. Washington also had two other code breakers called in, Elbridge Gerry and Colonel Elisha Porter. Washington had Gerry and Porter to work as a team and Samuel to work alone. The General wanted to see if each group would decipher the same hidden message.

A tent was prepared for Samuel, and a detail was assigned to guard his quarters while he worked at the message. Pastor began his study of the coded message as soon as lights out was shouted by the sentries. Samuel worked through the night, and by daybreak he sent a message to headquarters that he was ready to reveal the contents of the letter and who wrote it.

The code used in the letter was known as a "monalphabetic substitution" where one letter or in this case a symbol was substituted for a letter of the alphabet. Fortunately, for the Americans it was one of the easiest codes to break. In the English language some letters are consistently used more frequently than others. An example of a simple type of substitution.

Plain text alphabet: A B C D E F G H I J K L M N O P Q R S T U V W X Y Z
Ciphertext alphabet: Z E B R A S C D FG H I J K LM NO P Q T U V W X Y

American soldiers are here! (uncoded message) plain text alphabet
Zjaolgbzq plrfaop zoa daoa! (the coded message) cipher text alphabet

Washington received the coded message from the team of Porter and Gerry and the one from Samuel. When he compared the two messages they were identical. The coded letter revealed American casualties, troop strength, the mood of the people in many of the towns, and shipments of gunpowder. The original cipher letter was sent to Major Cane, a British officer in Boston, through a former mistress. After questioning the woman she admitted that the sender of the letter was Doctor Benjamin Church, who was serving as the Chief Physician and Director General of Medical Service of the continental Army.

On October 3, 1775, Church was taken before a court of inquiry with General Washington presiding. Church was visibly shaken when the court showed him the decoded message. He admitted he sent it, and he tried to defend his actions by saying that he sent exaggerated accounts of weapons and supplies to convince the British that to continue the war was a mistake. The court was not impressed with his story and found him guilty of criminal action and referred to the Continental Congress for its action.

Church was found guilty by Congress and could have been executed except for a loophole. The Congress had approved on November 7, 1775, to allow the death penalty for convicted spies, but because Church was convicted of spying before the death penalty had been authorized, it did not apply to him. Congress passed the following resolution: "That Doctor Church be close confined in some secure jail in the Colony of Connecticut, without use of pen, ink and paper, and that no person be allowed to converse with him except in the presence and hearing of a magistrate of the town or the sheriff of the county where he is confined, and in the English language, until further orders from this or a future Congress."

Dr. Church was sent to jail in Norwich, Connecticut and remained under guard until 1778. He was then banished and sailed from Boston, presumably for Martinique, and he was never heard from again. It was believed that the ship he was on was lost at sea.

In September of 1778 the British invaded Dartmouth and burned down West's parsonage, and some say it was in retaliation for his role in the Doctor Church affair. After the war Pastor Samuel West continued to preach at his church in Dartmouth. Over the years Samuel grew increasingly absent-minded.

On one occasion he preached the same sermon to the congregation three straight Sundays. No one was willing to upset him by telling him what he had done. On the fourth Sunday his daughter noticed that he had his Bible open to the same place. Before he went to the pulpit to preach the sermon for the fourth straight week, she opened the Bible to another place. When he returned to the pulpit he looked at the passage in the Bible and appeared a little confused. He then began to preach a different sermon for the first time in four weeks.

His absent-mindedness began to grow even worse, and he was forced to retire from the church in 1803. He went to live with a son in Tiverton, Rhode Island, where in died in 1807.

Sources: 1. *A History of the Town of Acushnet, Bristol County, State of Massachusetts* by Franklin Howland, page 78. 2. *The Writings of George Washington* by Jared Sparks, 1837, pages 504–506. 3. *The Original American Spies: Seven Covert Agents of the Revolutionary War* by Paul R. Misencik, pages 41–45. 4. Harvard Alumni Veterans of the American Revolutionary War.

John Woodhull

John Woodhull was born on January 26, 1744, at Long Island, New York, and he died on November 22, 1824, in New Jersey. He graduated

Woodhull　　　　　　THE CHAPLAINS

from Princeton in 1766 and was ordained in 1770. That same year he became pastor of Leacock Church in Lancaster, Pennsylvania, and he later became pastor of Old Tennent Church in New Jersey.

He served as chaplain in the 5th Lancaster Battalion Militia and he fought in the Battles of Germantown and Monmouth. During the battle at Monmouth he assisted at a cannon, when one of the men fell in battle. At the time he fought in clear view of the Old Tennent Church, where he would become pastor in 1779.

Sources: 1. *American Penny Magazine and Family Newspaper*, Vol. 1, page 533. 2. *The Chaplains and Clergy at the Battle of Monmouth* by Chaplain Stanley Cuyler, 1986, page 13. 3. Sons of the American Revolution Application.

* * *

"Soldiers, I look around upon your familiar faces with a strange interest. Tomorrow morning we will go forth to battle, for I need not tell you that your unworthy minister will march with you, invoking God's aid in the fight—we will march forth to battle."
—Prayer by Pastor Joab Trout who was killed
in battle at Brandywine on September 11, 1777.

Appendix
Other Chaplains Who Served in the American Revolution

The following is a list of chaplains who served in the American Revolution, from *The United States Army Chaplaincy by United States Department of the Army. Office of the Chief of Chaplains* published 1977.

James Aitkin—North Carolina, Denomination unknown, 4th North Carolina.

Slyvanus Ames—Probably born in Rhode Island in 1744. Served as a chaplain in the First Rhode Island Regiment and died at Valley Forge in 1778. Additional sources: 1. Athens County Ohio, Genealogy and History website. 2. *Sons of the American Revolution*, Vol. 1, page 441.

Ebenezer Baldwin—He was born on July 3, 1745, in Norwich, Connecticut, and he died on October 1, 1776, in Danbury, Connecticut. He graduated from Yale in 1763, and was ordained a minister on September 19, 1770, and became pastor of the first Church of Christ in Danbury. He served as chaplain of a militia regiment composed mostly of his own parishioners. A few months later he fell victim to sickness and died after he returned home. Additional sources: 1. *Biographical Sketches of the Graduates of Yale College, 1903*, Vol. 3. 2. *Yale and Her Honor-Roll in the American Revolution, 1775–1783* by Henry Phelps Johnson, page 232.

Samuel Baldwin—He served in Colonel John Cushing's Massachusetts Regiment for 15 days from June 13 to June 27, 1776, on an alarm at Bristol, Rhode Island. Additional Sources: 1. *Massachusetts Soldiers & Sailors of the Revolutionary War*, Vol. 1, page 522.

Alexander Balmaine—He was born in Scotland in 1741 and died on June 16, 1821. He married Lucy Taylor on October 31, 1786, and she applied for a widow's pension. He served in the 13th Virginia Regiment from February 1777 to May 1778 and he served as Brigade Chaplain under Brigadier General Muhlenberg from May 1778 to January 1782. He received over 6,000 acres of land in Virginia for his service. Additional source: 1. *Shenandoah Valley*

Appendix

Pioneers and Their Descendants: A History of Frederick County Virginia by Thomas Kemp Cartmell, page 183.

William Barton—He was born in 1754 and died in 1817 served as a chaplain in Colonel Benjamin Flower's Artillery Regiment.

Jeremy Belknap—He was born on June 4, 1744, in Boston and he died on June 20, 1798. He graduated from Harvard in 1762. He taught for several years before he became a minister. He was a minister in Dover, New Hampshire and when the Dover militia was called out in 1775 he accompanied them. Additional source: 1. *The Dover Pulpit During the Revolutionary War* by George Burley Spalding, 1876, page 18.

Joseph Bellamy—He was born in Cheshire, Connecticut, in 1719, and died in 1790. He graduated from Yale in 1735 and served as a chaplain in Connecticut.

Samuel Bird—He was chaplain of the 7th Connecticut Regiment under Colonel Charles Webb from April 1775 until December 1775. Additional Source: 1. *A Historical Collection from Official Records, Files of the Part Sustained by Connecticut during the War of the Revolution* by Royal Ralph Henman, 1842, pages 185–186.

Robert Blackwell—He was born on May 6, 1748, on Long Island, and he died on February 12, 1831, in Philadelphia. He was appointed chaplain of the 1st Pennsylvania Regiment by General Anthony Wayne. He later worked as a surgeon for a regiment at Valley Forge. He was an Episcopal minister. Additional source: 1. University of Pennsylvania Archives & Records Center.

Samuel Blair—He was born in 1741 in Pennsylvania, and he died on September 23, 1818. He graduated from Princeton and served as a chaplain to Thompson's Pennsylvania Rifle Brigade and later to the 1st Brigade of Artillery during the war. After the war he served for 2 years as the chaplain to the U.S. House of Representatives.

William Bland—He served in the 1st Virginia Regiment as a chaplain.

Abraham Blumer—He was born in 1736 and died in 1823. In 1781 he served as chaplain of the Northampton County Militia commanded by Colonel Stephen Balliet. When the British marched on Philadelphia the Liberty Bell was taken down and hid by the Reverend Blumer under the floor of the church.

Adam Boyd—On 4 January he enlisted as an ensign in the 1st North Carolina Battalion. He was promoted to second lieutenant in 1776. He was made chaplain to the 2nd North Carolina Battalion 18 months later and given the rank of brigade chaplain. He served under Colonel Thomas Clark and Colonel Edward Buncombe. After the war he was given 7,200 acres in Tennessee for his service. Additional sources: 1. *Chronology of the American Revolution:*

Other Chaplains Who Served in the American Revolution

Military and Political Actions Day by Day by Bud Hannings, page 289. 2. *Dictionary of North Carolina Biography*, edited by William S. Powell.

John Braidfoote (Bradfute)—He served as a chaplain in the 2nd Virginia State Regiment and possibly as a Navy Chaplain.

David Brady—He was a hospital chaplain from 1779 to 1781.

Joseph Buckminister—He was born on March 1, 1720, in Framingham, Massachusetts, and he died on 3 Nov. 1792 in Rutland, Massachusetts. He graduated from Harvard in 1739 and was ordained in 1742. He was chaplain of Colonel Webb's 19th Regiment in Captain Bostwick's Company. He was present for the crossing of the Delaware and Battle of Trenton. Additional sources: Sources: 1. *Yale and Her Honor-Roll in the American Revolution, 1775–1783* by Henry Phelps Johnson, page 38. 2. *D.A.R. Magazine*, Vol. 56, page 46.

John Carnes—He was born in 1723 in Boston, and he died on October, 20 1802, in Lynn, Massachusetts. On March 1, 1776, in was appointed chaplain of the 18th Continental Infantry under the command of Colonel Edmund Phinney.

Judah Champion—He was born on August 20, 1724, in Haddam, Connecticut, and he died on October 8, 1810, in Litchfield, Connecticut. He served during Burgoyne's Campaign. Additional sources: 1. *Yale and Her Honor-Roll in the American Revolution, 1775–1783* by Henry Phelps Johnson, page 201. 2. *Connecticut Men in the American Revolution*, page 631.

Hezekiah Chapman—He was born on August 31, 1746, in New Haven, Connecticut, and he died in 1794. He graduated from Yale in 1766 and he was ordinated on June 27, 1774. He went with several men to survey Western New York in 1792 and he became lost in the woods. He was later found partly eaten by wild animals. He was a chaplain in Colonel Reed's Massachusetts Regiment. Additional sources: 1. *Yale and Her Honor-Roll in the American Revolution, 1775–1783* by Henry Phelps Johnson, page 38. 2. *The Chapman Family* by the Rev. F.W. Chapman, 1854, page 197. *Biographical Sketches of the Graduates of Yale College*, Vol. III, 1778, page 175.

Jedidiah Chapman—He was born on September 27, 1741, East Haddam, Connecticut, and he died on May 22, 1813, Geneva, New York. He graduated from Yale and was pastor in Orange, New Jersey. He was chaplain in Colonel Martin's New Jersey Regiment. Because he was out spoken for the cause of liberty the Tories put a price on his head and he was referred to as the "Rebel High Priest." Additional source: 1. *Yale and Her Honor-Roll in the American Revolution, 1775–1783* by Henry Phelps Johnson, page 229.

Nicholas Cotton—He was born on March 24, 1742, in Delaware, and he died on March 20, 1826, in New Jersey. He was chaplain of the 1st Battalion of New Jersey from November 28, 1776, to September 26, 1780, He was prob-

Appendix

ably present at the battles of Brandywine, Germantown, Monmouth and camped at Valley Forge. Additional source: 1. Sons of the American Revolution Application.

Samuel Cotton—Served as chaplain in the 1st New Hampshire continental Regiment raised in 1776 under the command of Colonel Joseph Cilley. He was at Fort Ticonderoga until the approach of British General Burgoyne. Additional sources: 1. *Rolls of the Soldiers of the Revolutionary War*, 1885, page 391. 2. Harvard Alumni in the Revolutionary War.

Ebenezer David—He was a chaplain in the 9th Continental Infantry of the 2nd Rhode Island Infantry under the command of Colonel James Varnum. He died after his discharge in 1778. Additional source: *The Revolutionary War by Charles Patrick Neimeyer*, page 139.

Jedidiah Dewey—He was born on April 11, 1714, in Massachusetts, and he died on December 21, 1778, in Vermont. He helped to band together the men who successfully resisted the British and Hessians at the Battle of Bennington. Additional sources: 1. *D.A.R. Lineage Book*, Vol. 1, page 91. 2. Sons of the American Revolution Application.

George Duffield—He was born on October 7, 1732, in Lancaster County, Pennsylvania, and he died February 2, 1790, in Pennsylvania. He was pastor of Old Pine Street Presbyterian Church from 1772 to 1790. He served as a chaplain of the Continental Congress. Additional sources: 1. *D.A.R. Lineage Book*, Vol. 2, page 380. 2. *History of the Big Spring Presbyterian Church, Newville, Pa. 1737–1898*, page 217.

Francis Dunlap—He was appointed chaplain in Colonel Buckner's 6th Virginia Regiment early in the year 1776, and he died soon after his appointment. Some sources indicate that William Dunlap, the father of Francis, was the army chaplain. The obituary of Francis was in the Virginia Gazette, May 10, 1776, and read, "Mr. Francis Franklin Dunlap, an amiable youth, son of the Rev. Mr. Dunlap, and chaplain to the 6th Regiment." An ad ran in the same newspaper on 20, September 1776 which read, "Wanted in the 6th Regiment, a chaplain who will be allowed by congress 33 dollars per month & 2 rations per day. Mordecai Buckner Colonel of the 6th Regiment." Additional sources: 1. Claim for Land Bounty by heirs. 2. *Historical Register of Virginians in the Revolution*, page 241.

Samuel Eakin—He was a Princeton graduate in 1766 and served as a chaplain in the New Jersey Salem County Militia. Additional source: 1. *General Catalogue of Princeton University 1746–1906*, page 89. *D.A.R. Lineage Book*, Vol. 4, page 23.

Nathaniel Eells—He turned out for the Lexington alarm and later served as chaplain for the 8th Regiment which served in the New York campaign of 1776. Additional sources: 1. *D.A.R. Lineage Book*, Vol. 4, page 11. 2. *From*

Other Chaplains Who Served in the American Revolution

Its European Antecedents to 1791—The United States Army Chaplaincy by Parker C. Thompson, 1978, page 103.

Samuel Eells—In 1777 he read a notice from his pulpit that George Washington was in dire need of assistance. After he read the notice he left the pulpit and formed a company of militia and they made him their Captain. When he reached Washington's camp, the General appointed Samuel the chaplain. Additional sources: 1. *D.A.R. Lineage Book*, Vol. 4, page 269. 2. *From Its European Antecedents to 1791—The United States Army Chaplaincy* by Parker C. Thompson, 1978, page 103.

Robert Elder—Within half an hour, after prayer one Sunday, he recruited a company of his own church and he was chosen captain. Additional source: *D.A.R. Lineage Book*, Vol. 2, page 17.

John Eliot—He served as a chaplain in the Massachusetts militia.

John Elliot—He served as chaplain for the 2nd Connecticut form May 1, 1777, to February 20, 1778. After his service he defected to the British and two years later he returned to the American side.

Noble Everest—He served in Colonel Walbridge's Regiment of Vermont militia. Additional source: 1. *Rolls of the Soldiers in the Revolutionary War 1775-1783*, page 491.

Stephen Farrar—He was born in 1708 and died in 1783. On April 20, 1775, in marched to Boston leading 98 men from his church. Additional sources: 1. *New England Clergy & the American Revolution* by Alice Baldwin, 1928, pages 162-163. 2. *D.A.R. Magazine*, Vols. 48-49, page 167.

Elisha Fish—He was born in 1720 and died in 1795. He was a chaplain in the Massachusetts militia.

Hezekiah Foard—He was chaplain for the 5th North Carolina Regiment.

Perez Fobes—He was born in Bridwater, Massachusetts, and died in 1812 in Raynban, Massachusetts. He married Prudence Wales in 1775. He was in poor health most of his life but he did manage to graduate from Harvard in 1762 near the bottom of his class. He served as a chaplain in the Revolution.

Eli Forbes—He was a former enlisted man of King George's War (1744-1748) and in the Revolution he was chaplain in Colonel Timothy Ruggle's Regiment of Massachusetts troops. Additional sources: 1. *From Its European Antecedents to 1791—The United States Army Chaplaincy* by Parker C. Thompson, 1978, pages 73-74. 2. *D.A.R. Lineage Book*, Vol. 30, page 300.

Edmund Foster—He was a theological student when he went to fight at Bunker Hill. He had to borrow a gun before joining Captain Brooks in the action. Additional source: 1. *From Its European Antecedents to 1791—The United States Army Chaplaincy* by Parker C. Thompson, 1978, page 92.

William Foster—Chaplain that served in Pennsylvania and died in 1780.

Appendix

Daniel Fuller—Served as a chaplain in Massachusetts.

John Fuller—He was born in 1723 and died in 1777. He served as chaplain in the 8th Connecticut Regiment under Colonel Jedidiah Huntington in 1776. Additional Source: *Genealogy of Fuller Family*, 1898, page 13.

William Gordon—He was born in England in 1728 and died in 1807. He served as chaplain to both houses of the Massachusetts Provincial Congress and as a chaplain in the militia. He wrote a four volume book on the American Revolution. Additional source: 1. *From Its European Antecedents to 1791—The United States Army Chaplaincy* by Parker C. Thompson, 1978, page 81.

William Graham—He noticed that the young men in his church in Pennsylvania did not join the call to organize a new company of riflemen. So he joined the army which encouraged others to follow his example.

John Graham, Jr.—He was born in New Hampshire in 1722 and died in Connecticut in 1796. He served as a chaplain in the French and Indian War of 1754 and again served as a chaplain of the first Connecticut Regiment in 1777. Additional sources: 1. *From Its European Antecedents to 1791—The United States Army Chaplaincy* by Parker C. Thompson, 1978, pages 64, 68, and 225. 2. *Yale and Her Honor-Roll in the American Revolution, 1775–1783* by Henry Phelps Johnson, page 11.

Enoch Green—He graduated from Princeton in 1760 and was a chaplain in New Jersey. He died while in the service on December 2, 1776. Additional source: Presbyterian Heritage Center.

Enoch Hale—When his brother Nathan was hung as a spy on September 22, 1776, Enoch joined the army at White Plains and became a chaplain to the regiment recruited near his home. Additional source: 1. *D.A.R. Lineage book*, Vol. 5, page 86.

Samuel Hall—In 1775 he urged his congregation to enlist as minute men, and he followed his troops to Boston. Additional Source: 1. *D.A.R. Lineage Book*, Vol. 25, page 186.

Samuel Hart—He served as chaplain of the South Carolina 3rd Regiment under Colonel William Thompson. He is on the payroll in July 1779 and he received $40 a month. Additional sources: 1. U.S. Revolutionary War Rolls 1775–1783 for South Carolina.

Augustine Hibbard—He was born in 1748 in Windham, Connecticut, and he died in Stanstead, Canada in 1831. He served as chaplain under Colonel Timothy Bedell's Regiment, in Starks Brigade in 1776–77. He was at the Battles of Saratoga, Ticonderoga, and Bennington. Additional Sources: 1. *D.A.R. Lineage Book*, Vol. 31, page 6. 2. *Granite State Magazine*, edited by George Waldo Brown, Vol. 2, page 121. 3. *History of the Town of Claremont New Hampshire for a Period of One Hundred Thirty Years* by Otis Frederick Reed Waite, page 234.

Other Chaplains Who Served in the American Revolution

Ithmar Hibbard—He served as a chaplain in the Vermont State Militia.

Gad Hitchcock—Gad Hitchcock was born on February 12, 1719, and he died on August 8, 1803. He graduated from Harvard in 1747 and he settled in Pembroke, Massachusetts. In May 1774 he preached a sermon in support of liberty which greatly angered the British governor Gage who was in attendance. He served as a chaplain in Massachusetts. Additional Sources: 1. *Pembroke Chronicles* by Karen Cross Proctor. 2. D.A.R., *Catherine Hitchcock Avery*, Cleveland, Ohio, pages 7–10.

William Hollingshead—He was born in 1748 in Philadelphia and was ordained on July 29, 1773. He served as a chaplain with the New Jersey Militia. Additional sources: 1. *From Its European Antecedents to 1791—The United States Army Chaplaincy* by Parker C. Thompson, 1978, page 142.

John Holmes—He was born in 1747 and he married Chloe Bentley in 1767. John Enlisted as chaplain of the 1st Georgia Regiment, 8th Company under the command of Colonel McIntosh. Additional sources: 1. *Georgia's Roster of the Revolution* by Lucian L. Knight, 1920, page 10. 2. *D.A.R. Lineage Book*, Vol. 33, page 2.

John Hurst—He served as chaplain of the 1st and 2nd Virginia Brigades. John preached a sermon at Valley Forge and was later taken prisoner by the British. On March 3, 1791, he was appointed the first chaplain in the U.S. Regular Army by Washington. Additional source: 1. *From Its European Antecedents to 1791—The United States Army Chaplaincy* by Parker C. Thompson, 1978, pages 177, 206, 221, and 289.

Daniel Johnson—Daniel Johnson was born on May 27, 1746, in Bridgewater Massachusetts, and he died on September 23, 1776, in Massachusetts. He led the famous "Butter Rebellion" at Harvard in 1766 protesting rancid butter served at breakfast. In 1769 he became pastor of the First Congregational Church in Harvard, Massachusetts. He died from dysentery shortly after becoming a chaplain in 1776 during the Boston siege.

Stephen Johnson—He was born in 1724 in New Jersey and died November 8, 1786. He graduated from Yale and was chaplain to the 6th Connecticut Regiment under Colonel Samuel H. Parsons. Additional sources: 1. *D.A.R. Lineage Book*, Vol. 4, page 171. 2. *Yale and Her Honor-Roll in the American Revolution, 1775-1783* by Henry Phelps Johnson, page 190.

William Johnston—Served as a chaplain in New York and he died in 1783.

Samuel Jones—He was born in 1735 in Wales, and died in 1814 in Philadelphia. In 1776 he was appointed chaplain of a regiment in the Flying Camp under the command of Colonel Isaac Hughes. Source: 1. *D.A.R. Lineage Book*, Vol. 27, page 203–04.

David Judson—He served as a chaplain in Connecticut and died in 1776.

Appendix

Ephraim Judson—He was born in Connecticut in 1737 and graduated from Yale in 1763. He served as chaplain in Colonel Ward's Regiment in 1776. Additional sources: 1. *Connecticut Men in the War of the Revolution*, page 109. 2. *Sermon Preached on the 25th Anniversary of his settlement as Pastor by Erastus Maltby, 1851*, page 32.

Robert Keith—He graduated from Princeton in 1772 and was ordained in 1779 He married Mary Adams. He served as chaplain in Hart's Pennsylvania Battalion of the Flying Camp and he died in 1784.

Nathan Ker—He was born in 1736 in Freehold, New Jersey and he died in 1804 in Goshen, New York. He graduated from Princeton and was ordained in 1763. He served as a chaplain in New Jersey. Additional sources: 1. *D.A.R. Lineage Book*, Vol. 28, page 10. 2. *Annals of the American Pulpit: Presbyterian* by William B. Sprague, 1858, Vol. 4, page 394.

John King—He was a Presbyterian and served as a chaplain in Pennsylvania. Additional source: 1. *History of the Middle Spring Presbyterian Church* by Belle Swope, 1900, pages 208 and 217.

Thomas Lancaster—He was a graduate of Harvard and served as a chaplain in Colonel Jonathan Mitchell's Regiment of Massachusetts Militia from July to September of 1779. Additional source: 1. *History of Colonel Jonathan Mitchell's Cumberland County Regiment by Nathan Goold*, 1889, pages 7, 31, and 37.

James Latta—He was born in Ireland in 1732 and arrived in American in 1738. He entered the College of Philadelphia and graduated in 1757 and he was ordained 2 years later. He served as chaplain in Colonel Thomas Cooch's Battalion of Lancaster County Militia in 1776. He died in 1801 after a fall from a carriage. Additional sources: 1. *D.A.R. Lineage Book*, Vol. 23, page 141. 2. Sons of the American Revolution Application.

Andrew Lee—He was born on May 7, 1745, in Lyme, Connecticut, and he died there in 1832. He served in John Durkee's 4th Regiment of the Connecticut Line from 1 January until October 15, 1777. He was at the Battle of Germantown. Additional sources: 1. *Yale and Her Honor-Roll in the American Revolution* by Henry Phelps Johnston, page 249. 2. *D.A.R. Lineage Book*, Vol. 10, page 147.

Ichabod Lewis—He served as chaplain of Colonel Bradley's Regiment.

Joshua Lewis—He served as a chaplain in Georgia.

William Linn—He was born on February 27, 1752, and died on January 8, 1808. He was the first Chaplain of the U.S. House of Representatives and served as chaplain in the 5th and 6th Pennsylvania Battalions in 1776.

William Lockwood—He was born on January 21, 1753, in Wethersfield, Connecticut, and he died on June 23, 1828, in Glastenbury, Connecticut. According to his pension file he enlisted on October 12, 1780, and served

Other Chaplains Who Served in the American Revolution

until November 25, 1782. He was chaplain for the 1st Massachusetts Brigade and later the 3rd Massachusetts. He received $20 a month for his service. Additional sources: 1. Pension application S37635. 2. Pension Roll of 1835. 3. *Descendants of Robert Lockwood*, 1889, pages 246-247. 4. *Yale and Her Honor-Roll in the American Revolution* by Henry Phelps Johnston, page 301. 5. *D.A.R. Lineage Book*, Vol. 1, page 160.

John Lynd—He served as a chaplain in the 5th Pennsylvania Battalion.

John Lyth—He served in the 13th Virginia Regiment and was killed in the campaign against the Cherokee Indians January 15, 1778. He had the first verifiable religious service in Kentucky held under an elm tree on May 28, 1775.

Hugh McAlden—He served as a chaplain in North Carolina and died in 1781 while serving.

M'Clanahan—He raised a company of Baptist in Culpepper County, Virginia, and served both as chaplain and captain. Additional sources: 1. *The Baptist and the American Revolution* by William Cathcart, page 35. 2. *The People Called Baptist* by McDaniel, page 20. 3. *History of the Baptist* by Thomas Armitage, 1890, page 35.

Daniel McClure—He served in the 8th Pennsylvania Regiment.

William McKay—He was an Episcopal chaplain who served in the 11th and 15th Virginia Regiments.

Joseph Manning—He was a chaplain in the Rhode Island Militia.

Issac Mansfield—He was born on March 22, 1750, in Marblehead, Massachusetts, and he died on September 1, 1826, in Boston, Massachusetts. He was a 1767 graduate of Harvard College. In January of 1775 he joined Colonel Thomas's Regiment of militia. He later transferred the 6th Continental Infantry at Fort Ticonderoga and later served in the 27th Infantry until the end of 1777. Additional Sources: 1. *Pension List of 1792-1795*, page 112. 2. *Harvard Alumni in the Revolutionary War*. 3. *From Its European Antecedents to 1791—The United States Army Chaplaincy* by Parker C. Thompson, 1978, page 136. 4. *Massachusetts Soldiers and Sailors in the Revolutionary War*, page 198.

Daniel Marshall—He was a Baptist preacher that received no formal education. He served as a chaplain in the Georgia militia and his six sons also served. Daniel was arrested several times by the British because he refused to stop preaching for the patriot cause. He received land for his service. A friend described his as "a weak man, with a stammer, and no scholar." His second wife, Martha Stearns was also a preacher with no formal education. Additional sources: 1. *The Georgians: Genealogies of Pioneer Settlers* by Jeannette Holland Austin, page 249. 2. *Roster of Revolutionary Soldiers in Georgia*, page 123. 3. *Georgia Revolutionary Soldiers & Sailors, Patriots & Pioneers*, page 170. 4. *D.A.R. Lineage Book*, Vol. 57, page 63.

Appendix

John Mason—He was born in 1734 in Scotland and he died on June 3, 1792, in New York City. He was chaplain in 1776 of Colonel Peter Gansevoort's 3rd New York Regiment. In 1778 he was the chaplain of posts on the Hudson where he served to the close of the war. Additional sources: 1. *D.A.R. Lineage Book*, Vol. 16, page 82. 2. *The Military Chaplain's Review, 1987*, pages 26, 27, and 58. 3. *From Its European Antecedents to 1791—The United States Army Chaplaincy* by Parker C. Thompson, 1978, pages 205 and 215.

Eleazer May—He was born in Connecticut in 1733 and marched to Boston with one hundred men.

Silas Mercer—He was born in North Carolina in 1745, and he died from a skull fracture when he was kicked by a hose on August 1, 1796, in Wilkes County, Georgia. He served as a chaplain with the rank of major to North Carolina troops. Additional sources: 1. Sons of the American Revolution Application. 2. *Roster of Revolutionary Soldiers in Georgia*, Vol. I, page 200. 3. *Father Mercer: The Story of a Baptist Statesman* by Anthony L. Chute, page 3.

Philip Jacob Michael—He was born in Switzerland and came to America as a young man. He was minister in the German Reformed Church in Pennsylvania. He was appointed chaplain of the First Battalion of Berks County Militia during the Revolution. Additional source: 1. *The Pennsylvania-German* by Philip Columbus Croll & Henry Addison Schuler, Vol. 8, page 190.

Henry Miller—He was chaplain to all Germans in the entire American Army. He was at Valley Forge and the Battle of Monmouth. At the battle his job was to be an interpreter and to encourage the German soldiers to fight. He was probably used to communicate with the Hessian deserters from the British. Additional source: 1. *The Chaplains and Clergy at the Battle of Monmouth June 28, 1778* by Stanley W. Cuyler, pages 3 and 16.

Joseph Montgomery—He was born on September 23, 1733, in Pennsylvania, and he died on October 14, 1794, in Harrisburg, Pennsylvania. He was commissioned as chaplain of Colonel Smallwood's Maryland Regiment and was at the Battles of Brandywine, Germantown, and Monmouth. He spent the harsh winter at Valley Forge. Additional source: 1. *D.A.R. Lineage Book*, Vol. 6, page 11.

Edward Morris—He was born in 1756 in Virginia and died in 1830 in Tennessee. He enlisted in the army but General Washington relieved him from military duty and gave him the position of chaplain. He married Elizabeth Witaker. Additional sources: 1. *D.A.R. Lineage Book*, Vol. 11, page 335. 2. *Some Prominent Virginia Families, Vols. 1-2* by Lousie Peoquet de Bellet, page 127.

Other Chaplains Who Served in the American Revolution

Philip Mulkey—He was born in 1732 in Halifax, North Carolina, and he died in 1800 in Tennessee. He served as a chaplain in the North Carolina Militia. Additional source: *D.A.R. Lineage Book*, Vol. 40, page 227.

James Murdock—He served in Colonel Ira Allen's Regiment of the Vermont Militia in the fall of 1781.

John Wesley Gilbert Nevelling—He was born in 1750 in Germany and died in 1844 in Pennsylvania. He converted all his property into money, amounting to about 5,000 pounds and loaned it to the government. He later lost his certificate of receipt and was never repaid. He served as a chaplain in New Jersey and he died in poverty. Additional sources: 1. *From Its European Antecedents to 1791—The United States Army Chaplaincy* by Parker C. Thompson, 1978, page 191. 2. *D.A.R. Lineage Book*, vol. 35, page 288.

Samuel Newell—He was born on March 1, 1714 in Connecticut, and died there on 10 February 1789. He graduated from Yale in 1739 and served as a chaplain in the army for brief periods of time. Additional sources: 1. *Thomas Newell and His Descendants by Mary A. (Newell) Hall*, 1878, pages 27–28. 2. *D.A.R. Lineage Book*, Vol. 15, page 173.

Robert Nixon—He served as chaplain of the Onslow Regiment of Militia in North Carolina. He was paid ten pounds for his service.

Obediah Noble—He was born in 1739 in Connecticut and he died on February 19, 1829 in Vermont. He served as chaplain and is on the roll of Colonel Hobart's Regiment of New Hampshire Militia. They marched in September 1777 to reinforce the army at Saratoga. Additional sources: 1. *U.S. Revolutionary War Rolls 1775-1783*, page 4–256. 2. *D.A.R. Lineage Book*, Vol. 19, page 270.

Oliver Noble—He served as chaplain of Colonel Little's Regiment at the siege of Boston in 1775. After January 1, 1776 he was chaplain for both Little's and Hitchcock's Rhode Island Regiments, which were in the same brigade. He died in 1792. Additional source: 1. *Yale and Her Honor-Roll in the American Revolution* by Henry Phelps Johnston, page 211.

David Osgood—He was the chaplain of the 1st New Hampshire Regiment under the command of Colonel Stark. He was at the Battle of Bunker Hill.
Additional source: 1. *Medford in the War of the Revolution* by Helen T. Wild.

Joshua Payne—He served as chaplain in the 3rd Continental Infantry of New Hampshire.

Joseph Perry—He was born on August 13, 1731 in Sherborn, Massachusetts, and he died on August 21, 1783 in Windsor, Massachusetts. He was chaplain in Colonel Wolcott's Regiment from December 1775 to February 1776. He graduated from Harvard in 1752. Additional sources: 1. Tombstone. 2. *Harvard Alumni in the Revolutionary War*.

Appendix

Joseph Pope—He served as a chaplain in Connecticut.

Nathaniel Porter—He was born in 1745 in Massachusetts and died in 1810 in New Hampshire. He was chaplain in Wingate's Militia and the 3rd New Hampshire Regiment from July 1776 to July 1777. Additional source: 1. *D.A.R. Lineage Book*, Vol. 20, page 14.

Isaiah Potter—He served as a chaplain from Connecticut in 1777.

Thomas Prentiss—He was born in 1747 in Holliston, Massachusetts and he died February 28, 1814. He died from congestion of the lungs brought about by exposure during a violet snowstorm. He was visiting a sick family in a neighboring town. Thomas served as a chaplain in the American Army and was stationed at Roxbury. He was at the Siege of Boston in April 1775 to March 1776. Additional source: 1. *Annals of the American Pulpit: Trinitarian Congregational* by William Buell Sprague, 1857, page 678-9.

Henry Purcell—He was born in 1739 in England and died on March 11, 1802 in South Carolina. He was chaplain of the 2nd and 5th Infantry of South Carolina and he was commissioned on May 7, 1776.

John Reed—He was born on November 11, 1751 in Farmington, Connecticut, and he died on February 17, 1831 in Bridgewater, Massachusetts. He was a graduate of Yale and a personal friend of George Washington. He served as chaplain on the ship *Warren* in 1777. Additional sources: 1. *D.A.R. Lineage Book*, Vols. 59-60, page 243. 2. Sons of the American Revolution Application.

Thomas Reed—In 1776 he took his musket and with 40 to 50 others he marched to Philadelphia to help defend it against British General Howe. In 1777 just before the Battle of Brandywine Thomas, because of his knowledge of the country, saved Washington from being overwhelmed at Elk Ferry. Additional source: 1. *The Chaplains and Clergy of the Revolution* by Joel Tyler Headley, 1864, page 69.

Elisha Rexford—He was born on October 14, 1737 in New Haven, Connecticut, and he served as pastor of the New Strafford Church for 44 years. He was chaplain for Colonel Elmore's Regiment in Connecticut in 1776. Additional sources: 1. *The Record of Connecticut Men in the Military & Naval Service during the American Revolution* by Henry Phelps Johnston, page 113. 2. *Biographical Sketches of the Graduates of Yale College*, 1903, pages 43-44.

John Rogers—He served in Heath's Brigade in Connecticut and he died in 1811. Additional source: 1. *From Its European Antecedents to 1791—The United States Army Chaplaincy* by Parker C. Thompson, 1978, page 153.

William Rogers—He was born on July 22, 1751, in Newport, Rhode Island, and died on April 7, 1824, in Philadelphia. He was a chaplain in the Sullivan Expedition. Additional source: 1. *From Its European Antecedents to 1791—The United States Army Chaplaincy* by Parker C. Thompson, 1978, pages 186-190.

Other Chaplains Who Served in the American Revolution

Ezra Sampson—He was born in February 1745 in Middleboro, Massachusetts, and he died on December 12, 1823, in New York City. In 1775 he was a volunteer chaplain in the camp at Roxbury, and in July he preached a sermon before Col. Cotton's regiment, of patriotic and inspiring that it was immediately printed by request of the army. Additional sources: 1. *Yale and Her Honor Roll in the American Revolution* by Henry Phelps Johnston, page 292. *Collections, Historical and Miscellaneous: and Monthly Literary of the American Revolution*, Vol. 2, page 103.

Loveless Savage—He was a chaplain and one of the field officers of the "Regiment of Refugees" of Richmond County, Georgia. This regiment was the name given to a group of citizen soldiers who took to the back country after the fall of Savannah and several other Georgia towns. He died about 1815. Additional source: 1. *Georgia Baptists* by Jesse Harrison Campbell.

Martinus Schoonmaker—After the occupation of Long Island by the British he often carried letters sewed in his shirt. He was watched by the British who considered him a spy, and one time narrowly escaped capture. He died in 1824. Additional source: 1. *D.A.R. Lineage Book*, vol. 12, page 54.

Alexander Scott—His wife taught him to spell, but she died before he could read. He served as chaplain in the 1st Georgia Regiment under Colonel Caleb Howell. Additional sources: 1. *Georgia's Rosters of the Revolution*, 1920, pages 156 and 391. 2. *Georgia Baptists* by Jesse Harrison Campbell.

Daniel Sere—He served as chaplain for Smallwood's Battalion of Maryland Regular Troops. Additional sources: 1. *A Vagabond Army: A Novel of Maryland in the American Revolution; Vol. 2* by John Conradis, page 6. 2. *Maryland Historical Magazine* by William Hand Browne, 1906, page 173.

William Seward—He was born on February 11, 1745, in Connecticut, and he died there on July 13, 1822, in Fishkill, New York. He married Thankful Parmelee on November 20, 1771. He was a chaplain in Colonel David Waterbury's Regiment in Connecticut.

Josiah Sherman—He was born in 1734 in Connecticut, and he died there on November 24, 1789. He served in the 7th Connecticut Line and was the brother of Roger Sherman a signer of the Declaration of Independence. Additional sources: 1. *The Heroes of the American Revolution & Their Descendants* by Henry Whittemore, 1897, page 36. 2. *D.A.R. Lineage Book*, Vol. 13, page 239.

Thomas Smiley—He served as a chaplain in Pennsylvania. Additional source: *D.A.R. Lineage Book*, Vol. 1, page 34.

Cotton M. Smith—He served as a chaplain with the 4th Connecticut Regiment.

Elias Smith—He was born in 1731 in reading Massachusetts, and he died on October 17, 1791, in Middleton, Massachusetts. He served as a chaplain

Appendix

in the 19th Connecticut Infantry from January until December 1776 and was probably was at the Battle of White Plains. Additional sources 1. *Harvard Alumni in the Revolutionary War.*

John Blair Smith—He was born on June 6, 1756 in Pequea, Pennsylvania, and he died 22 August 1799 in Philadelphia, Pennsylvania. He served as a captain of a militia company in Virginia that helped support the American army after the Battle of Cowpens. Additional source: 1. *The National Cyclopedia of American Biography*, page 327.

Manassah Smith—He was born in 1748 in Leominister, Massachusetts, and he died on 21 May 1825 in Wiscasset, Maine. He served as a chaplain in Colonel Asa Whitcomb's Regiment. He was at the siege of Boston in 1776, serving for 34 days. He was a graduate of Harvard and later became a lawyer. Additional sources: 1. *D.A.R. Lineage Book*, Vol. 29, page 357–358. 2. *Massachusetts Soldiers and Sailors in the War of the Revolution*, Vol. 14, page 496.

Alexander Stewart—He served as a chaplain in Knox's Regiment Continental Artillery of Massachusetts.

Philip Stockton—His brother Richard signed the Declaration of Independence and he was at the Battle of Princeton. Source: *D.A.R. Lineage Book*, Vol. 4, page 52.

John Storrs—He served as a chaplain in North Carolina and died in 1781 while serving.

He was born on December 1, 1735, in Mansfield, Connecticut, and he died there in 1799. He served as a chaplain in Colonel Fisher Gay's Regiment in Wadsworth's Brigade in the campaign around New York in 1776. He also served in General David Waterbury's Brigade in Connecticut. Additional sources: 1. *The National Cyclopedia of American Biography*, page 111. 2. *Yale and Her Honor-Roll in the American Revolution* by Henry Phelps Johnston, page 210. 3. *D.A.R. Lineage Book*, Vol. 31, page 247.

Christian Streit—He was born in 1749 in New Jersey, and he died March 10, 1812, in Virginia. He served as chaplain in the 3rd Virginia Regiment in 1776. When he was pastor of a church in Charleston he was taken prisoner by the British when they capture Charleston. He was soon exchanged. Additional sources: 1. *The Lutheran World Almanac*, 1926, page 217. 2. *From Its European Antecedents to 1791—The United States Army Chaplaincy* by Parker C. Thompson, 1978, page 129. 3. *Ohio History*, Vol. 23, page 213.

Joseph Strong—He was born on March 19, 1729, in Coventry, Connecticut, and he died on January 1, 1803, in Goshen, Massachusetts. He graduated from Yale in 1749 and he married Jane Gelston in 1749. He served as chaplain in the 20th Continental Infantry with troops on Long Island from March to December 1776. Additional sources: *D.A.R. Lineage Books*, Vol. 49, page

Other Chaplains Who Served in the American Revolution

331 2. U.S. Revolutionary War Rolls 1775–1783. 3. *The History of Elder John Strong, of Northampton* by Benjamin Woodbridge Dwight, Vol. 1, page 355. 4. *Yale and Her Honor-Roll in the American Revolution* by Henry Phelps Johnston, page 200.

Nathan Strong—He was born on October 17, 1748, and he died on December 25, 1816. He graduated from Yale in 1769 and he served as pastor of the First Church in Hartford, Connecticut from 1774–1816. He was chaplain of the 22nd Continental Infantry in 1776 and he was at the Battle of Long Island. He is listed on the October 1776 rolls as "absent sick." Additional source: 1. *Yale and Her Honor-Roll in the American Revolution* by Henry Phelps Johnston, page 261–2.

Joseph Swain—He served as a chaplain in the French and Indian War and in the revolution he served in Pennsylvania. He fell into chronic alcoholism after the death of his wife. Source: 1. *From Its European Antecedents to 1791—The United States Army Chaplaincy* by Parker C. Thompson, 1978, page 216.

Eleazer Sweetland—He died on March 25, 1777. He served as chaplain in Sargent's Massachusetts Regiment, 17th Continental Infantry. Additional source: 1. *D.A.R. Magazine*, 15 July 1915, page 22.

Job Swift—He was born on October 3, 1711 in Wareham, Massachusetts, and he died on 14 February 1801 in Sharon, Connecticut. He answered the Lexington alarm on April 19, 1775 at the age of 64. He also alerted others in the community of the advancing British troops. He served under Captain Ebenezer Tisdale for 16 days. His three sons also served in the war. Additional sources: 1. Sons of the American Revolution Application. 2. *Massachusetts Soldiers and Sailors in the Revolutionary War*, page 315.

William Tennent—He served as chaplain in Swift's and Mott's Connecticut State Regiments in 1776 at Fort Ticonderoga. Additional sources: 1. *Record of Service of Connecticut Men in the War of Revolution*, page 391. 2. *The Chaplains and Clergy of the Revolution* by Joel Tyler Headley, 1864, pages 376–379.

John Peter Tetard—He was born in Switzerland and preached to a French Congregation in New York City. He served as chaplain for General Montgomery during the invasion of Canada and he served for the 4th New York Regiment. He became the first translator for the new State Department and he translated the Articles of Confederation for distribution throughout Europe. Additional sources: 1. *From Its European Antecedents to 1791—The United States Army Chaplaincy* by Parker C. Thompson, 1978, page 176. 2. *The Story of the Bronx* by Stephen Jenkins, 1912, pages 101 and 277.

Peter Thacher—He was born in 1753 in Attleboro, Massachusetts, and he died there on December 4, 1814. He served as a private and a chaplain

Appendix

in Colonel Timothy Walker's Regiment for three months starting on May 1, 1775. Additional sources: 1. *Massachusetts Soldiers and Sailors in the War of the Revolution*, Vol. 14, page 503. 2. *D.A.R. Lineage Book*, Vol. 27, page 110.

Jabez Thayer—He served as a chaplain for the 14th Massachusetts from January 1, 1777, until September of 1777. He died of smallpox while in the service. Additional sources: 1. *Historical Register of Officers of the Continental Army During the War of Revolution* by Francis Bernard Heitman, page 396. 2. *Massachusetts Soldiers and Sailors in the War of the Revolution*, page 535.

Amos Thompson—He was born on August 7, 1731 in New Haven, Connecticut, and he died on September 8, 1804, Loudoun County, Virginia. He served as chaplain in Stephenson's Maryland and Virginia Rifleman Regiment in 1776.

James Hampden Thomson—After the surrender of Charleston to the British James was arrested for refusing to become a British subject and he was taken to St. Augustine. He was put into prison and he acted as chaplain to the other prisoners. Source: 1. *D.A.R. Lineage Book*, Vol. 12, page 124.

Jonathan Todd—He marched from East Guilford, Connecticut to Boston with 83 of the men in his congregation. Source: 1. *The New England Clergy and the American Revolution* by Alice Baldwin, 1928, page 162.

Samuel Todd—He was born on March 6, 1716, in North Haven, Connecticut, and he died on June 10, 1789, in Oxford, New Hampshire. He married Mercy Evans on August 31, 1739. Samuel served as a chaplain during the war. Additional source: Sons of the American Revolution Application.

Joseph Treat—He was born in 1734 in Abington, Pennsylvania, and he died in 1797 in New Jersey. He was a chaplain in Colonel William Malcolm's Regiment in 1776. The Colonel raised and paid for his regiment with his own money. Joseph may have been at the Battle of White Plaines. Additional source: *D.A.R. Lineage Book*, Vol. 19, page 276.

Joab Trout—The night before the Battle of Brandywine Chaplain Trout gave a sermon to the men before the battle. This is a small part of what he said, "Soldiers, I look around upon your familiar faces with a strange interest. Tomorrow morning we will go forth to battle, for I need not tell you that your unworthy minister will march with you, invoking God's aid in the fight—we will march forth to battle." Pastor Joab Trout was killed in battle at Brandywine on September 11, 1777. Additional sources: 1. California Society of the Sons of the American Revolution. 2. *From Its European Antecedents to 1791—The United States Army Chaplaincy* by Parker C. Thompson, 1978, page 155 and Appendix VIII.

John Tuck—He was born in 1740 in Hampton, New Hampshire, and he died February 9, 1777, in Salem, New York. He was a graduate of Harvard

Other Chaplains Who Served in the American Revolution

and in 1777 he was appointed as a chaplain. As he was traveling to join his regiment he was seized with smallpox and died. Additional source: 1. *D.A.R. Lineage Book*, Vol. 18, page 282.

William Van Horne—He was born in Pennsylvania in 1747 and he died in 1807 in Pittsburgh while on a journey to Ohio. He served as Brigade Chaplain in the Pennsylvania Brigade of General Glover in 1779. Additional source: 1. *D.A.R. Lineage Book*, Vol. 43, page 304.

William Waite—He fought at the Battle of Bennington, which took place on his farm. The Hessian soldiers were confined in his church. Additional source: 1. *D.A.R. Lineage Book*, Vol. 6, page 247.

Samuel Wales—He was a professor of Divinity at Yale, and he died on February 18, 1794. He served as chaplain for the Connecticut State Troops for a short time in 1775–76. Additional source: 1. *Yale and Her Honor-Roll in the American Revolution* by Henry Phelps Johnston, page 252.

John Warren—He was a Congregationalist and served as a chaplain in Rhode Island.

Samuel Webster—Served as a chaplain in New Hampshire.

Whitman Welch—He served as pastor at Williamstown, Massachusetts from 1765 to 1776. In the early part of 1776 he was chaplain of one of the militia regiments of Western Massachusetts which was sent to reinforce the defeated army at Quebec. Smallpox broke out in the camp and he died from it in March 1776. Additional source: 1. *Yale and Her Honor Roll in the American Revolution* by Henry Phelps Johnston, page 232.

Noah Wells—He was a chaplain for British prisoners of war and he died from jail fever on 31 December 1776. His type of ministry was the first of its kind in the American Army. Additional sources: 1. *Yale and Her Honor-Roll in the American Revolution* by Henry Phelps Johnston, page 189. 2. *From Its European Antecedents to 1791—The United States Army Chaplaincy* by Parker C. Thompson, 1978, page 145.

Benjamin Wildman—He served as a chaplain in Connecticut.

Joseph Willard—He was born on December 29, 1738, in Biddeford, Maine, and he died on September 25, 1804, in New Bedford, Massachusetts. He served as president of Harvard from 1781 until 1804. He led two companies of soldiers to fight in the Revolution. Additional source: 1. *Much Preached At: The Early Ministers of First Parish Church in Beverly 1667–1958* by Charles E. Wainwright.

Samuel Williamson—He was a chaplain in the 4th Continental Moylan's Dragoons in 1777 and he was at the Battles of Germantown and Brandywine.

Francis Winter—He was born on December 3, 1744, in Middlesex, Massachusetts, and he died on December 20, 1826 in Bath, Maine. He served as

Appendix

chaplain in a Connecticut Regiment under Colonel Ichabod Alden, who was the brother of Abigail, the wife of Francis. Additional sources: 1. Tombstone. 2. *Massachusetts Soldiers and Sailors in the Revolutionary War*, page 647.

Samuel Wood—He was born in 1724 in Massachusetts and he died in 1777 in Brooklyn, New York. He was a chaplain in the 5th Connecticut Regiment and was captured at Fort Washington on November 16, 1776. He died on the British prison ship *Asia* in 1777. Additional sources: 1. *Revolutionary War Records of Fairfield, Connecticut* by Donald Lines Jacobus, Katie S. Curry, page 361. 2. *From Its European Antecedents to 1791—The United States Army Chaplaincy* by Parker C. Thompson, 1978, page 144–145.

Samuel Woodbridge—He served as a chaplain in Connecticut. Additional source: 1. *Yale and Her Honor-Roll in the American Revolution* by Henry Phelps Johnston, page 236.

Matthew Woodson—He was born on July 17, 1731, in Virginia, and he died in 1800 in Kentucky. He served as chaplain in the 1st Virginia Regiment. When he died he owned well over 231 slaves. Additional sources: 1. *Virginia Soldiers of 1776*, Vol. 1. 2. *D.A.R. Lineage Book*, Vol. 16, page 292.

William Worth—He was born on April 21, 1745, in Basking Ridge, New Jersey, and he died on January 2, 1808. He served as chaplain in the 2nd Battalion New Jersey Militia for four years. Additional sources: 1. "New Jersey Chaplains in the Army of the Revolution" by F.R. Brace, *Proceedings of the New Jersey Historical Society*, Vol. 6, no. 1, page 9. 2. *Official Register of the Officers and Men of New Jersey in the Revolutionary War* by New Jersey Adjutant-General Office, page 346.

Johann Yeager—He served as a chaplain in the war. Source: 1. *D.A.R. Lineage Book*, Vol. 1, page 46.

Bibliography

Alderman, Pat. *One Heroic Hour at King's Mountain.* Johnson City, TN: Overmountain Press, 1968.

Alexander, Samuel Davies. *Princeton College During the 18th Century.* New York: Anson D. F. Randolph & Company, 1872.

The American Revolution in South Carolina. Website.

Armitage, Thomas. *History of the Baptist.* New York: The Christian Literature Company, 1890.

Armstrong, Zella. *Notable Southern Families Vol II.* Chattanooga: The Lookout Publishing Co., 1922.

Asher, Brad. *Athens County Ohio, Genealogy and History.* Website.

_____. *Cecelia and Fanny: The Remarkable Friendship Between an Escaped Slave and Her Former Mistress.* Lexington: University Press of Kentucky, 2011.

Austin, Jeannette Holland. *The Georgians: Genealogies of Pioneer Settlers.* Baltimore: Clearfield, 1984.

Avery, Mrs. Elroy M. *The American Monthly Magazine, Vol. 37.* New York, 1910.

Baldwin, Alice M. *The New England Clergy and the American Revolution.* New York: F. Ungar, 2013.

Bartlett, George B. *The Concord Guide Book.* Boston: D. Lothrop and Company, 1880.

Bell, James B. *The Imperial Origins of the King's Church in Early America 1607–1783.* New York: Palgrave Macmillan, 2004.

Benedict, David. *A General History of the Baptist Denomination in America.* New York: Lewis Colby and Company, 1848.

Blake, Rev. Mortimer. *A Centurial History of the Mendon Association of Congregational Ministers.* Boston: Seawall Harding, 1853.

Bolles, Albert S. *Pennsylvania Province and State History, 1609–1790, Vol. II.* Philadelphia: William Stanley Ray the State Printer, 1900.

Bond, Dr. Henry. *Genealogies of the Families and Descendants of the Early Settlers of Watertown, Massachusetts.* Boston: Little, Brown, 1885.

Brace, F.R. *Brief Sketches of the New Jersey Chaplains in the Continental Army.* Paterson, NJ: The Press Printing and Publishing Company, 1909.

Bridge, William Dawson. *Genealogy of the John Bridge Family in America.* Cambridge, MA: Murray Publishing Company, 1924.

Brown, Fred. *Marking Time: East Tennessee Historical Markers and the Stories Behind Them.* Knoxville: University of Tennessee Press, 2005.

Brown, George Waldo, ed. *Granite State Magazine Vol. 2.* 1905.

Browne, William Hand. *Maryland Historical Magazine.* 1906.

Butler, Jon. *New World Faiths: Religion in Colonial America.* New York: Oxford University Press, 2008.

Byrd, James P. *Sacred Scriptures, Sacred War: The Bible and the American Revolution.* New York: Oxford University Press, 2013.

Campbell, Jesse H. *Georgia Baptist: Historical and Biographical.* Richmond: H.K. Ellyson, 1847.

Cartmell, Thomas Kemp. *Centennial Memorial of the Presbytery of Carlisle.* Harrisburg, PA: Meyers Publishing Company, 1829.

_____. *Shenandoah Valley Pioneers and Their Descendants: A History of Frederick County Virginia.* Winchester, VA: The Eddy Press Corp., 1909.

Bibliography

Chambers, John Whiteclay. *Cranbury: A New Jersey Town from the Colonial Era to the Present.* New Brunswick: Rivergate Books, 2012.

Clemens, William M. *Hunter Family Records.* New York: William Clemens Publisher, 1914.

Cleveland, Edmund J., and Horace G. Cleveland. *The Genealogy of the Cleveland and Cleveland Families.* Hartford, MA: The Case, Lockwood, and Garinard Company, 1899.

Chapman, Rev. F.W. *The Chapman Family.* Hartford, CT: Case, Tiffany Company, 1854.

Chute, Anthony L. *The Story of a Baptist Statesman.* Macon: Mercer University Press, 2011.

Clyde, Rev. John C. *Congregational Quarterly Vol. 19.* Wales, 1932.

_____. *Rosbrugh, Tale of the Revolution or Life, Labors and Death of Rev. John Rosbrugh.* Easton, PA, 1880.

Conradis, John. *A Vagabond Army: A Novel of Maryland in the American Revolution; Vol. 2.* Westminster, MD: Heritage Books, 2009.

Coulter, Ann. *The Liberal Mob Is Endangering America.* New York: Crown Forum, 2011.

Crane, Ellery Bicknell. *Historic Homes & Institutions and Personal Memoirs of Worcester County.* New York: Lewis Publishing Company, 1907.

Crockell, Walter Hill. *Soldiers of the Revolutionary War Buried in Vermont.* Baltimore: Clearfield, 1904.

Croll, Philip Columbus, and Henry Addison Schuler. *The Pennsylvania-German Vol. 8.* Lancaster: The Pennsylvania-German Society, 1911.

Cutler, William Parker, and Julia Perkins Cutler. *Life Journals and Correspondence of Rev. Manasseh Cutler, LL.D. by William Parker Cutler and Julia Perkins Cutler, Vol. 1.* Cincinnati: Robert Clarke and Company, 1888

Cutter, William Richard. *New England Families, Genealogical & Memorial.* New York: Lewis Historical Publishing Company, 1914.

Cuyler, Chaplain Stanley W. *The Chaplains and Clergy at the Battle of Monmouth.* U.S. Army Chaplain Center and School Library, 1986.

Dandridge, Danske. *American Prisoners of the Revolution.* Charlottesville: Michie Company, 1911.

Dann, John C., ed. *The Revolution Remembered: Eyewitness Accounts of the War for Independence.* Chicago: University of Chicago Press, 1977.

Daughters of the American Revolution. *Lineage Books.* Washington, D.C.: D.A.R., 1921.

_____. *Roster of Soldiers from North Carolina in the American Revolution.* Durham: D.A.R., 1932.

Davis, Matthew. *Memoirs of Aaron Burr Vol. 1.* New York: Harper and Brothers, 1837.

Dawson, Henry Barton. *This Day in Presbyterian History, Daily Devotional Readings in Scripture, July 25, Rev. James Hall.* Presbyterian website.

_____. *Westchester County, New York, During the American Revolution.* New York: private publisher, 1886.

De Bellet, Lousie Peoquet. *Some Prominent Virginia Families, Vols. 1–2.* Lynchburg, VA: J.P. Bell Publishing Company, 1907.

Derby, George, and James Terry White. *The National Cyclopedia of American Biography, Vol. 1–Vol. 13.* New York: James T. White, 1898.

Dexter, Franklin Bowditch. *Biographical Sketches of the Graduates of Yale College, Annals 1768–69.* New York: Henry Holt, 1896.

Dickens, William E., Jr. *Answering the Call: The Story of the U.S. Military Chaplaincy from the Revolution through the Civil War.* Dissertation.com, 1999.

Duggan, Lawrence. *Armsbearing and the Clergy in the History and Cannon Law of Western Christianity.* Rochester: Boydell Press, 2013.

Dury, Clifford. *The History of the Chaplain Corps, United States Navy Vol. 1 1778–1939.* Washington, D.C.: U.S. Government Printing Office, 1974.

Dwight, Benjamin Woodbridge. *The His-

Bibliography

tory of the Descendants of John Dwight of Dedham, Mass. New York: John F. Trow, and Son, 1874.

———. *The History of Elder John Strong, of Northampton Vol. 1.* Albany: Joel Munsell, 1871.

Dwight, Theodore. *American Penny Magazine, and Family Newspaper, Vol. 1.* New York, 1847.

Edwards, Morgan. *Materials Towards a History of the Baptists.* Philadelphia: American Baptist Publication Company, 1898.

Ege, Ralph. *Pioneers of Old Hopewell: with Sketches of Her Revolutionary Heroes.* Hopewell, NJ: Race and Savidge, 1908.

Egle, William H. *Pennsylvania in the War of the Revolution: Battalions and Line, 1775–1783.* Harrisburg, PA: E.K. Meyers, 1890.

Emerson, Mary H. *Betty Allen and Her Six Sons.* Amherst, MA: D.A.R., 1896.

Erskine, Rev. Ebenezer. *The Centennial Memorial of the Presbytery of Carlisle, Vol. 2.* Harrisburg, PA: E.K. Meyers, 1889.

Farmer, John, and Jacob Bailey Moore. *Collections, Historical and Miscellaneous: and Monthly Literary of the American Revolution, Vol.1.* Concord, MA: Hill & Moore, 1824.

Felt, Joseph Felt. *History of Ipswich, Essex, and Hamilton.* Cambridge, MA: Charles Folsom, 1834.

Fisher, Dan. *Bringing Back the Black Robed Regiment, Vols. I and II.* Mustang, OK: Tate Publishing, 2013

Foote, W.H. *Sketches of North Carolina, Historical and Biographical.* New York: Robert Carter, 1846.

Foster, Joseph. *The Soldiers' Memorial 1893–1921 Storer Post, No. 1.* Portsmouth, NH: self published, 1921.

Flower, Dennis. *Hartland in the Revolutionary War.* Hartland, VT: Solitarian Press, 1914.

Fuller, Newton. *Genealogy of Fuller Family.* Boston: Palmer, 1898.

Gano, Rev. John. *Biographical Memoirs of the Late Rev. John Gano of Frankfort.* New York: Southwick and Hardcastle, 1806.

Garden, Alexander. *Anecdotes of the Revolutionary War.* Charleston, SC: A.E. Miller, 1822.

Germain, Aidan Henry. *Catholic Military and Naval Chaplains, 1776–1917.* Washington, D.C.: Catholic University of the American Press, 1917.

Germann, Rev. William. *The Crisis in the Early Life of General Peter Muhlenberg, from Pennsylvania Magazine of History and Biography, Vol. 37.* Philadelphia: Historical Society, 1913.

Goodrich, John, ed. *Rolls of the Soldiers of the Revolutionary War.* Rutland, VT: Tuttle Company, 1885.

Goold, Nathan. *History of Colonel Jonathan Mitchell's Cumberland County Regiment.* Portland, ME: Thurston Press, 1889.

Gragg, Rod. *By the Hand of Providence.* New York: Howard Books, 2011.

Griffin, Simon. *The History of Keene, New Hampshire.* Keene, NH: Sentinel Press, 1904.

Guild, Reuben Aldridge. *Chaplain Smith and the Baptist.* Philadelphia: American Baptist Publication Company, 1885.

Gwathmey, John H. *Historical Register of Virginians in the Revolution.* Richmond: Dietz Press, 1938.

Hall, Mary A. (Newell). *Harvard Soldiers and Sailors in the American Revolution, Harvard Alumni Graduates Magazine.* Boston: Harvard University Press, 1924.

———. *Harvard Alumni Veterans of the American Revolutionary War.* Boston: Harvard University Press, 1921.

———. *Thomas Newell and His Descendants.* Southington, CT: Cochrane Brothers, 1878.

Hannings, Bud. *Chronology of the American Revolution: Military and Political Actions Day by Day.* Jefferson, NC: McFarland, 2008.

Harvey, Oscar Jewell. *A History of Wilkes-Barre.* Philadelphia: Raeder Press, 1909.

Headley, J.T. *The Chaplains and Clergy of the Revolution.* New York: Charles Scribner, 1864.

Heckewelder, Rev. John. *History and Customs of The Indian Nations Who Once Inhabited Pennsylvania and the Neigh-*

Bibliography

boring States. Philadelphia: Publication Fund of the Historical Society of Pennsylvania, 1881.

Heitman, Francis Bernard. *Historical Register of Officers of the Continental Army during the War of Revolution.* Washington, D.C.: Government Printing Office, 1892.

Henderson, Helen. *Matawan and Aberdeen: Of Town and Field.* Charleston, SC: Arcadia Publishing, 2003.

Hinman, Royal Ralph. *A Historical Collection from Official Records, Files of the Part Sustained by Connecticut during the War of the Revolution.* Hartford, CT: E. Gleason, 1842.

_____. *Historical Collection of the Part Sustained by Connecticut during the War of the Revolution, complied by Royal Hinman.* Hartford, CT: E. Gleason, 1842.

Holden, Frederick A., and James Lockwood, *Descendants of Robert Lockwood.* Philadelphia: Printed by the Family, 1889.

Homor, Wi8lliam S. *This Old Monmouth of Ours.* Freehold, NJ: Moreau Brothers, 1932.

Howard, R.H., and Henry E. Crooker, eds. *A History of New England: Containing Historical and Descriptive Sketches.* Boston: Crocker and Company, 1880.

Howes, Barnabas. *Historical Sketches of the Times and Men in Ashfield, Mass., During the Revolutionary War.* North Adams, MA: Mrs. W.B. Walden, Book and Job Printer, 1883.

Howland, Franklin. *A History of the Town of Acushnet, Bristol County, State of Massachusetts.* New Bedford, MA: F. Anthony and Sons, 1907.

Hudson, Charles. *History of Lexington by Charles Hudson.* Boston: Houghton Mifflin, 1913.

Humphrey, Carol Sue, ed. *Voices of Revolutionary America: Contemporary Accounts of Daily Life.* Santa Barbara, CA: Greenwood, 2011.

Hunter, C.L. *Sketches of Western North Carolina.* Raleigh: The Raleigh News Steam Job Print, 1877.

Hurd, Duane Hamilton. *History of New London County, Connecticut.* Philadelphia: J.W. Lewis and Company, 1882.

Jenkins, Stephen. *The Story of the Bronx.* New York: Knickerbocker Press, 1912.

Johnston, Henry Phelps. *The Campaign of 1776 around New York and Brooklyn.* Brooklyn: Long Island Historical Society, 1878.

_____. *Connecticut Men in the Revolutionary War.* Clearfield, 1889.

_____. *Yale and Her Honor-roll in the American Revolution, 1775–1783.* New York: privately printed, 1888.

Kidd, Thomas S. *God of Liberty: A Religious History of the American Revolution.* New York: Basic Books, 2010.

Knight, Lucian Lamar. *Georgia's Roster of the Revolution.* Atlanta: Index Printing Company, 1920.

_____. *A Standard History of Georgia and Georgians.* Chicago: Lewis Publishing Company, 1917.

Lamb, Martha, J., ed. *The Magazine of American History with Notes and Queries, Vol. 6.* New York, 1886.

Lennox, Herbert John. *Samuel Kirkland's Mission to the Iroquois by Herbert John Lennox.* Chicago: University of Chicago, 1935.

Logusz, Michael O. *With Musket and Tomahawk: The Saratoga Campaign and the Wilderness War of 1777.* Havertown, PA: Casemate, 2010.

Lohrenz, Otto. *Anglican and Episcopal History.* Historical Society of the Episcopal Church, 2007.

_____. "The Reverend Abner Waugh: The 'Best Dancer of the Minuet in the State of Virginia.'" *The Kentucky Review* 15, no. 2 (2003).

Lossing, Benson J. *Pictorial Field Book of the Revolution Vol. II.* New York: Harper and Brothers, 1850.

Lurie, Maxine N., and Marc Mappen, eds. *Encyclopedia of New Jersey.* New Brunswick: Rutgers University Press, 2004.

Mallory, Charles D. *Memoirs of Elder Botsford.* Charleston, SC: W. Riley, 1832.

Malone, Dumas, ed. *Dictionary of American Biography.* Boston: Houghton Osgood and Company, 1879.

Bibliography

Maltby, Erastus. *Sermon on the 25th Anniversary of His Settlement as Pastor.* Boston: Phillips, Sampson, and Company, 1851.

_____. *Magazine of the D.A.R. Vol. 2, Issues 2-4.* Washington, D.C.

Maness, Michael Glenn. *Character Counts: Freemasonry Is a National Treasure and a Source of our Founders Constitutional Original Intent.* Bloomington: AuthorHouse, 2010.

McCall, Mrs. Howard H. *Roster of Revolutionary Soldiers in Georgia, Vol III.* Baltimore: Clearfield, 1968.

McClish, Eli. *The Twentieth Century Biographical Dictionary of Notable Americans Vol. VII.* Boston: The Biographical Society, 1904.

McDaniel, George W. *People Called Baptist.* Franklin, TN: North Valley Publications, 1919.

McKendree, Avery, and Catherine Hitchcock (Tilden). *The Groton Avery Clan, Vol. 1.* Cleveland: Wentworth Press, 1912.

_____. *The Minute Man, Vol. 11-20.* Sons of the Revolution in the State of Illinois, 1921.

Misencik, Paul R. *The Original American Spies: Seven Covert Agents of the Revolutionary War.* Jefferson, NC: McFarland, 2013.

Moore, Frank. *Diary of the American Revolution: from Newspapers and Original Documents.* New York: Charles Scribner, 1860.

_____. *The Patriot Preachers of the American Revolution: With Biographical Sketches 1776-1783.* New York: Printed for the Subscribers, 1860.

Mudge, Alfred. *Memorials: A Genealogical Account of the Name of Mudge in America.* Boston: Alfred Mudge and Sons for the Family, 1868.

Muzzey, A.B. *Reminiscences and Memorials of Men of the Revolution and Their Families.* Cambridge, MA: John Wilson and Son, 1883.

Neimeyer, Charles Ratrick. *The Revolutionary War.* Westwood, CT: Greenwood Press, 2007.

Nelson, James L. *With Fire and Sword: The Battle of Bunker Hill and the Beginning of the American Revolution.* New York: Saint Martin's Press, 2011.

New Jersey Historical Society. *Proceedings of the New Jersey Historical Society, Vol. 6, No. 1.* Newark: New Jersey Historical Society, 1898.

Norlie, Olaf Morgan, comp. *The Lutheran World Almanac.* New York: The Lutheran Council, 1926.

O'Brien, Steve. *Blackrobe in Blue: The Naval Chaplaincy of John P. Foley, S.J.* Lincoln, NE: Writers Club Press, 2002.

_____. *Ohio History, Vol. 23.* Columbus: F.J. Feer Printing Company, 1918.

Patton, Jacob Harris. *The Pennsylvania Magazine of History & Biography* XIII (1889).

_____. *Pennsylvania Magazine of History and Biography* XXVII, no. 1 (1903).

_____. *A Popular History of the Presbyterian Church.* New York: R.S. Mighill and Company, 1900.

Perry, Max. *The Descendants of Simpson-Roach Families of South Carolina.* Midland, TX: Published by Perry, 1974.

Peterson, Clarence Stewart. *Known Military Deaths in the American Revolution 1775-1783.* Baltimore: Clearfield, 1959.

Phinney, Elias. *History of the Battle of Lexington: on the Morning of the 19th April, 1775.* Boston: Phelps and Farnham, 1825.

Porter, Colonel Elisha. *Diary of Colonel Porter.* Pittsburg, TX, Library, 2001.

Potaski Michael. *Blackstone Valley Tribune* II, no. 10.

Powell, William S. *Presbyterian Heritage Center at Montreat.* Website.

_____, ed. *Dictionary of North Carolina Biography: Vol. 3 H-K.* Chapel Hill: University of North Carolina Press, 1991.

Price, Carl F. *Yankee Township by Carl F. Price.* East Hampton, CT: Citizens Welfare Club, 1941.

Proctor, Karen Cross. *Pembroke Chronicles by Karen Cross Proctor.* Charleston, SC: The History Press, 2015.

_____. *The Pennsylvania German Society.* Pennsylvania German Society, 1901 and 1903.

_____. *Princeton Alumni Weekly, Vol. 65*

Bibliography

December, 1, 1904. Princeton: The Princeton Publishing Company, 1964.

_____. *Princeton Alumni Weekly, Vol. 9*. Princeton: The Princeton Publishing Company, 1906.

_____. *Quarter Millennial Celebration of the City of Taunton, Massachusetts*. Taunton, MA: Published by the City Government, 1889.

Raymond, Marcius Denison. *Gray Genealogy: Being a Genealogical Record and History of the Descendants of John Gray of Beverly, Mass*. Tarrytown, NY: M.D. Raymond, 1887.

_____. *Sketch of Rev. Blackleach Burritt and Related Stratford Families: a Paper Read before the Fairfield Historical Society*. Fairfield, CT: Fairfield Historical Society, 1892.

Reed, Newton. *The Early History of Amenia*. Amenia, NY: DeLacey and Wiley, 1875.

Ripley, Rev. Ezra. *A History of the Fight at Concord of the 19th of April, 1775*. Concord, MA: Herman Atwill, 1832.

Robbins, Rev. Ammi R. *Journal of Rev. Ammi R. Robbins in the Northern Campaign of 1776*. New Haven: B.L. Halmen, 1850.

Rose, Alexander. *Washington's Spies: The Story of America's First Spy Ring*. New York: Bantam Books, 2007.

Root, Mary Philotheta, ed. *Chapter Sketches, Connecticut Daughters of the American Revolution by the Connecticut D.A.R.* New Haven: Connecticut Chapter of the D.A.R., 1901.

Russell, David Lee. *The American Revolution in the Southern Colonies*. Jefferson, NC: McFarland, 2000.

Saffell, William. *Records of the Revolutionary War*. Baltimore: Charles C. Saffell, 1894.

Sakowski, Carolyn. *Touring the East Tennessee Backroads*. Winston-Salem, NC: John F. Blair, 1993.

Salley, A.S., Jr. *South Carolina Historical and Genealogy Magazine 58, no. 44*. Charleston, SC: Walker, Evans, and Cogswell, 1957.

Savas, Theodore P., and J. David Dameron. *A Guide to the Battles of the American Revolution*. New York: Savas-Beatie, 2010.

_____. *The New American Revolution Handbook: Facts and Artwork for Readers of All Ages, 1775-1783*. New York: Savas-Beatie, 2010.

Scharf, Thomas, and Thompson Westcott. *Philadelphia History 1609-1884*. Philadelphia: L.H. Everts, 1884.

Scoggins, Michael. *The Day it Rained Militia: Huck's Defeat and the Revolution in the South Carolina Backcountry, May-July 1780*. Charleston, SC: The History Press, 2005.

Sewall, Samuel. *The History of Woburn, Middlesex County, Mass*. Boston: Wiggin and Lunt, 1868.

Shipton, Clifford K. *Sibley's Harvard Graduates, Vol. 16, 1764-1767*. Cambridge, MA, Historical Society, 1971.

Smith, Frances M. *Colonial Families of America, Volume 1*. Baltimore: Seaforth Press, 1909.

Smith, Robert. *The American Revolution and Righteous Community*. Columbia: University of South Carolina Press, 2007.

Society of the Sons of the American Revolution. *Manual of the Rhode Island Society of the Sons of the American Revolution*. New York: The Republic Press, 1892.

Sons of the American Revolution Applications. Ancestry.com database.

Spalding, George Burley. *The Dover Pulpit during the Revolutionary War*. Dover, NH: Morningstar Steam Job Printing House, 1876.

Sparks, Jared. *The Writings of George Washington*, Washington, D.C.: U.S. Government Printing Office, 1837.

Sprague, William Buell. *Annals of the American Pulpit Vol. 3*. New York: Robert Carter and Brothers, 1856.

Stacey, James. *History and Published Records of the Midway Congregational Church, Liberty County, Georgia*. Reprint Company, 1951.

Stark, Caleb, *Memoir and Official Correspondence of General Stark*. Concord, NH: Steam Press of McFarland and Jenks, 1860.

Bibliography

_____. *The State Society of the Cincinnati of Pennsylvania*. Website.

Stevens, Leon G. *One Nation Under God: A Factual History of America's Religious Heritage*. New York: Morgan James, 2013.

Stryker, William S., comp. *Official Register of the Officers and Men of New Jersey in the Revolutionary War by New Jersey Adjutant-General Office*. Trenton: William T. Nicholson and Company, 1872

Swope, Belle McKinney Hays. *History of Middle Spring Presbyterian Church, Middle Spring, Pa. 1738–1900*. Newville, PA: Times Steam Printing House, 1900.

Swope, Gilbert Earnest. *History of the Big Spring Presbyterian Church, Newville, Pa*. Newville, PA: Times Steam Printing House, 1898.

Symonds, Craig L., and William J. Clipson. *A Battlefield Atlas of the American Revolution*. Annapolis: The Nautical & Aviation Publishing Company of America, 1986.

Thompson, John R. *The Southern Literary Messenger: Devoted to Every Department of Literature and the Fine Arts, Vol VI*. Richmond: MacFarlane, Fergusson, and Company, 1835.

Thompson, Parker C. *From Its European Antecedents to 1791: The United States Army Chaplaincy*. Office of the Chief of Chaplains Department of the Army, Washington, D.C.: Department of the Army, 1978.

Tonsetic, Robert L. *Special Operations in the American Revolution*. Havertown, PA: Casemate, 2013.

Townsend, Leah. *South Carolina Baptists, 1670–1805*. Columbia: University of South Carolina, 1935.

Trumbull, Benjamin. *Collections of the Connecticut Historical Society Vol. VII, Journal of Benjamin Trumbull*. Hartford, CT: Hartford Historical Society, 1898.

Trumbull, Rev. J. Hammond. *The Memorial History of Hartford County, Connecticut, 1633–1884: Town Histories*. Boston: Edward L. Osgood, 1886.

Tsesis, Alexander. *For Liberty and Equality: The Life and Times of the Declaration of Independence*. New York: Oxford University Press, 1986.

Tyler, Lyon Gardiner. *Encyclopedia of Virginia Biography, Vol. II*. New York: Lewis Historical Publishing Company, 1915.

_____. *University of Pennsylvania Archives & Records Center*. Website.

Waddell, Jos. A. *Annals of Augusta County*. Staunton, VA: C. Russell Caldwell, 1886.

Wainwright, Charles, E. *Much Preached At: The Early Ministers of First Parish Church in Beverly 1667–1958*. Website.

Waite, Otis Frederick Reed. *History of the Town of Claremont New Hampshire for a Period of One Hundred Thirty Years*. Manchester, NH: The John B. Clarke Company, 1895.

Wallace, Paul A. *The Travels of John Heckewelder in Frontier America*. Pittsburgh: University of Pittsburgh Press, 1958.

Weeks, Lyman Horace, ed. *Prominent Families of New York*. New York: The Historical Company, 1897.

Werneer, Emmy E. *In Pursuit of Liberty: Coming of Age in the American Revolution*. Westport, CT: Praeger, 2006.

Whittemore, Henry. *History of the Adams Family*. New York: Willis McDonald and Company, 1893.

Wilcoxson, William Howard. *History of Stratford, Connecticut 1639–1939*. Stratford, CT: Stratford Tercentenary Commission, 1939.

Wild, Helen T. *Medford in the War of the Revolution*. Medford, MA: J.C. Miller Jr., 1898.

Wilson, James Grant, and John Fiske. *Appleton's Cyclopaedia of American Biography, Vol 8*. New York: D. Appleton, 1918.

Wing, Rev. C.P. *Rev. C. P. Wing's History of Cumberland County*. New York: Published by the Society, 1879.

Wright, Robert K., and Morris J. MacGregor. *Soldier-Statesman of the Constitution*. Honolulu: University Press of the Pacific, 2004.

Bibliography

Manuscripts and Archival Sources

Dwight Family Papers. Yale collection, 1788.
General Catalogues of Princeton University 1746-1906. New Jersey, 1908.
John Cleveland Papers 1722-1799. Peabody Essex Museum, Massachusetts.

Government Records

Census records. Ancestry.com database.
Connecticut Town Birth Records. Ancestry.com database.
Federal Warrant No. 1495 for bounty land issued 18 May, 1799. Ancestry.com database.
Founders online National Archives. National Archives.
Index of Obituaries, Massachusetts 1740-1800. Ancestry.com database.
Massachusetts Soldiers & Sailors in the War of Revolution Vols. 1. Boston 1902.
Massachusetts Soldiers & Sailors in the War of Revolution Vols. 12. Boston 1904.
Massachusetts, Wills & Probate Records 1635-1999, Vol. 74-75. Ancestry.com database.
The Military Chaplain's Review, 1987. U.S Army, 1992.
New Hampshire, Death & Burial Records 1654-1949. Ancestry.com database.
New Jersey Marriage Records 1683-1802. Ancestry.com database.
Pennsylvania Veterans Burial Cards 177-2012. Ancestry.com database.
Pennsylvania Province and State History, 1609-1790, Vol II. Ancestry.com database.
Pension List of 1792-1795. Ancestry.com database.
Service of Connecticut Men in the War of the Revolution. Ancestry.com database.
State of North Carolina Archives, Revolutionary Army Accounts, 1995.
The United States Army Chaplaincy by United States Department of the Army. Office of the Chief of Chaplains. 1977.
U.S. Pension Records. Ancestry.com database.
U.S. Pensioners 1818-1872. Ancestry.com database.
U.S. Revolutionary War Rolls 1775-1783. Ancestry.com database.
Valley Forge Muster Roll Project. Valley forge Park Alliance website.
Virginia Claims for Land Bounty Lands. 1840, Ancestry.com database.
Virginia Soldiers of 1776, Vol 1. Ancestry.com database.

Index

Adams, the Rev. Amos 7
Adams, John 13, 93
Adams, the Rev. John 4
Adams, John Q. 132
Adams, Samuel 39–40
Aitkin, the Rev. James 151
Allen, Ethan 68
Allen, the Rev. Moses 8–12, 15
Allen, the Rev. Thomas 11–15
Alliance (frigate) 19
Ames, the Rev. Slyvanus 151
Andre, Maj. John 17; trial and execution 80
Arlington 19
Armstrong, the Rev. James Francis 15–16
Arnold, Gen. Benedict 17, 20–21 24, 80, 99, 131–132
Asia (prison ship) 168
Avery, the Rev. David 6, 71, 116

Balch, the Rev. Benjamin 18–19
Balch, the Rev. Hezehiah 63
Baldwin, the Rev. Abraham 19–20
Baldwin, the Rev. Ebenezer 151
Baldwin, the Rev. Samuel 151
Balmaine, the Rev. Alexander 151
Baptists 3, 6, 44, 65, 70, 79, 104, 124, 140, 159
Barlow, the Rev. Joel 20–21
Barnet, the Rev. John 21–22
Barnum, the Rev. Caleb 22–23
Barrett, Col. James 66–67
Bartlett, the Rev. Nathaniel 23–24
Barton, the Rev. William 152
battles: Bennington 14–15, 154, 167; Brandywine 6, 46, 60, 93, 107, 113, 162; Breed's Hill 16, 100, 136; Briar Creek 10; Bunker Hill 16, 43, 51, 100–101, 106, 111, 135–137; Butt's Hill 56; Charleston 16, 121, 130; Chatterton Hill 144; Concord 66–68, 135–136; Connecticut Farms 36–37; Cowan's Ford 77; Elizabethtown 35–36; Fishing Creek 123; Fort Ann 105; Fort Chambly 140; Fort Clinton 71–72; Fort John 140–141; Fort Montgomery 71–72; Fort Ticonderoga 13, 17, 24, 42–43, 68, 79, 92–93; Fort Washington 69–70; Germantown 60, 93, 107, 135; Great Bridge 146; Greenville 93; Greenwich 34; Harlem Heights 70; Kings Mountain 44, 62–63, 113; Lexington 4, 19, 22, 41–42, 109; Lexington & Concord 50–51, 67–68; Long Island 12, 25–28, 43, 69, 126; Mobley's Meeting House 122; Monmouth 65, 76, 93, 103, 107; Montreal 23, 140; New Haven 59–60, 145; New London 32; Newport 53; Paoli 93–94; Princeton 47, 71, 101, 137; Quebec 24, 51, 99, 132; Red Bank 138; Rhode Island 53–56; Saratoga 15, 17, 22, 53, 64, 128–129; Savannah 9, 29; Springfield 37; Stillwater 127–128; Sullivan's Island 150, 107; Trenton 15, 43, 46–47, 71, 95, 119, 137; Wateree Ferry 122–123; White Plains 12–13, 21, 71, 137, 142–144
Beaty, the Rev. Charles 4
Beck, the Rev. Daniel 24–25
Beebe, the Rev. James 25–26
Belknap, Jeremy 152
Bellamy, the Rev. Joseph 152
Benedict, the Rev. Abner 26–27
Bennington (battle of) 14–15, 154, 167
Bird, the Rev. Samuel 152
Blackwell, the Rev. Robert 152
Blair, the Rev. Samuel 152
Bland, the Rev. William 152
Blanket Hill 134
Blumer, the Rev. Abraham 152
Boardman, the Rev. Benjamin 4, 27
Boston: evacuation 23; siege of 51–52, 67, 125–126
Boston (frigate) 19
Boston Tea Party 80
Botsford, the Rev. Edmund 28–29
Boyd, the Rev. Adam 152
Brackenridge, the Rev. Hugh Henry 30
Brady, the Rev. David 153
Braidfoote, the Rev. John 153
Brandywine (battle of) 6, 46, 60, 93, 107, 113, 162
Breed's Hill (battle of) 16, 100, 136
Briar Creek (battle of) 10
Bridge, the Rev. Matthew 30–31
British Navy 53

177

Index

Brock, the Rev. Thomas 31
Bucher, the Rev. John Conrad 32
Buckminister, the Rev. Joseph 153
Bunker Hill (battle of) 16, 43, 51, 100–101, 106, 111, 135–137
Burgoyne, Gen. John 15, 17, 53, 80, 112, 127–128
Burritt, the Rev. Blackleach 4, 33–35
Butt's Hill (battle of) 56

Caldwell, Hannah 35–37
Caldwell, the Rev. James 6, 35–38
Cambridge 16, 51–52, 77, 104
Canada Expedition 42
Carnes, the Rev. John 153
Catholicism 3, 98–99
Champion, Judah 153
Champman, the Rev. Hezekiah 153
chaplains: duties 4–6, 111; in hospitals 110, 131, 133; pay 5; as recruiters 3; sermons 3–4; taken prisoner 6; uniforms 4, 94
Chapman, the Rev. Jedidiah 153
Charleston (battle of) 16, 121, 130
Chatterton Hill (battle of) 144
Cherokee Indians 48, 61
Church, Dr. Benjamin 148–149
Church, German Reformed 160
Church of England 3, 42
Clark, Gen. George Rogers 74, 92
Clark, the Rev. Jonas 4, 38–42
Cleveland, the Rev. Ebenezer 42–43
Cleveland, the Rev. John (Mass.) 42–44
Cleveland, the Rev. John (Va.) 44–45
Clinton, Gen. George 71
Clinton, Gen. Henry 36
Clinton, Gen. James 71–74
coded message 147–148
College of New Jersey *see* Princeton
Concord (battle of) 66–68, 135–136
Congregational 3, 7–8, 12, 17, 22, 33, 45, 49, 80, 100, 132, 147, 167
Connecticut Farms (battle of) 36–37
Continental Congress 20
Continental Navy 19, 92
Cooke, the Rev. Noah 45
Cooper, the Rev. Robert 45–46
Cordell, the Rev. John 46
Cornwallis, Gen. Charles 5, 77; second Battle of Trenton 119; at Yorktown 94
Cotton, the Rev. Nicholas 153–154
Cowan's Ford (battle of) 77
Craighead, the Rev. John 47
Cummings, the Rev. Charles 47
Cutler, the Rev. Manassah 49–59

Daggett, the Rev. Naphtali 59–60
Darthmouth 21, 95

David, the Rev. Ebenezer 97, 154
Davis, the Rev. Thomas 60–61
Declaration of Independence 5, 35, 81, 163–164
Dewey, the Rev. Jedidiah 154
Doak, the Rev. Samuel 61–62
Duffield, the Rev. George 154
Dunlap, the Rev. Francis 154
Dunmore, Lord 146
Dwight, the Rev. Timothy 63

HMS *Eagle* 82
Eakin, the Rev. Samuel 154
Eells, the Rev. Nathaniel 154
Eells, the Rev. Samuel 155
Elder, the Rev. Robert 155
Eliot, the Rev. John 155
Elizabethtown (battle of) 35–36
Elliot, the Rev. John 155
Ellis, the Rev. John 65
Ely, the Rev. David 4
Emerson, Ralph Waldo 67
Emerson, the Rev. William 66–69, 135
Episcopalian 46, 61, 75, 152, 159
Evans, the Rev. Israel 65
Everest, the Rev. Noble 155
executions 131

Farrah, the Rev. Stephen 155
Ferguson, Maj. Partick 62
Fish, the Rev. Elisha 155
Fishing Creek (battle of) 123
Fithian, the Rev. Philip Vickers 69–70
Foard, the Rev. Hezekiah 155
Fobes, the Rev. Perez 155
Forbes, the Rev. Eli 155
Fort Ann (battle of) 105
Fort Chambly (battle of) 140
Fort Clinton (battle of) 71–72
Fort John (battle of) 140–141
Fort Montgomery (battle of) 71–72
Fort Moultrie *see* Sullivan's Island (battle of)
Fort Pitt 78
Fort Ticonderoga (battle of) 13, 17, 24, 42–43, 68, 79, 92–93
Fort Washington (battle of) 69–70
Fort Stanwix 96
Foster, the Rev. Edmund 155
Foster, the Rev. William 155
France: aid to colonies 129; King Louis XVI 53; Navy 54–56; treaty with U.S. 74; at Yorktown 108
Franklin, Benjamin 48, 92
French and Indian War 25, 32, 42–43, 100, 111, 134, 138, 156
Fuller, the Rev. Daniel 156

Index

Fuller, the Rev. John 156
Furman, the Rev. Richard 5

Gano, the Rev. John 70-74
Gates, Gen. Horatio 53, 68, 110, 112, 128, 136
Geagen, the Rev. James 19
George III, King 14
German Reform Church 32
Germantown (battle of) 60, 93, 107, 135
Gibault, the Rev. Pierre 74-75
Gordon, the Rev. William 156
Graham, the Rev. John 156
Graham, the Rev. William 156
Grayson, the Rev. Spencer 75
Great Bridge (battle of) 146
Greater State of Franklin 46
Green, the Rev. Enoch 156
Greene, Gen. Nathanael 5, 20, 54, 77, 107, 109
Greenville (battle of) 93
Greenwich (battle of) 34
Greenwich Tea Party 80
Griffith, the Rev. David 75-76
Grosvenor, the Rev. Daniel 76-77

Hadley, the Rev. Samuel 156
Hale, the Rev. Enoch 156
Hall, the Rev. James 77-78
Hamilton, Alexander 30, 108
Hancock, John 38-40
Harlem Heights (battle of) 70
Hart, the Rev. Samuel 156
Harvard 7, 12, 18, 22, 31, 38, 45, 79, 109, 112, 135, 147, 152-153, 155, 157-158, 161, 164, 166-167
Hayes, Mary *see* Pitcher, Molly
Heckewelder, the Rev. John 78-79
Henry, Patrick 48
Hessians 53, 93, 98, 107, 119, 131, 138, 154, 160; at Trenton 17, 118
Hibbard, the Rev. Augustine 156
Hibbard, the Rev. Ithmar 157
Hill, the Rev. William 79
Hitchcock, the Rev. Enos 79-80
Hitchcock, the Rev. Gad 157
Hollingshead, the Rev. William 157
Holmes, the Rev. John 157
Howe, Gen. William 54, 93, 117, 141
Hunter, the Rev. Andrew 70, 80-92
Hurst, the Rev. John 157

Indians: battles with 48; scalping 48
Iroquois Indians 86
Irving, Washington 34

Jackson, Andrew 134, 139
Jefferson, Thomas 83

Johnson, the Rev. Daniel 157
Johnson, the Rev. Stephen 157
Johnston, the Rev. William 157
Jones, the Rev. David 6, 92-94
Jones, the Rev. Samuel 157
Judaism 3, 10
Judson, the Rev. David 157
Judson, the Rev. Ephraim 158

Keith, the Rev. Robert 158
Kendall, the Rev. Thomas 95
Ker, the Rev. Nathan 158
King, the Rev. John 158
Kings Mountain (battle of) 44, 62-63, 113
Kirkland, the Rev. Samuel, 95-96
Knox, Gen. Henry 51

Lafayette, Marquis de 38, 54, 76
Lancaster, the Rev. Thomas 158
Latta, the Rev. James 158
Lee, the Rev. Andrew 158
Lee, Gen. Charles 71, 73
Leonard, the Rev. Abiel 96, 97
Lewis, the Rev. Ichabod 158
Lewis, the Rev. Isaac 98
Lewis, the Rev. Joshua 158
Lexington 40; alarm 27, 68, 76; British advance 39; British retreat 68, 109; deaths 41-42
Lexington (battle of) 4, 19, 22, 41-42, 109
Lexington & Concord (battle of) 50-51, 67-68
Linn, the Rev. William 158
Lockwood, the Rev. William 158
Long Island (battle of) 12, 25-28, 43, 69, 126
Lotbiniere, Father Louis Eustace 98-99
Lutherans 3, 106
Lynd the Rev. John 159
Lyth, the Rev. John 159

MacCalla, the Rev. Daniel, 99
MacClintock, the Rev. Samuel, 100-101
Madison, James 94
Manning, the Rev. Joseph 159
Mansfield, the Rev. Issac 159
Marion, Gen. Francis 5
Marshall, the Rev. Daniel 159
Mason, the Rev. John 159
Martin, the Rev. John Nicholas 5
May, the Rev. Eleazer 160
McAlden, the Rev. Hugh 159
M'Clanahan, the Rev. 159
McClintock, the Rev. Samuel 5
McClure, the Rev. Daniel 159
McKay, the Rev. William 159
McKnight, the Rev. Charles 101-102

Index

McMordie, the Rev. Robert 102
McWhorter, Alexander 102
Mercer, the Rev. Silas 160
Metomeny *see* Arlington
Michael, the Rev. Philip Jacob 160
Miller, the Rev. Henry 160
Mobley's Meeting House (battle of) 122
Monmouth (battle of) 65, 76, 93, 103, 107
Monroe, James 21
Montgomery, the Rev. Joseph 160
Montgomery, Gen. Richard 24, 132
Montreal (battle of) 23, 140
Morgan, Gen. Daniel 46
Morgan, James 38
Morris, the Rev. Edward 160
Mudge, the Rev. John 104–105
Muhlenberg, the Rev. John Peter Gabriel 4, 105–108
Mulkey, the Rev. Philip 161
Murdock, the Rev. James 161
Murray, the Rev. John 108–109

Nancy (prison ship) 8–11
Nevelling, the Rev. John Wesley Gilbert 161
New Haven (battle of) 59–60, 145
New Jersey (prison ship) 101
New London (battle of) 32
New York Campaign 81–86, 114, 141–142
New York City 12, 27–28, 31; burning of 84
Newell, the Rev. Samuel 161
Newport (battle of) 53
Nixon, Gen. John 129
Nixon, the Rev. Robert 161
Noble, the Rev. Obediah 161
Noble, the Rev. Oliver 161
North Bridge *see* Lexington & Concord (battle of)
Norwalk Battle of 98

Oneida Indians 95–96
Osgood, the Rev. David 161

Paoli (battle of) 93–94
Parish, the Rev. Elijah 43
Parker, Capt. John 41–42
Payne, the Rev. Joshua 161
Payson, the Rev. Samuel Phillips 109–110
Perry, the Rev. Joseph 161
Petersburg battle of 107
Pitcher, Molly 103
Plumbe, the Rev. William 110–111
Pomeroy, the Rev. Benjamin 111–112
Pope, the Rev. Joseph 162
Porter, the Rev. Nathaniel 162
Porter, the Rev. Nehemiah 112
Potter, the Rev. Isaiah 162
Prentiss, the Rev. Thomas 162

Presbyterians 3, 16, 34–35, 37, 59, 62, 69, 133–134, 136, 158
Prime, the Rev. Ebenezer 4
Princeton (battle of) 47, 71, 101, 137
Princeton College 8, 22, 24, 30, 35, 45, 47, 61, 63, 69, 77, 80, 95, 100, 117, 121, 124, 131, 154, 156, 158
prison ships: *Asia* 168; *Nancy* 8–11; *New Jersey* 101
Purcell, the Rev. Henry 162
Putnam, Gen. Israel 24, 64, 104, 129, 136

Quaker Hill
Quakers 3, 5, 18
Quebec (battle of) 24, 51, 99, 132

Red Bank (battle of) 138
Reed, the Rev. John 162
Reed, the Rev. Thomas 162
Revere, Paul 39–40
Rexford, the Rev. Elisha 162
Rhea, the Rev. Joseph 112–113
Rhode Island (battle of) 53–56
Ripley, the Rev. Hezekiah 113–115
Robbins, the Rev. Ammi Ruhamah 115–116
Roe, the Rev. Azel 116
Rogers, the Rev. John 162
Rogers, the Rev. William 162
Rosenbrugh, the Rev. John 117–120

St. Clair, Gen. Arthur 13, 93
Sampson, the Rev. Ezra 163
Sanford the Rev. David 120
Saratoga (battle of) 15, 17, 22, 53, 64, 128–129
Savage, the Rev. Loveless 163
Schoonmaker, the Rev. Martinus 163
Savannah (battle of) 9, 29
Schuyler, Gen. Philip 93, 124, 127
Scott, the Rev. Alexander 163
Seneca Indians 95
Separatists 42–43
Sere, the Rev. Daniel 163
Seward, the Rev. William 163
Sherman, the Rev. Josiah 163
Simpson, the Rev. John 121–123
Six Nations 95
slaves 49, 64, 146
smallpox 23–24, 97, 167
Smiley, the Rev. Thomas 163
Smith, the Rev. Cotton M. 163
Smith, the Rev. Cotton Mather 123–124
Smith, the Rev. Elias 163
Smith, the Rev. Hezekiah 124–130
Smith, the Rev. John Blair 164
Smith, the Rev. Manasseh 164
Smith, the Rev. Robert 130

Index

Society of Friends *see* Quakers
Spencer, the Rev. Elihu 130-131
Spring, the Rev. Samuel 131-133
Springfield (battle of) 37
Sproat, the Rev. James 133
spy 163
Stark, Gen. John 14, 45, 100-101
Steel, the Rev. John 134
Stewart, the Rev. Alexander 164
Stillwater (battle of) 127-128
Stockton, the Rev. Philip 164
Stony Point battle of 107
Storrs, the Rev. John 164
Streit, the Rev. Christian 164
Strong, the Rev. Joseph 164
Strong, the Rev. Nathan 165
Sugar House Prison 5, 33, 117
Sullivan, Gen. John 53-54, 56, 96, 125
Sullivan Expedition 50, 73, 81, 86-92
Sullivan's Island (battle of) 150, 107
Sumter, Gen. Thomas 5, 122-123
Swain, the Rev. Joseph 165
Sweetland, the Rev. Eleazer 165
Swift, the Rev. Job 165

Tarleton, Lt. Col. Banastare 123
Tate, the Rev. James 134-135
Tennent, the Rev. William 165
Tetard, the Rev. John Peter 165
Thacher, the Rev. Peter 165
Thaxter, the Rev. Joseph 135-137
Thayer, the Rev. Jabez 166
Thompson, the Rev. Amos 166
Thompson, the Rev. Charles 137-138
Thomson, the Rev. James Hampden 166
Thruston, the Rev. Charles Mynn 138-139
Todd, the Rev. Jonathan 4, 166
Todd, the Rev. Samuel 166
Tories 14, 102; battles with 33-34, 36, 60, 116, 122; Kings Mountain 44
Treat, the Rev. Joseph 166
Trenton (battle of) 17, 43, 46-47, 71, 95, 119, 137
Trout, the Rev. Joab 6, 150, 166
Trumbull, the Rev. Benjamin 139-145
Tuck, the Rev. John 166
Turtle (submarine) 82-83
Tyron, Gov. William 144-145

United States Navy 19
Univeralist 108

Valcour Islans, 408
Valley Forge 5, 17, 65, 72, 103, 107, 138, 152

Van Horn, the Rev. William 167
Von Steuben, Baron 107

Wadden, the Rev. James 47
Waite, the Rev. William 167
Wales, the Rev. Samuel 167
Walnut Street prison 46
War of 1812 94
Ware, Rev William 39
Warren, the Rev. John 167
Washington, George 5, 16-18, 21, 26, 30-31, 34, 43, 47, 51, 61, 83, 85-86, 104, 107-109, 114, 129, 136; appeal for help 117, 155; appointed commander 114; baptized 72-73; code breakers 147-148; crossing the Delaware 71; donations 38; end of war 74; French and Indian War 138; funeral 61; letters 97, 103; New York campaign 83, 141-142; president 75; problems with General Lee 76; retreat from Long Island 126; Siege of Boston 52; spy ring 78; spy trial 104; surveyor 134; at Trenton 102, 118-119; at Valley Forge 72, 93; White Plains 144; Yorktown 94
Wateree Ferry (battle of) 122-123
Waugh, the Rev. Abner 145-146
Wayne, Gen. Anthony 88, 92-94, 152
Webster, the Rev. Samuel 167
Welch, the Rev. Whitman 167
Wells, the Rev. Noah 167
West, the Rev. Samuel 146-149
West Point 64, 80
Whiskey Rebellion 30
White Plains (battle of) 12-13, 21, 71, 137, 142-144
Wildman, the Rev. Benjamin 167
Willard, the Rev. Joseph 167
Williamson, the Rev. Samuel 167
Winter, the Rev. Francis 167
Wood, the Rev. Samuel 168
Woodbridge, the Rev. Samuel 168
Woodhull, the Rev. John 149-150
Woodson, the Rev. Matthew 168
Worth, the Rev. William 168

Yale 21-22, 25-27, 31, 43, 49, 59, 63-65, 76, 111, 113, 115, 120, 130, 151-153, 157-158, 161, 164-165, 167-168
Yeager, the Rev. Johann 168
Yorktown 15, 65, 74, 79, 94, 123; redoubts 107-108

www.ingramcontent.com/pod-product-compliance
Ingram Content Group UK Ltd.
Pitfield, Milton Keynes, MK11 3LW, UK
UKHW042014140426
5217IPUK00015B/1174